T0207287

Lecture Notes in Computer Science 14199

The series Lecture Notes in Computer Science (LNCS), including its subseries Lecture Notes in Artificial Intelligence (LNAI) and Lecture Notes in Bioinformatics (LNBI), has established itself as a medium for the publication of new developments in computer science and information technology research, teaching, and education.

LNCS enjoys close cooperation with the computer science R & D community, the series counts many renowned academics among its volume editors and paper authors, and collaborates with prestigious societies. Its mission is to serve this international community by providing an invaluable service, mainly focused on the publication of conference and workshop proceedings and postproceedings. LNCS commenced publication in 1973.

Hideyuki Takada · D. Moritz Marutschke ·
Claudio Alvarez · Tomoo Inoue · Yugo Hayashi ·
Davinia Hernandez-Leo
Editors

Collaboration Technologies and Social Computing

29th International Conference, CollabTech 2023
Osaka, Japan, August 29 – September 1, 2023
Proceedings

Springer

Editors
Hideyuki Takada ⓘD
Ritsumeikan University
Shiga, Japan

D. Moritz Marutschke ⓘD
Kyoto University of Advanced Science
Kyoto, Japan

Claudio Alvarez ⓘD
Universidad de los Andes
Las Condes, Santiago, Chile

Tomoo Inoue ⓘD
University of Tsukuba
Tsukuba, Japan

Yugo Hayashi ⓘD
Ritsumeikan University
Ibaraki, Japan

Davinia Hernandez-Leo ⓘD
Pompeu Fabra University
Barcelona, Spain

ISSN 0302-9743   ISSN 1611-3349 (electronic)
Lecture Notes in Computer Science
ISBN 978-3-031-42140-2   ISBN 978-3-031-42141-9 (eBook)
https://doi.org/10.1007/978-3-031-42141-9

This Springer imprint is published by the registered company Springer Nature Switzerland AG
The registered company address is: Gewerbestrasse 11, 6330 Cham, Switzerland

Preface

This volume contains the papers presented at the 29th International Conference on Collaboration Technologies and Social Computing. The conference was held during August 29–September 1, 2023, in Osaka, Japan, in hybrid format.

This year we received 32 submissions, including 20 full papers and 4 Work-in-Progress (WIP) contributions. Each paper was carefully reviewed by 3 to 4 Program Committee members in a double-blind process. As a result, the Committee decided to accept 8 full papers and 12 as WIP papers. The accepted papers present relevant and interesting research works related to theory, models, design principles, methodologies, and case studies that contribute to a better understanding of the complex interrelations that exist at the intersection of collaboration and technology. The program also included a keynote presentation.

As editors, we would like to thank the authors of all CollabTech 2023 submissions and the members of the Program Committee for carefully reviewing the submissions. Our thanks also go to our sponsors who allowed us to make CollabTech 2023 attractive to participants with rich opportunities to socialize with each other. In addition, we attribute the success of the conference to the efforts of the Special Interest Group (SIG) on Collaboration and Network Services of the Information Processing Society of Japan, the SIG on Cyberspace of the Virtual Reality Society of Japan, and the SIG on Communication Enhancement of the Human Interface Society. Last but not least, we would like to acknowledge the effort of the organizers of the conference and thank the Steering Committee for the opportunity to organize the conference and all the help provided during the process.

August 2023

Hideyuki Takada
D. Moritz Marutschke
Claudio Alvarez
Tomoo Inoue
Yugo Hayashi
Davinia Hernandez-Leo

Organization

General Chairs

Tomoo Inoue   University of Tsukuba, Japan
Yugo Hayashi   Ritsumeikan University, Japan
Davinia Hernandez-Leo   Universitat Pompeu Fabra, Spain

Program Chairs

Hideyuki Takada   Ritsumeikan University, Japan
D. Moritz Marutschke   Kyoto University of Advanced Science, Japan
Claudio Alvarez   Universidad de los Andes, Chile

Steering Committee

Nelson Baloian   Universidad de Chile, Chile
Heinz Ulrich Hoppe   RIAS-Institute, Germany
Tomoo Inoue   University of Tsukuba, Japan
Minoru Kobayashi   Meiji University, Japan
Hideaki Kuzuoka   University of Tokyo, Japan
Hiroaki Ogata   Kyoto University, Japan

Finance Chairs

Nobutaka Kawaguchi   Hitachi, Ltd., Japan
Kazuyuki Iso   NTT, Japan

Publicity Chair

Kouyou Otsu   Ritsumeikan University, Japan

Local Arrangement Chairs

Takafumi Tanaka   Tamagawa University, Japan
Yuji Wada   Ritsumeikan University, Japan
Shigen Shimojo   Ritsumeikan University, Japan
Tzu-Yang Wang   Japan Advanced Institute of Science and
                            Technology, Japan

Local Arrangement Chair (Social Event)

Mondheera Pituxcoosuvarn   Ritsumeikan University, Japan

Publication Chairs

Akihiro Miyata   Nihon University, Japan
Arinobu Niijima   NTT, Japan

Registration Chair

Tomohiro Kokogawa   International Professional University of
                            Technology in Tokyo, Japan

Liaison Chairs

Chihiro Takayama   NTT, Japan
Takashi Yoshino   Wakayama University, Japan

Program Committee

Carlos Alario-Hoyos   Universidad Carlos III de Madrid, Spain
Ishari Amarasinghe   Universitat Pompeu Fabra, Spain
Nelson Baloian   University of Chile, Chile
Sonia Guadalupe Mendoza Chapa   CINVESTAV, Mexico
Irene-Angelica Chounta   University of Duisburg-Essen, Germany
Cesar A. Collazos   Universidad del Cauca, Colombia
Yannis Dimitriadis   University of Valladolid, Spain
Orlando Erazo   Universidad Técnica Estatal de Quevedo, Ecuador

Chi-Lan Yang   University of Tokyo, Japan
Mika Yasuoka   Roskilde University, Denmark
Takashi Yoshino   Wakayama University, Japan
Takaya Yuizono   Japan Advanced Institute of Science and
                        Technology, Japan
Alejandro Zunino   CONICET-ISISTAN, UNICEN, Argentina

Contents

Work-in-Progress Papers

Full Papers

HelaDepDet: A Novel Multi-class Classification Model for Detecting the Severity of Human Depression

Y. H. P. P. Priyadarshana$^{(\boxtimes)}$ (ID), Zilu Liang (ID), and Ian Piumarta (ID)

Kyoto University of Advanced Science (KUAS), Kyoto, Japan
{2022md05,liang.zilu,ian.piumarta}@kuas.ac.jp

Abstract. Depression-driven suicide is a serious social problem. Early identification of depression is vital for the well-being of society. Clinical diagnosis of depression takes a significant amount of time and requires highly skilled medical staff, which greatly limits its accessibility. Social media analysis for depression detection is therefore a rapidly growing research area. However, most of the available methods can only detect the presence or absence of depression, not the severity of depression. On the other hand, a few recently developed models for depression severity detection have not been validated on large datasets due to fundamental issues such as data sparsity. In this study, we proposed a novel method based on confidence vectors for detecting the severity of depression. We evaluated our method using a large dataset consisting of more than 40,000 annotated statements extracted from multiple social network services. To our knowledge, this is the largest and most well-balanced dataset for depression severity classification to date. Preliminary results showed that our models outperformed the existing state-of-the-art models by 5%, achieving a micro-averaged F1 score of 66% for human depression severity detection.

Keywords: Depression Severity Detection · Multi-class Classification · Natural Language Processing · Affective Computing

1 Introduction

Human depression has been identified as a severe mental illness throughout the entire world. According to the latest statistics of the World Health Organization, nearly 350 million people suffer from this mental disorder while over 700,000 people die due to suicide as a result of depression [1, 2]. Even though sufficient attention has been given to physical illnesses such as cancer, diabetes, allergies, etc., still most of the mental disorders such as schizophrenia, anxiety and depression have been neglected [3]. Among these, depression has been categorized as the most critical type of mental disorder globally [4]. The reason behind this situation is that more than 70% of depressed people do not seek early treatment due to various circumstances [5]. Even though many clinical approaches were established for diagnosing depression, the early identification of the severity of human depression remains a challenging task [6].

H. Takada et al. (Eds.): CollabTech 2023, LNCS 14199, pp. 3–18, 2023.
https://doi.org/10.1007/978-3-031-42141-9_1

At the same time, the response to COVID-19 has played a major role in reshaping human society and working culture. Significant research has revealed that the major symptoms of human anxiety and depression can be elevated with sudden changes to our working culture [7]. Even though working from home has been one of the major impacts of the COVID-19 pandemic, serious mental health consequences have been reported due to the lack of social relationships and communication [8]. Evidence for this has been seen in the extraordinary increase in social media use in response to isolation from loved ones [9]. Considering all these factors, an early depression identification screening tool can be considered as a critical social need.

Multiple research challenges can be determined such as:, *"How can the early identification of human depression be further enhanced?"* and, *"How can the categorization of the severity of human depression be further improved?"* In this study we evaluated a novel method for detecting depression severity based on social media analysis. The main contributions of this study can be summarized as follows:

- We proposed a novel method for human depression severity detection. Severity is formulated as a confidence vector representation of depression mentions such as words and/or phrases.
- We created a balanced dataset, which has been properly annotated according to the guidelines of the depression severity annotation scheme [10] and BDI-3 [11] clinical levels.
- We validated our method on the largest dataset consisting of more than 40,000 annotated statements extracted from multiple social media platforms. Our model was compared with state-of-art baselines for depression detection under several benchmarking strategies to show that the proposed methodology performs well at depression severity detection.

The overall organization of the paper is as follows: Sect. 2 critically reviews related work in this area while Sect. 3 explains the data construction and the overall methodology. Experimental results are presented in Sect. 4 and then discussed in Sect. 5.

2   Related Work

The literature can be grouped into two main segments which are analyzing human depression detection and analyzing the severity detection of human depression. Although human depression detection approaches can be identified as clinical, emotional, or linguistic based, this research work has focused only on linguistic based depression detection. When considering any text based linguistic approach, a significant public corpus is essential. Losada, et al., [12] were the first to publish a corpus related to human depression detection. A further enhancement was made by revealing the nature of human depression and language usage as the first in a series of eRisk challenges [13]. Shen, et al., [14] were able to extract depression related feature groups on Twitter. After 2017, a new trend arose where human depression detection benefitted from natural language processing (NLP) and a novel approach has been proposed for extracting the linguistic relationships for depression detection [15]. Skaik, et al., [16] presented a systematic review on the significant progress of human depression identification based on social media.

Suhara, et al., [17] proposed a machine learning driven approach for forecasting human depressive moods using logs extracted from personal devices as inputs. Orabi, et al., [18] demonstrated a convolutional neural network (CNN) based approach for obtaining features of language that are useful in depression detection. The first attempt has been made to use transfer learning to implement a computational model for human depression identification [19]. Burdisso, et al., [20] introduced a novel binary classification machine learning model to detect depression identification using social media postings. A specific study on depression detection using text summarization has been released as a deep neural based framework [21].

Since severity detection of human depression is the focus of our approach, investigating such attempts is important. Even though there is a long history of detecting the severity of human depression based on clinical or emotional procedures, little work has been conducted using text based linguistic methods. An ensemble machine learning approach has been introduced for depression severity detection where a Bidirectional Encoder Representations from Transformers (BERT) model has been applied as a pre-trained language model (PLM) [22]. Wu, et al., [23] demonstrated an enhanced version of the previous attempt for measuring the early signs of depressive severity disorders. In the same year, a constructive survey has been conducted on listing the trending NLP approaches in depression severity identification [24]. Recently, Naseem, et al.,[25] introduced a deep neural based approach for depression severity classification using social media posts. Although different approaches have been devised, major issues remain to be addressed such as the shortage of text based linguistic public corpora and unbalanced data distribution issues in the prevailing corpus.

3 Methodology

We can divide our methodology into two phases, data construction and algorithmic development.

3.1 Data Construction

Depression severity annotation is diversified considering the clinical depression categorization. As per the text based linguistic approach, the depression severity annotation has been conducted considering BDI-3 [11] and the depression severity annotation scheme of Mowery, et al., [10] as the ground truth. According to the criteria, depression can be categorized into four levels: *minimal, mild, moderate*, and *severe*. Two such publicly available annotated corpora have been considered, namely DEPTWEET [26] and the depression severity annotated dataset of Naseem, et al. [25]. These datasets were developed using the extracted social media posts from Twitter and Reddit users, although both suffer from structural issues such as insufficient size and unbalanced data distribution among the pre-defined classes. To overcome these issues, an aggregated larger corpus has been introduced as a part of the present work. The NearMiss [27] undersampling technique has been used to balance data tuples optimally. Common features of both datasets such as *id, reply_count, reply_comment, reply_addressee, target_label,*

Table 1. Class-wise corpora distribution.

Dataset	Depression class	Corpus size
Depression severity annotated corpus	Minimal	2,587
	Mild	290
	Moderate	394
	Severe	282
DEPTWEET	Minimal	32,401
	Mild	5,243
	Moderate	1,810
	Severe	741
Our aggregated corpus	Minimal	10,549
	Mild	10,661
	Moderate	9,473
	Severe	11,176

and *confidence_score* were used for corpora aggregation. The class-wise distribution statistics of the corpora are shown in Table 1.

It can be seen that the tuple distribution of the aggregated corpus is well balanced after applying the NearMiss undersampling strategy which is one significant contribution of our study. A sample of the constructed aggregated corpus is shown in Fig. 1.

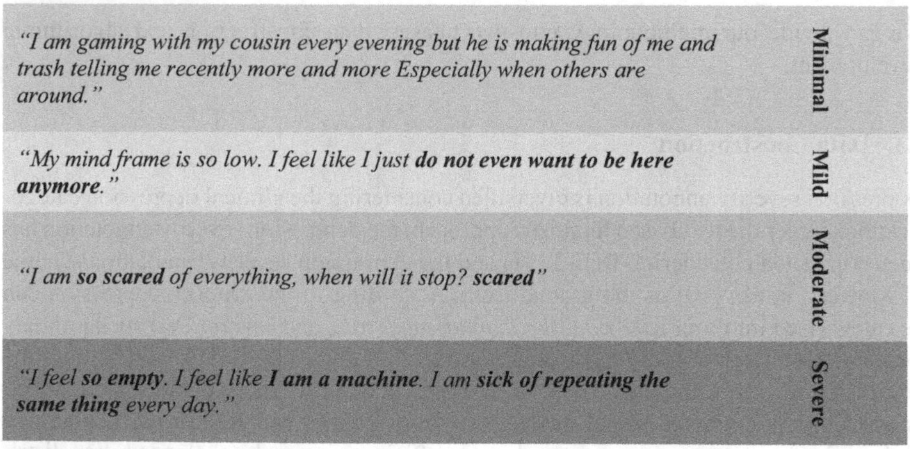

Fig. 1. Sample of the aggregated constructed dataset

The labelling procedure has been conducted considering the highlighted depression related terms. The original dataset labels were used as the annotations of the aggregated dataset so that combining them would not have any impact on the fundamentals of corpus construction.

3.2 Methodological Development

A high-level conceptual overview of our methodology is shown in Fig. 2.

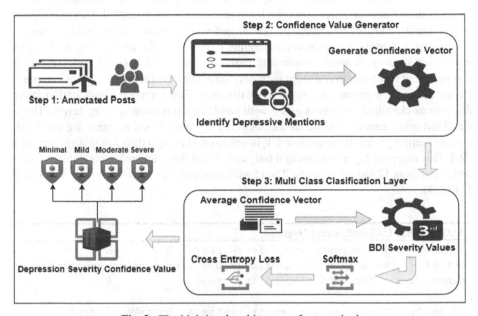

Fig. 2. The high-level architecture of our method

The entire approach can be divided into three main steps. In the initial step, the annotated social media posts were fed to the system. The pre-annotation tasks such as preprocessing are performed in this step. Identification of the depressive words/phrases and generating the confidence vectors are the tasks of step 2: *confidence value generator*. Identifying depressive mentions is facilitated by prior work on extracting hate speech related mentions [28]. The respective depression severity categories (*minimal, mild, moderate,* and *severe*) g and the potential depressive mentions (*words* and/or *phrases*) m are mapped to form a dictionary. Considering these, the depression confidence vector cv of a particular social media conversational post can be obtained as in Eq. 1.

$$cv = \{cv(m_1g_1), cv(m_2g_2), cv(m_3g_3), \ldots, cv(m_ng_n)\} \qquad (1)$$

Generating the confidence vectors for the determined depressive words/phrases is another novel contribution of our work. Once the confidence vector for each user post is obtained, the third section *multi-class classification layer* commences. This section is responsible for deriving the multi-class depression severity classification. The average confidence vector CV can be determined as in Eq. 2.

$$CV = \sum_{mg \in t_s} cv(m_n g_n) \tag{2}$$

The set t_s denotes the conversation history of a particular user. In a text-based multi-party conversation, conversation history (or interaction history) is essential for the semantic mapping of each follow-up utterance of the same conversation to identify the transition of conversation topics and for dynamic topic tracking [29]. This mapping is done using the above-mentioned *reply_count* and *reply_comment* features. Once the CV is obtained, it is converted to the corresponding BDI-3 score for determining the level of depression severity. A novel approach to multi-class depression severity classification was used that involved several steps including sentence classification, n-gram mapping, classification of n-grams, and layer normalization. The sentence classification layer determines classified utterances along with labels of depression severity levels. These classified utterances are tokenized for obtaining n-grams. Once n-grams are obtained, n-gram mapping with the respective CV is determined using a direct mapping approach [30]. This mapping layer consists of a fully connected deep network with a hidden layer which contains 12 hidden neurons. The classification of n-grams is shown in Algorithm 1 (Fig. 3).

ALGORITHM 1: Classification of n-grams

```
Input -> self, x_test, prep, leave_pbar
Output -> cv: a list of numeric values representing the confi-
dence levels for each element in x_test

If self.__categories__ is empty, raise an EmptyModelError
If self.get_ngrams_length() and self.get_nword_slices() is true
then
   return self.__predict_fast__(x_test, prep=prep,
leave_pbar=leave_pbar, proba=True) End If
Set x_test to be a list of x_test
Set classify to be self.classify()
for each element x in x_test
     Return a list of classifications cv
     Iterate over each element x in x_test
END FOR
RETURN cv
```

Fig. 3. Classification of n-grams

N-gram classification is conducted using N-word slices. This helps to obtain BDI-3 scores for respective depressive words and/or phrases which are generated as in Fig. 2 by converting the determined CV into the respective BDI-3 score. A softmax activation function and a normalization layer enhance this process while normalizing mappings. This enables smoother gradients, a faster training process, and ultimately better accuracy

[31]. Cross entropy [32] is used as the loss function for minimizing the loss between the generated and predicted results of the system. The loss function LV can be determined as:

$$LV = -\sum_{g=1}^{M} y_{mg} log(p_g)$$ (3)

where $M = |\{Minimal, Mild, Moderate, Severe\}|$ is the number of depressive severity levels, y is a binary value indicating whether g is the correct classification and p is the probability of an exact depressive category. Assuming the respective severity level is s, the depression severity confidence value $DSCV$ can be obtained as in Eq. 4.

$$DSCV = \left[softmax(CV\{s, M\}), -\sum_{g=1}^{M} y_{mg} log(p_g) \right]$$ (4)

The obtained $DSCV$ lies in the range 0 to 63, aligning with the range of the BDI-3 scale. Considering the range of $DSCV$, the depression severity levels can be determined as: *minimal* (0–9), *mild* (10–18), *moderate* (19–29) or *severe* (30–63), aligning with the levels of BDI-3 scale.

For the implementation, *Python 3.8* was used for core model development and *TensorFlow 2.10* was used as the backend machine learning framework. Several NLP related Python packages such as *NLTK* were used to support various pre-processing related tasks. The model training was performed for 10 epochs using a Nvidia GeForce RTX 3060 Ti GPU by setting the batch size to 4.

4   Experimental Results

Experiments on inter-annotator reliability and depression severity confidence value are discussed in this section.

4.1   Inter-annotator Reliability

Since multiple raters and multiple categorical ratings were employed in the construction of the original two corpora, the annotator's reliability must be determined. The objective is not to re-annotate but to re-evaluate the labelled corpora after corpora aggregation. A sample of the annotated aggregated corpus is shown in Table 2.

Annotators 1, 2 and 3 represent the panel of annotators while Trust 1, 2 and 3 are confidence coefficients on a scale of 0 to 1 for the obtained annotator values. Annotator values range from 1 to 4 representing the depression severity classes from *minimal*, to *severe*, respectively. The most appropriate depression severity class has been determined considering the maximum number of votes from the panel of annotators. The respective severity labels and confidence scores for social media statements can be found as follows in Table 3.

The inter-annotator agreement was determined by calculating the Kappa coefficient (K) [33] which measures the pairwise agreement among a set of annotators to obtain a

Table 2. Samples of the aggregated corpus.

Post	Annotator 1	Annotator 2	Annotator 3	Trust 1	Trust 2	Trust 3
He said he had not felt that way before, suggested I go rest...	1	1	2	0.967	0.967	1
I decided to stop taking it for a few days to see if it was really helping. Now, about 40 h...	3	2	3	1	1	0.933

Table 3. Samples of confidence scores and target labels.

Post	Target label	Confidence score
He said he had not felt that way before, suggested I go rest...	Minimal	0.647
I decided to stop taking it for a few days to see if it was really helping. Now, about 40 h since my last dose...	Moderate	0.667

reliability measure for a manual labelling task under a computational task. The above confidence value was used as an average agreement of all annotators. Considering these, the K coefficient is determined as follows.

$$K = \frac{observed\ \ agreement - chance\ \ agreement}{1 - chance\ \ agreement} \tag{5}$$

The inter-annotator reliability can be classified as a *fair, moderate, substantial*, or *almost perfect* for values of K in the ranges *0.21 - 0.40, 0.41 - 0.60, 0.61 - 0.80* or *0.81– 0.99* respectively [34]. The observed agreement indicates the proportion of times that the annotators agreed where chance agreement is considered as the maximum proportion of times that annotators could agree. In our case, the obtained confidence score can be taken as the observed agreement. The individual Kappa values K for the four depression severity categories are shown in Table 4.

Table 4. Kappa values for depression severity categories.

Class	Probability	Kappa	Error	Z value	P value
Minimal	0.82	0.75	0.13	3.42	0.04
Mild	0.77	0.68	0.13	3.86	0.04
Moderate	0.69	0.72	0.13	4.21	0.03
Severe	0.57	0.71	0.13	3.58	0.03

Here, *probability* is the chance of being annotated by all annotators which is important for obtaining the probability of chance agreement. *Error* is for the standard error of the calculated K which measures the overall precision of the estimation. The Z *value* represents an approximate normal testing statistic, and the P *value* is the probability of measuring evidence against the null hypothesis. Considering the obtained individual Kappa and P values, we can conclude that all individual class level inter-annotator reliability shows a substantial good agreement with statistical significance.

4.2 Depression Severity Confidence Value

The next analysis examines the performance of our models on *DSCV*. The model was evaluated using three performance measures: *Precision, Recall,* and the *F1 Score*. These measures were calculated using the following equations where *TP, FP, TN, FN* represent true positives, false positives, true negatives, and false negatives respectively. Additionally, the micro-average Precision, micro-average Recall and micro-average F1 score were also calculated from the confusion matrix shown in Table 5.

$$Precision = \frac{TP}{TP + FP} \tag{6}$$

$$Recall = \frac{TP}{TP + FN} \tag{7}$$

$$F1Score = 2 * \frac{Precision * Recall}{Precision + Recall} \tag{8}$$

Table 5. Confusion matrix.

	Annotated as depressed	Annotated as non-depressed
Are recognized as depressed	True Positives	False Negatives
Are recognized as non-depressed	False Positives	True Negatives

We used a one-versus-rest strategy where the positive class refers to one of the depression levels and the negative class refers to all the other levels. The set of evaluation metrics were calculated for each of the four cases where each depression level was considered as the positive class, and the average values of the metrics were used as the results.

Ten-fold cross validation was used to avoid overfitting and selection bias. The grid search optimization technique [35] was used to optimize the hyper-parameters. The warm-up proportion, learning rate, epoch rate, and batch size were set to 0.1, 0.005, 10, and 4 respectively. The obtained experimental results for *DSCV* are shown in Table 6. *P, R,* and *F1* stand for Precision, Recall, and F1 Score respectively.

The micro-averaged values of the above statistical experimental results were obtained since *micro-averaged Precision, micro-averaged Recall,* and *micro-averaged F1 Score*

Table 6. Class-wise experimental results for each fold of the cross-validation process.

		k=1	k=2	k=3	k=4	k=5	k=6	k=7	k=8	k=9	k=10
Minimal	P	0.692	0.693	0.693	0.696	0.698	0.703	0.712	0.718	0.722	0.724
	R	0.676	0.677	0.678	0.677	0.678	0.678	0.679	0.681	0.681	0.682
	F1	0.688	0.688	0.689	0.689	0.689	0.691	0.691	0.692	0.692	0.693
Mild	P	0.686	0.686	0.682	0.683	0.685	0.687	0.687	0.688	0.689	0.691
	R	0.627	0.627	0.628	0.628	0.628	0.629	0.629	0.63	0.631	0.632
	F1	0.643	0.643	0.645	0.646	0.647	0.647	0.648	0.649	0.649	0.651
Moderate	P	0.663	0.664	0.665	0.665	0.666	0.667	0.667	0.668	0.668	0.669
	R	0.602	0.603	0.604	0.604	0.605	0.605	0.605	0.606	0.607	0.607
	F1	0.576	0.577	0.577	0.578	0.579	0.579	0.581	0.582	0.582	0.583
Severe	P	0.716	0.716	0.717	0.717	0.718	0.719	0.719	0.72	0.721	0.722
	R	0.637	0.637	0.638	0.638	0.639	0.639	0.64	0.641	0.641	0.642
	F1	0.655	0.655	0.656	0.657	0.657	0.658	0.659	0.659	0.661	0.662

Table 7. Average results for DSCV generation.

Class	Precision	Recall	F1 Score
Minimal	0.71	0.68	0.69
Mild	0.69	0.63	0.65
Moderate	0.67	0.61	0.58
Severe	0.72	0.64	0.66
Micro Avg	0.68	0.65	0.66

have been considered as the optimal evaluation metrics for evaluating multi-class classification models [10]. The class-wise micro-averaged results shown in Table 7.

These experimental results were used for benchmarking purposes. Our results were compared with the results of the existing state-of-the-art baselines for text-based depression severity detection. These baselines have been introduced for addressing downstream tasks such as depression detection and self-harming detection using text-based corpora. These baselines were set up locally and we conducted several evaluation cycles using our novel aggregated corpus to satisfy the fundamental requirements of benchmarking. Regarding baselines, *DEPTWEET* [26] and *DepressionNet* [21] were used as depression classification machine learning models. *SVM + LBFs, RF + LBFs* and *MLP +*

LBFs were used as self-harming detection models. *LBFs* stands for language-based features such as term frequency-inverse document frequency (*TF-IDF*), parts of speech, etc. Such features were used as inputs to different machine learning classifiers such as support vector machines (*SVM*), random forest (*RF*), and multi-layer perceptron (*MLP*). The benchmarking results are shown in Table 8.

Table 8. Comparison to prior studies.

Model	Precision	Recall	F1 Score
DepressionNet	0.61	0.59	0.60
DEPTWEET	0.62	0.61	0.61
SVM + LBFs	0.51	0.56	0.52
RF + LBFs	0.59	0.54	0.56
MLP + LBFs	0.56	0.54	0.56
Ours - *HelaDepDet*	**0.68**	**0.65**	**0.66**

Considering the benchmarking results, we can conclude that our novel model performed better than existing baselines in *micro-average Precision, micro-average Recall,* and *micro-average F1 Score.* The benchmarking was conducted considering only publicly available baselines for depression detection tasks since some baselines are private and their implementation cannot be accessed.

To summarize the benchmarking results, the hand-crafted feature-centric models such as *SVM + LBFs, RF + LBFs,* and *MLP + LBFs* performed slightly worse than the linguistic feature-based models such as *DepressionNet, DEPTWEET,* and our novel model -- *HelaDepDet.* The linguistic feature-based models performed well due to their ability to capture and categorize mental health state efficiently. Considering *Depression-Net, DEPTWEET,* and our novel model *HelaDepDet, HelaDepDet* performed well at capturing the exact depression severity level considering the overall loss of multi-class classification which is relevant to how exactly the predicted depression severity level differs from the real depression severity level.

Additionally, measuring the accuracy of our *DSCV* model for training the aggregated corpus is necessary. Model accuracy is one of the most popular metrics in multi-class classification and it is directly generated using the confusion matrix [36]. The accuracy indicates an overall evaluation of the quality of the model's predictions considering the entire corpus. The evaluation metric for accuracy can be calculated as follows.

$$Accuracy = \frac{TP + TN}{TP + TN + FP + FN} \tag{9}$$

The accuracy values of the overall model training process are shown in Fig. 4.

We can conclude that the accuracy increased with the number of epoch cycles of the training process. The maximum accuracy obtained after 10 epoch cycles was 0.678.

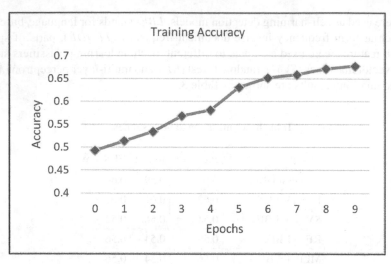

Fig. 4. Training accuracy

5 Discussion

Depression severity determination has been identified as essential for the well-being of human beings. With the impact of recent circumstances, the number of reported cases of human depression has increased at an alarming rate. Even though plenty of clinical depression detection practices are established, a significant number of depression-driven suicides are still reported worldwide. This reminds us of the high demand for an early identification depression detection tool. Since humans are social creatures, cases of human depression can be identified from recent behavioral changes more effectively than by traditional clinical depression detection [37]. In this study, we suggest a novel, multi-class classification approach to linguistic text-based depression severity detection, which can be used as an early depression detection screening tool based on social media analytics. Even though human depression can be analyzed using clinical, emotional, and linguistic techniques, we have concentrated on linguistic text-based depression severity detection in this study.

The initial contribution of our work is a novel aggregated dataset[1] for depression severity detection using BDI-3 [11] and the depression severity annotation scheme of Mowery, et al., [10] as the ground truth. Multiple depression severity annotated corpora were used for the novel dataset construction. Our aggregated corpus consists of more than 40,000 user posts and comments which were extracted from multiple social media networks including Twitter and Reddit. Four levels of clinical depression severity, *minimal, mild, moderate,* and *severe,* were used as labels to annotate the contents of the original datasets that we considered. Introducing this novel aggregated corpus helped to mitigate the existing issues with the available annotated corpora such as data sparsity and unbalanced data distribution among depression severity classes. Optimal undersampling techniques were used to balance data tuples. The depression severity annotations of the

---

[1] https://github.com/CyraxSector/Depression_Severity_Levels_Dataset.

original corpora were used as the annotations of the aggregated dataset so that combining them would not have any impact on the fundamentals of the corpus. Our novel corpus has been contributed back to the original authors and is stored in a public repository for research related purposes.

To address the two main research questions, *"How can the early identification of human depression be further enhanced?"* and *"How can the categorization of the severity of human depression be further improved?"*, we introduced a novel multi-class classification approach for human depression severity detection. Here, *early identification of human depression* can be identified as the most important result when using our novel model to classify text-based chat conversations for human behavioral analysis. On social media platforms there is a high tendency for users to express feelings and emotions without hiding anything and therefore analyzing that content could lead to the detection of abnormal behavior sooner than would analyzing the same cohort clinically at a later stage. We formulated depression severity as a confidence vector considering depression related words and/or phrases. To map the generated confidence vector to the corresponding BDI-3 score, several steps such as sentence classification, n-gram mapping, classification of n-grams, and layer normalization were used. The process as a whole can be recognized as a novel approach to multi-class depression severity classification and the research question, *"How can the early identification of human depression be further enhanced?"* can be considered answered. Our novel model was implemented[2] using *Python 3.8* as the main programming language.

Our model was evaluated using multiple experimental metrics. The main novelty, which is obtaining the depression severity confidence value *DSCV*, was evaluated according to *Precision, Recall, F1 score,* and *accuracy*. From the evaluation results, we conclude that our model outperformed the existing state-of-the-art models for depression severity detection as a multi-class classification task by a considerable margin. Considering our benchmark results we can say that the next research question, *"How can the categorization of the severity of human depression be further improved?"*, has also been addressed.

Regarding ethical concerns, since the annotated tuples of original corpora which were used for aggregation purposes were already published, an additional ethical approval is not needed. However, to avoid the risk of information leakage, all extracted social media posts were anonymized. The results of inter-annotator reliability re-evaluations will be made available in the near future with a corresponding non-disclosure agreement.

6   Limitations and Future Work

Considering the sustainability of corpora aggregation, several issues may occur such as biases due to multiple annotators and demographic or other social factors. Most of these issues have been mitigated by re-evaluating the inter-annotator reliability of the aggregated corpora following a constructive evaluation process. We are working on mitigating other issues and limitations as far as possible before this study is converted into a finished system. Although we conducted experiments on a large and well-balanced dataset,

---

[2] https://github.com/CyraxSector/HelaDepDet. The code will be released publicly in the near future for research purposes.

the experiments were limited to depression classification machine learning models and hand-crafted feature-centric models. In future, we hope to conduct further experiments on larger pre-trained language models for constructive benchmarking purposes. Additionally, this research is limited to a screening tool for depression severity detection that must not be used for clinical diagnosis purposes.

In future we will focus on analyzing multi-party conversations in social media and investigate how multi-party conversations can be used to determine the severity of human depression. Additionally, experiments with clinical and emotional based approaches in multi-model human depression detection would be valuable future work.

Acknowledgements. We thank the anonymous reviewers for their valuable comments and suggestions.

References

1. Hsu, C.W., Tseng, W.T., Wang, L.J., Yang, Y.H., Kao, H.Y., Lin, P.Y.: Comparative effectiveness of antidepressants on geriatric depression: real-world evidence from a population-based study. J. Affect Discord. **296**, 609–615, 1 January 2022. https://doi.org/10.1016/j.jad.2021.10.009. Epub 14 October 2021 PMID: 34655698 (2022)
2. Kaplan, C., Zhang, Y.: Assessing the comparative-effectiveness of antidepressants commonly prescribed for depression in the US Medicare population. J. Ment. Health Policy Econ. 171–178. PMID: 23525835; PMCID: PMC3608926 (2012)
3. Wang, D., Liu, L.: The depression of Chinese and the reflection related to their society and culture. Chin. General Pract. **7**(5), 315–317 (2004)
4. Zafar, A., Chitnis, S.: Survey of depression detection using social networking sites via data mining. In: 10th International Conference on Cloud Computing, Data Science and Engineering (Confluence), pp. 88–93 (2020)
5. Shen, G., et al.: Depression detection via Harvesting social media: a multimodal dictionary learning solution. In: International Joint Conference on Artificial Intelligence (2017)
6. Ríssola, E.A., Aliannejadi, M., Crestani, F.: Beyond modelling: understanding mental disorders in online social media. In: Jose, J., et al. Advances in Information Retrieval. ECIR 2020. Lecture Notes in Computer Science, vol. 12035. Springer, Cham (2020). https://doi.org/10.1007/978-3-030-45439-5_20
7. Li, H.Y., Cao, H., Leung, D.Y., Mak, Y.W.: The psychological impacts of a COVID-19 outbreak on college students in China: a longitudinal study. Int. J. Environ. Res. Public Health **17**(11), 3933 (2020)
8. Gruber, J., et al.: Mental health, and clinical psychological science in the time of COVID-19: challenges, opportunities, and a call to action. Am. Psychol. (2020). Advance online publication. https://doi.org/10.1037/amp0000707
9. Karhu, M., Suoheimo, M., Häkkilä, J.: People's perspectives on social media use during COVID-19 pandemic. In: 20th International Conference on Mobile and Ubiquitous Multimedia (MUM 2021). Association for Computing Machinery, New York, NY, USA, pp. 123–130 (2022)
10. Mowery, D.L., Bryan, C., Conway, M.: Towards developing an annotation scheme for depressive disorder symptoms: a preliminary study using twitter data. In: Proceedings of the 2nd Workshop on Computational Linguistics and Clinical Psychology: From Linguistic Signal to Clinical Reality, pp. 89–98 (2015)

11. Jackson-Koku, G.: Beck depression inventory. Occup. Med. **66**(2), 174–175 (2016)
12. Losada, D.E., Crestani, F.: A test collection for research on depression and language use. In: Fuhr, N., et al. (eds.) CLEF 2016. LNCS, vol. 9822, pp. 28–39. Springer, Cham (2016). https://doi.org/10.1007/978-3-319-44564-9_3
13. Losada, D.E., Crestani, F., Parapar, J.: eRISK 2017: CLEF lab on early risk prediction on the internet: experimental foundations. In: Jones, G.J.F., et al. (eds.) CLEF 2017. LNCS, vol. 10456, pp. 346–360. Springer, Cham (2017). https://doi.org/10.1007/978-3-319-65813-1_30
14. Shen, G., et al.: Depression detection via harvesting social media: a multimodal dictionary learning solution. In: International Joint Conference on Artificial Intelligence, pp. 3838–3844 (2017)
15. Burdisso, S., Errecalde, M.L., Montes y Gómez, M.: To-wards measuring the severity of depression in social media via text classification. In: XXV Congreso Argentino de Ciencias de la Computación (CACIC) (Universidad Nacional de Río Cuarto, Cór-doba (2019)
16. Skaik, R., Inkpen, D.: Using social media for mental health surveillance: a review. ACM Comput. Surv. (CSUR) **53**(6), 1–31 (2020)
17. Suhara, Y., Xu, Y., Pentland, A.S.: DeepMood: forecasting depressed mood based on self-reported histories via recurrent neural networks. In: Proceedings of the 26th International Conference on World Wide Web, pp. 715–724 (2017)
18. Orabi, A.H., Buddhitha, P., Orabi, M.H., Inkpen, D.: Deep learning for depression detection of twitter users. In: Proceedings of the Fifth Workshop on Computational Linguistics and Clinical Psychology: From Keyboard to Clinic, pp. 88–97 (2018)
19. Abed-Esfahani, P., et al.: Transfer learning for depression: early detection and severity prediction from social media postings. CLEF (working notes) **1**, 1–6 (2019)
20. Burdisso, S.G., Errecalde, M.L., Montes y Gómez, M.: Using text classification to estimate the depression level of Reddit users. J. Comput. Sci. Technol. (2021)
21. Zogan, H., Razzak, I., Jameel, S., Xu, G.: DepressionNet: a novel summarization boosted deep framework for depression detection on social media. arXiv preprint arXiv:2105.10878 (2021)
22. Rao, G., Peng, C., Zhang, L., Wang, X., Feng, Z.: A knowledge enhanced ensemble learning model for mental disorder detection on social media. In: Li, G., Shen, H.T., Yuan, Y., Wang, X., Liu, H., Zhao, X. (eds.) KSEM 2020. LNCS (LNAI), vol. 12275, pp. 181–192. Springer, Cham (2020). https://doi.org/10.1007/978-3-030-55393-7_17
23. Wu, S.H., Qiu, Z.J.: A RoBERTa-based model on measuring the severity of the signs of depression. In: CLEF (Working Notes), pp. 1071–1080 (2021)
24. Ríssola, E.A., Losada, D.E., Crestani, F.: A survey of computational methods for online mental state assessment on social media. ACM Trans. Comput. Healthcare **2**(2) (2021)
25. Naseem, U., Dunn, A.G., Kim, J., Khushi, M.: Early identification of depression severity levels on Reddit using ordinal classification. In: Proceedings of the ACM Web Conference, pp. 2563–2572 (2022)
26. Kabir, M., et al.: DEPTWEET: a typology for social media texts to detect depression severities. Comput. Hum. Behav. **139**, 107503 (2023)
27. Yang, Z., Gao, D.: An active under sampling approach for imbalanced data classification. In: 2012 Fifth International Symposium on Computational Intelligence and Design, vol. 2, pp. 270 273. IEEE (2012)
28. Priyadarshana, Y.P., Ranathunga, L., Amalraj, C.R.J., Perera, I.: HelaNER: a novel approach for nested named entity boundary detection. In: IEEE EUROCON 2021-19th International Conference on Smart Technologies, pp. 119–124. IEEE (2021)
29. Gu, J.C., Tao, C., Ling, Z.H.: WHO Says WHAT to WHOM: a survey of multi-party con-versations. In: Proceedings of the Thirty-First International Joint Conference on Artificial Intelligence, IJCAI, pp. 5486–5493 (2022)

30. Chen, S., Wang, J., Jiang, F., Lin, C.Y.: Improving entity linking by modeling latent entity type information. In: Proceedings of the AAAI Conference on Artificial Intelligence, vol. 34, No. 05, pp. 7529–7537 (2020)
31. Zhu, Q., He, Z., Zhang, T., Cui, W.: Improving classification performance of softmax loss function based on scalable batch-normalization. Appl. Sci. 10(8), 2950 (2020)
32. Gordon-Rodriguez, E., Loaiza-Ganem, G., Pleiss, G., Cunningham, J.P.: Uses and abuses of the cross-entropy loss: case studies in modern deep learning (2020)
33. Sim, J., Wright, C.C.: The Kappa Statistic in Reliability Studies: Use, Interpretation, and Sample Size Requirements. Phys. Ther. 85(3), 257–268 (2005)
34. Chen, B., Zaebst, D., Seel, L.: A macro to calculate kappa statistics for categorizations by multiple raters. In: Proceeding of the 30th Annual SAS Users Group International Conference, pp. 155–130 (2005)
35. Pontes, F.J., Amorim, G.F., Balestrassi, P.P., Paiva, A.P., Ferreira, J.R.: Design of experiments and focused grid search for neural network parameter optimization. Neurocomputing 186, 22–34 (2016)
36. Grandini, M., Bagli, E., Visani, G.: Metrics for multi-class classification: an overview. arXiv preprint arXiv:2008.05756 (2020)
37. Guntuku, S.C., Yaden, D.B., Kern, M.L., Ungar, L.H., Eichstaedt, J.C.: Detecting depression and mental illness on social media: an integrative review. Curr. Opin. Behav. Sci. 18, 43–49 (2017)

Analyzing Peer Influence in Ethical Judgment: Collaborative Ranking in a Case-Based Scenario

Claudio Álvarez[1,2]([✉]) [iD], Gustavo Zurita[3] [iD], and Andrés Carvallo[4] [iD]

[1] Facultad de Ingeniería y Ciencias Aplicadas, Universidad de los Andes, Santiago, Chile
calvarez@uandes.cl
[2] Centro de Investigación en Educación y Aprendizaje, Universidad de los Andes, Santiago, Chile
[3] Facultad de Economía y Negocios, Universidad de Chile, Santiago, Chile
gzurita@fen.uchile.cl
[4] National Center for Artificial Intelligence, Santiago, Chile

Abstract. Peer influence is how an individual's beliefs, actions, and choices can be influenced by the opinions and behaviors of their peers. Peer influence can affect the moral behavior of individuals. In this study, we analyze peer influence in the context of case-based learning activity in ethics education. To conduct this type of activity, we introduce EthicRankings, a groupware environment that enables students to analyze an ethical case and reason about it by ranking the actors involved according to some ethical criteria. A study with a sample of 64 engineering students was conducted at a Latin American university to analyze peer influence from a dual standpoint in an activity comprising an individual response phase followed by a collaborative phase with anonymous chat interaction. Firstly, we determine how likely a student is to change their rankings in the collaborative phase when observing their peers' rankings and interacting with them anonymously. Secondly, we compare positive, neutral, and negative sentiment variations in students' written justifications for rankings before and after collaborating. Results show that students are highly likely to change their responses in the collaborative phase if their responses differ significantly from their peers' in the individual phase. Also, sentiments in written ranking justifications vary in ways consistent with changes in ranking. The pedagogical implications of these findings are discussed.

Keywords: Peer Influence · Ethical Judgment · Case-Based Learning · Groupware

1 Introduction

Peer influence is the concept of how an individual's beliefs, actions, and choices can be influenced by the opinions and behaviors of their peers. According to [1], peer influence can affect moral behavior. In collaborative learning environments, peer influence can have benefits such as exposure to diverse perspectives, encouragement of critical thinking and debate, and validation and support for one's ideas and contributions. However, there are also potential drawbacks, such as conformity, where students may feel compelled to

H. Takada et al. (Eds.): CollabTech 2023, LNCS 14199, pp. 19–35, 2023.
https://doi.org/10.1007/978-3-031-42141-9_2

adopt their peers' opinions or decisions even if they disagree, as well as domination by stronger voices and deviation from educational objectives.

In this study, we analyze peer influence in the context of a case-based learning activity in ethics education. To conduct this type of activity, we introduce EthicRankings, a groupware environment that enables students to analyze an ethical dilemma or conflict and reason about it by ranking the actors involved in the situation according to some ethical criteria. An EthicsRanking activity was conducted with a cohort of engineering students (N = 63). The activity consists of an individual work phase followed by a collaborative one. In the former, the learner ranks a set of actors according to a given question and justifies the assigned rankings using short written responses. In the collaborative phase, learners interact anonymously via chat to discuss and revise their answers, with the answers of their peers from the previous phase presented to them.

To analyze the students' responses and changes in them considering possible peer influence in the collaborative phase of the activity, specific metrics are considered, including the difference in ranking steps for a given case actor between a student and their group peers, the difference between a student's responses in successive phases, and the difference between successive phases of variables associated with the automated analysis of sentiment expressed in students' justifications for rankings (i.e., positive, negative, or neutral).

Two research questions drive the current study regarding peer influence phenomena: (1) Will the EthicRankings activity promote social influence among students in the collaborative phase after they have seen their peers' responses in the individual phase and interacted anonymously with them? (2) Are there statistically significant differences in the sentiment of students' responses in the individual and collaborative phases of the activity? Are these differences consistent with variations in character rankings?

The following sections present theoretical background, research hypotheses, materials and methods, results, a discussion of these results, and conclusions and future work.

2 Theoretical Background

2.1 Ethics Education and Case-Based Learning

Ethics is the study of moral judgment and conduct, providing a systematic approach to distinguish between good and bad, and admirable or deplorable behavior. As unethical conduct has become more common in the workplace and academia, accreditation institutions have required ethics education to be included in higher education curricula. However, teaching ethics is challenging due to students' and teachers' differences in perception about the subject and limited student participation that is possible in traditional classroom settings and courses. Practical courses in ethics education are needed in various fields, such as business, social sciences, engineering, and medicine. Common methods involve using codes, case studies, and discussions, but learning experiences that involve actors and situations are necessary for ethical reasoning skill development, [1].

Case-Based Learning (CBL) is a methodology that utilizes real or hypothetical cases to promote problem-solving and decision-making. By presenting students with simulated or actual situations and encouraging them to analyze, discuss, and apply prior knowledge, CBL aims to equip students with practical skills and knowledge for real-life scenarios, [2, 3]. CBL also supports social constructivism and active learning by stimulating critical thinking and problem-solving. Empirical studies have shown that CBL is effective in various fields, including ethics, [4–6].

CBL can also be carried out by means of technology-enhanced environments [7–10]. Sharipova [11] reviewed several of such approaches. Some systems, like Ethos [12] and PETE [13], focus on supporting students' case analysis process by providing a structure or scaffolding system for ethical decision-making. Similarly, the Agora system [14] permits customizing the structure of ethical analysis, allowing for greater flexibility. Belvedere and LARGO [15] are systems aiming to improve students' argumentative skills by having them diagram their arguments and provide feedback based on argument structure. Serious games like Conundrum [16] aim to provide students with realistic experiences and a deeper understanding of ethical issues. Adaptive systems, such as AEINS [17] personalize the ethical learning experience by adjusting the storyline of a case based on the student's existing skills.

Research has shown that collaborative learning environments can facilitate the construction of shared knowledge and meanings, as well as enhance the development of argumentation skills in the context of ethics education [18, 19]. Goldin et al. [20] proposed a system to assist in framing a case by aiding students in identifying and defining ethical issues within a case study, with peer reviewing and a proposed "Reviewer Aide" functionality enhancing the process. Tools like AGORA-net [21] have utilized CSCL scripts to engage students in ethical case analysis through interactive, computer-mediated discussions. The Value Exchange software [22] and the system proposed by Goldin et al. [13] further highlights the importance of collaboration, demonstrating benefits when learners view each other's ideas or engage in peer-reviewing activities. EthicApp is a CSCL script platform developed by the present authors' [23], which is based on many of these principles, promoting discussion and reflection through a user-friendly interface, anonymous interactions, and real-time chat discussions. Despite these promising tools, research into CSCL-supported CBL in ethics education remains limited and calls for further exploration to optimize design and implementation strategies for more effective teaching and learning processes.

2.2 Peer Influence in Ethical Decision Making

Peer influence refers to how an individual's attitudes, behaviors, and decisions can be affected by the opinions and actions of their peers [1]. According to [1], moral behavior is susceptible to peer influence. They arrived at this conclusion by investigating how peer information affects moral preferences and decision-making, through two studies: in the first one, participants accurately inferred the goals of prosocial and antisocial peers by observing their ethical decisions. In the second study, participants made moral decisions before and after observing the decisions of a prosocial or antisocial peer, which led to participants' preferences becoming more like those of their peers. The researchers demonstrated that peer influence changes the value of moral behavior, prioritizing choice attributes that align with peers' goals. Additionally, they found that participants were

more aware of prosocial influence than antisocial influence. These findings have implications for strengthening and blocking the effects of prosocial and antisocial influence
on moral behavior. Peer influence can positively and negatively affect students' learning
and decision-making. Some notable positive effects are the following:

- Exposure to different perspectives: Peer influence can enrich the discussion by expos-
  ing students to different opinions and approaches to ethical cases. This can help students develop a broader and more nuanced understanding of the problem and learn
  from the experiences and knowledge of their peers.
- Encouragement of critical thinking and debate: Interaction and exchange of ideas
  among students can stimulate critical thinking and encourage constructive debates.
  This can improve the quality of decision-making and help students understand and
  articulate their viewpoints.
- Validation and support: Peer influence can validate and support students, especially
  if they struggle with a difficult ethical concept or decision. Peer support can increase
  students' confidence in their abilities and motivate them to participate more actively
  in the activity.

Possible negative effects are the following:

- Conformity and suppression of opinions: Peer influence can also lead to conformity,
  where students may feel pressured to adopt their peers' opinions or decisions even if
  they don't agree. This can suppress the diversity of opinions and limit the quality of
  debate and decision-making.
- Domination of stronger voices: In some cases, students with stronger opinions or
  more dominant personalities can exert disproportionate influence in the group, which
  could silence more reserved students or those with less popular opinions.
- Deviation from educational objective: Peer influence can divert students from the
  main aim of the activity, especially if the discussion focuses on unrelated issues or
  if students feel pressured to make decisions based on popularity rather than a solid
  ethical evaluation.

2.3   Use of Rankings in Group Decision Making

According to [2], effective communication within a group is essential for decision-
making. In the context of communication within a group, both verbal and nonverbal
communication are important and can affect members' perceptions and the overall group
dynamic. In turn, group discussions may disproportionately reflect information known
to all group members at the expense of information known only to one group member.
This can lead to suboptimal group decisions.

The way group discussion is conducted, and the communication technology used
can affect the quality of decisions made by the group [2]. Groups that use face-to-face
communication may have better decision quality than computer-mediated groups. This
may be because face-to-face communication allows for greater expression of nonverbal
communication, facilitating greater understanding and consideration of all presented
viewpoints. Similarly, access to information during group discussions can also affect the
quality of group decision-making. The study found that access to information during

group discussion increased discussion of unique and common information under face-to-face conditions but did not affect the quality of group decisions. This suggests that while access to information can improve discussion, it does not necessarily guarantee better decision-making. Procedural aspects of group discussion, such as instructing groups to rank alternatives instead of choosing the best alternative, can help overcome the impact of pre-discussion preferences on information processes and group decisions.

2.4 Sentiment Analysis

Natural language processing (NLP) has emerged as a powerful tool for analyzing human language and automating various tasks such as sentiment analysis [24], named entity recognition [25], and question answering [26].

Sentiment analysis, also known as opinion mining, is a natural language processing (NLP) technique used to determine the sentiment expressed in a text, whether positive, negative, or neutral [27]. It uses computational algorithms to extract and analyze subjective information from large volumes of text data, such as social media posts, customer reviews, news articles, and more [28]. The importance of sentiment analysis lies in its ability to provide insights into how people feel about a particular topic. Sentiment analysis is a rapidly developing field, with advances in machine learning and natural language processing enabling more accurate and efficient sentiment analysis models.

Most research in this area has focused on the English language and social media platforms [29], with limited attention given to other languages like Spanish. Fortunately, recent developments in NLP have led to the creation of state-of-the-art pre-trained language models, such as BETO [30] and DistillBETO [31], specifically for the Spanish language. In this study, the approach proposed by Perez et al. [32] is preferred, which leverages the advanced pre-trained language model, BETO, to perform sentiment analysis on Spanish text data. This approach has demonstrated superior performance over other state-of-the-art models in several benchmark datasets [32, 33], making it a reliable and effective option for analyzing the sentiment of student comments during collaborative activities.

To the present authors' best knowledge, sentiment analysis has not been previously reported in the literature for analyzing students' justifications in a case-based scenario in ethics education, which is the context in which sentiment analysis is applied in this research.

3 Collaborative Ranking Activity

This article presents EthicRankings, an activity based on the pre-existing groupware platform [23]. With EthicRankings, students can analyze an ethical case in several successive phases (Fig. 1). The student is presented with an ethical case, usually based on an ethical dilemma or an ethical conflict situation involving two or more characters. Then, the student is prompted with a question, in which they are asked to rank the actors according to a certain criterion, e.g., "rank the actors based on who behaved most justly. Place the most just actor at the top of the ranking." The following phases can be individual or collaborative, maintaining the question, or changing it, also with the possibility of modifying the actors that the student must rank. The following parameters are available to the teacher to define phases of an activity with EthicRankings:

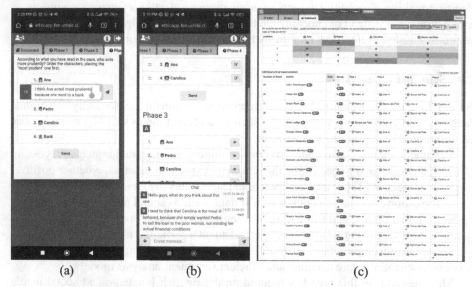

(a)   (b)   (c)

Fig. 1. (a) Students' interface in the individual phase. (b) Students' interface in the group phase, with chat, and showing previous students' responses. (c) Teacher's dashboard.

- Question and actor list: In any phase of the activity, the teacher enters a question that the students must analyze in relation to the case, along with a list of actors. The teacher can define whether students are required to provide justification in certain ranking positions (e.g. justify the first and second place in the ranking), or whether the justification should be linked to an actor (e.g. justify John's rank, regardless of the assigned ranking). In addition, the teacher can define a minimum number of words for each justification.
- Individual or group interaction: In the case of group interaction, groups of any size can be defined. Groups of three are commonly preferred.
- Anonymous or identified interaction: Anonymous communication allows students to discuss and debate their decisions without fear of being judged or singled out. This fosters openness and the exchange of ideas, leading to a better understanding of ethical issues and more informed decision-making. It is also possible for students to interact by revealing their identities.
- Including students' responses from a previous phase: The teacher can allow students in a group to see their classmates' responses from one or more previous phases.
- Interaction through text-based chat: Students can communicate through text chat in group phases, like those found in instant messaging applications such as Telegram and WhatsApp. They can quote messages from others when responding and use emojis.

- Group composition: It is possible to form groups using different algorithms, including random, heterogeneous, and homogeneous grouping. The latter two are based on the difference or similarity of students' responses to form the groups. Groups can be maintained or recomposed between successive phases.

While students perform a phase of the activity, the teacher has a dashboard, in which they can configure the next phase according to the options listed above and review the students' and groups' responses. The teacher can also see the interaction that group peers have through chat. The dashboard at the top contains a matrix updated in real-time, through which the teacher can observe the rankings that the students have given to the actors, and the frequencies of those rankings. Below the matrix, the list of students' responses appears, ordered by groups of student responses where the actors are ranked in the same order.

To explore the effects of peer influence on students' responses, in this study, we incorporated a three-phase instructional design with EthicRankings: the first phase is individual, the second is collaborative with anonymous interaction via chat, and the third is a debriefing exercise involving the entire class, guided by the teacher.

In phase 1, each student reflects on the case and their beliefs, values, and prior knowledge to make a personal, informed decision. Working individually helps students identify their strengths and weaknesses in ethical decision-making.

In phase 2, students collaborate in groups to reconsider alternatives and anonymously share responses from phase 1. This allows for exposure to different perspectives, discussion and reasoning, thus can lead to interpersonal skill development, reinforcement of learning, broadening of perspectives, practical application of knowledge and judgment, and ultimately, active and meaningful learning.

With the results of the first two phases of the activity, this study aims to determine how likely students are to change their responses in the second collaborative phase, provided that they see the responses their peers gave in the first individual phase. Additionally, we are interested in knowing if there are statistically significant variations in students' sentiment in ranking justifications before and after the collaborative phase.

4 Hypotheses

The following hypotheses are defined since in the collaborative phase (i.e., phase 2) of the instructional design under study, groups are formed, and each student can see what their peers answered in the individual phase (i.e., phase 1) before re-elaborating their response:

- H_1: The greater the difference that the student has with their peers in ranking an actor in phase 1, the greater the probability that the student changes ranking of such an actor in phase 2.
- H_2: The sentiment in the students' responses in phase 2 will differ from that in phase 1, per each case actor.

Considering the above hypotheses, the probability of a change in response observed according to H_1 can be understood as a proxy for the outcome of the social influence that a student receives from their peers, both passively, that is, by reading peer responses in phase 1, and actively, through anonymous chat discussion. In addition, about H_2, variation of sentiment is a means for capturing differences in students' justification for their ranking decisions.

5 Method and Materials

5.1 Educational Context and Sample Description

The present study was conducted in the Professional Ethics Seminar course for fifth-year engineering students at a Universidad de los Andes, Chile. The course includes students from five engineering majors, including Computer Science, Electrical, Environmental, and Civil Engineering. A cohort of 64 students participated in the EthicRankings activity, of which 16 were female and 48 were male, mostly aged between 22 and 24. Student participation was voluntary and rewarded with bonus points in a reading quiz that accounted for 20% of the final grade for the course.

5.2 Ethical Case

The case used in this study was obtained from a compendium of ethics cases developed by numerous academics and students in a Latin American business school. The case involves two protagonists: Pedro, a recent graduate of business school, who works as an executive at a bank, and Ana, a person with no higher education who is a young mother of a girl suffering from a high-cost disease. With little knowledge of finance, Ana turns to Pedro at the bank to request a loan to cover the medical expenses for her daughter's illness. Ana does not have the profile of a solvent person, as although she has a stable job, her income could be higher. The bank has designed an incentive policy to reward executives who achieve loan approvals at higher rates and those who manage to grant a certain number of loans per month. Pedro feels conflicted because, on the one hand, Ana barely meets the requirements to obtain the loan and needs the money for something important; on the other hand, likely, Ana will not be able to repay her debt well and end up refinancing it, increasing the payment for accumulated interest. Therefore, Pedro turns to his boss Carolina to decide what to do. His boss suggests that he should grant the loan because Ana meets the requirements, and if the loan is not granted, she could eventually get it from another bank, and Pedro would lose the benefits of acquiring a new client.

Finally, tempted by the monetary benefits he could receive and motivated by Ana's extreme need, Pedro decides to grant her the loan. As a risky client, the interest rate to which she will be subject will be higher. Pedro prefers to offer her a long-term loan, that is, with attractive low-value installments, but ensuring that the bank obtains profits from the accumulation of interests. Thanks to the loan, Ana can pay for her child's surgeries and treatments, however, her solvency and liquidity worsen day by day.

5.3 Variables

Independent Variables. Hypothesis H_1 requires calculating the differences between each student's and classmates' rankings in phase 1. To measure these differences, we start by considering that in phases 1 and 2 of the activity, each student orders the actors in the case [A]na, [P]edro, [C]arolina, and [B]ank, according to the criterion of the presented question. Then, for each phase i and each student j, we consider $rank_{ijk}$ as the ranking position in phase i, in which student j ranks actor k (i.e., k in $\{A,P,C,B\}$). For example, $rank_{11A}$ is the integer value in the range 1–4 corresponding to the position in which student 1 ranks actor Ana in phase 1. To calculate the differences, for each student j, their groupmates v and w (i.e., considering groups of three students), and actor k in the case, we define $rank\_diff_{jk} = |rank_{1jk} - rank_{1vk}| + |rank_{1jk} - rank_{1wk}|$, that is, as the sum of the ranking differences between a student and their groupmates, for a particular actor in the case.

Dependent Variables. To validate hypothesis H_1, it is necessary to operationalize the variation of an actor's ranking by a student between phases 1 and 2. For this, we formally define, for each student j and actor k, the dependent variable $rank\_delta_{jk} = |rank_{1jk} - rank_{2jk}|$. In addition, we define $rank\_changed_{jk}$ as a binary variable that takes a value of 1 if $rank\_delta_{jk}$ is greater than zero and 0 otherwise. Finally, to validate H_2, it is necessary to contrast differences in variables associated with the sentiments in the students' justifications to rank each actor in each phase. For this, we consider variables pos_{ijk}, neu_{ijk}, and neg_{ijk} related to positive, neutral, and negative sentiments, respectively, in the written justification in phase i by student j for actor k. All these variables are continuous in the interval $[0,1]$.

5.4 Procedure

In a class in the last week of the Professional Ethics Seminar course, the ranking activity with EthicRankings previously described, was carried out in 50 min. Student participation was online, through EthicRankings, and in a Zoom session. In the first phase, the task was individual and was based on the following question: "*According to the case, who acts in the most prudent way? Rank the characters, putting the most prudent one in first place.*" Each student had to rank actors Ana, Pedro, Carolina, and the Bank. In addition, for each character, the student had to justify the assigned ranking with a brief comment. The time allotted for this phase was 15 min.

The second phase was collaborative, with a duration of 20 min. For this, groups of three students were formed using heterogeneous groups based on phase 1 responses. The task presented to the students was the same as in the previous phase. However, each student could see their classmates' responses of the prior phase, and group members were allowed to interact via anonymous chat. Each student was free to maintain their responses given in the previous phase or to change their answer, rearranging the characters and re-elaborating the justifications to give each character a determined ranking. After the collaborative phase of the activity, the teacher led a 15-min debriefing exercise which included a whole-class discussion of several students' responses submitted in the previous phases of the activity.

5.5 Analyses

All analyses in this study are computed in an environment based on R 4.2.3. The following analyses are performed to validate hypotheses H_1 and H_2:

Actor Rankings. The Shapiro-Wilk normality test is computed with $rank\_diff_k$ and $rank\_delta_k$ variables, considering all students' responses per each actor k. Then, correlation, that is, parametric or non-parametric depending on fulfillment of normality assumption, is computed among $rank\_diff_k$ and $rank\_delta_k$ variables, in order to determine whether a relationship exists among these variables as expected considering hypothesis H_1. Furthermore, to validate hypothesis H_1, a logistic regression model is developed using a Bayesian approach [34], with $rank\_changed$ as predicted variable, and $rank\_diff$ as predictor variable. In addition, the Bayesian approach is based on non-informative (uniform) prior distributions for model parameters, as the present authors have no prior knowledge about students' behavior in the analyzed context. However, a Bayesian approach is preferred to estimate model parameters, due to the limited sample size available, especially regarding observation of highest values of $rank\_diff_k$, which turn out to be infrequent. The model is computed with data of all case actors, that is, without stratifying data per each actor. In this way, the model is expected to provide a general indication on the probability of students changing their responses concerning the differences they hold with their peers. The runjags package in R, and JAGS ("Just Another Gibbs Sampler") [35] are used to estimate model parameters with Markov Chain Monte Carlo (MCMC) simulation, with 10.000 iterations. With the mode of estimated logistic regression parameters, the logistic function in R's psych package is used to compute probability of $rank\_changed = 1$, for all possible values of $rank\_diff$, that is, considering all students' responses and case actors.

Sentiment Variables. In this study, we employed a Spanish sentiment classification model proposed by Perez et al. [32] to analyze text and discern whether it conveyed a neutral, negative, or positive sentiment. Continuous variables in the [0,1] range, namely neu, neg and pos are operationalized for this intent. Shapiro-Wilk test for normality is conducted with these variables, considering all students' written justifications in the two phases of the EthicRankings activity. Next, correlation analyses are conducted. Lastly, Wilcoxon or Student's t tests are conducted to detect significant differences among sentiment variables in phases 1 and 2 of the EthicRankings activity, thus validating H_2.

Position / Actor	🐱 Ana	🐧 Pedro	🏦 Bank	🏛 Carolina
1	12	45	6	0
2	24	15	18	6
3	18	2	23	20
4	9	1	16	37

Position / Actor	🐱 Ana	🐧 Pedro	🏦 Bank	🏛 Carolina
1	12	48	3	0
2	31	15	12	5
3	16	0	32	15
4	4	0	16	43

Fig. 2. Frequency of students' rankings of case actors in phase 1 (left), and phase 2 (right).

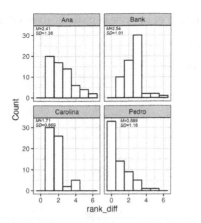 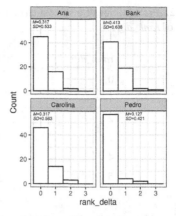

Fig. 3. Histograms for *rank_diff_k* and *rank_delta_k*, based on all students' responses.

6 Results

6.1 Student Participation

Sixty-three students participated in the activity, that is, almost all the students available in the course (64). Twenty-one groups were formed in the second phase of the activity.

6.2 Actor Rankings

In Fig. 2, the ranking decisions of the students are illustrated in relation to the four actors of the ethical case. Pedro is consistently ranked first as the actor who is best rated according to the question of who acts most prudently. In second place, Ana is considered, followed by the Bank, and lastly, Carolina. It can be appreciated that the trends in phase 1 are reinforced in phase 2. That is to say, the preferences for Pedro and Ana in the top positions increase, while the preferences for the Bank and Carolina have a downward result.

Shapiro-Wilk normality tests for both *rank_diff_k* and *rank_delta_k*, that is, considering all students' responses and each case actor k, all resulted in significant p-values at the 0.001 level, thus the data is highly non-normal, as it can also be seen in Fig. 3.

Table 1. Spearman rank correlation among *rank_diff_k* and *rank_delta_k* variables. All coefficients are significant at the 0.01 level.

Actor (k)	ρ	p-value
Ana	0.331	*0.007*
Pedro	0.451	*0.000*
Carolina	0.274	*0.03*
Bank	0.357	*0.004*

Table 2. Probabilities of a student changing the ranking of an actor in phase 2, given different values of *rank_diff*.

rank_diff	P(rank_change = 1)
0	0.214
1	0.353
2	0.521
3	0.685
4	0.813
5	0.897
6	0.945

Table 3. *p*-values of Wilcoxon tests for mean rank differences in sentiment. Variables for case actors, and Cliff's delta effect sizes for significant *p*-values.

Actor	neg *p*-value	neg Cliff's δ	neu *p*-value	neu Cliff's δ	pos *p*-value	pos Cliff's δ	n
Ana	0.005	-0.143	0.003	0.243	0.053	0.178	63
Carolina	n.s	-	n.s	-	n.s		63
Pedro	0.007	-0.126	n.s	-	n.s		63
Bank	n.s	-	0.028	0.172	n.s		63

Table 1 shows Spearman correlation among $rank\_diff_k$ and $rank\_delta_k$. A positive correlation is observed among them, per actor, and highly significant for each case actor k.

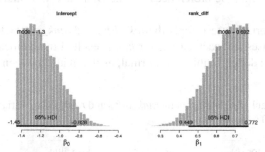

Fig. 4. Posterior distributions for logistic regression model parameters. Mode for $\beta_0 = -1.3$, and mode for $\beta_1 = 0.692$.

The posterior distributions of the parameters of the Bayesian regression model can be seen in Fig. 4. With these parameters and the logistic function in R, the probabilities of a student changing the ranking of an actor have been computed, considering the different values of *rank_diff* (see Table 2).

The probabilities in Table 2 indicate that the probability of a student changing the ranking of an actor is relatively high when they have no differences with their peers (in phase 1) regarding that specific actor. Note that for *rank_diff* $= 0$, the probability percentage of a student changing their response in phase 2 is of 21.4%. This is because an actor's ranking can change when the rankings of other actors are modified. For example, if the actor who was ranked last in phase 1 moves to the first place in phase 2, then all other actors change their ranking. For this reason, the larger the difference a student has with their peers in phase 1, the probability of the student changing their ranking in phase 2 grows rapidly. According to Fig. 3 (left), the average value of *rank_diff* varies for the different actors in the case, between 0.9 and 2.5, approximately, so in these average cases, the probability of a student changing an actor's ranking varies between 30 and 60%, which is considerable. However, ranking changes are generally small, as shown in *rank_delta* histograms in Fig. 3 (right).

6.3 Sentiment Analysis

The distributions of the sentiment variables in the written responses of the students, considering all their responses, are presented in Fig. 5 (left). It can be observed that the variables *neu* ($M = 0.442$, $SD = 0.291$, Median $= 0.47$) and *neg* ($M = 0.423$, $SD = 0.36$, Median $= 0.321$) tend to be more uniform in the interval $[0,1]$, compared to the variable *pos* ($M = 0.133$, $SD = 0.206$, Median $= 0.05$), which concentrates its observations in a small range up to the third quartile ($q3 = 0.137$). Figure 5 (right) shows a correlogram with the sentiment variables, where the correlations are significant at the 99% level. Consistently, the *neg* and *pos* variables have a high negative correlation. The *neu* variable, on the other hand, has correlations with both variables, positive in the case of *pos* and negative in the case of *neg*.

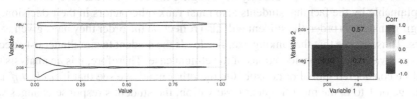

Fig. 5. Violin plots for neu, neg and pos variables (left). Correlogram for these variables based on Spearman rank correlation (right), significant at the 0.01 level.

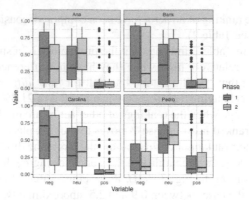

Fig. 6. Variations of sentiment variables in phases 1 and 2, per actor.

7   Discussion

According to the results obtained, for cases where the ranking difference between a student and their peers in phase 1 is higher, i.e., higher values of *rank_diff*, it becomes very likely that the response in phase 2 will change, however, there are differences among the case actors. For example, with respect to Pedro, we saw that the number of students who change their response is minority, even though the correlation between *rank_diff* and *rank_delta* is 0.45. This means that the students who change their response could potentially be influenced by the distance that their phase 1 response has from their peers' responses. In the case of the Bank, the mode of $rank\_diff_B$ is 3, which corresponds to 30 students, and it is observed that about 20 students, practically 2/3 of them, change the ranking of this actor by one position. This is consistent with the probability of 0.68 in Table 3, for the case where *rank_diff* is 3.

The estimated parameters for the logistic regression model indicate that if *rank_diff* is 0, there is around a 20% probability of changing the actor's order (see Table 3). This is explainable by the fact that students also must rank other actors in their decision. By changing an actor's order, the student will also reflect on the order they have given to the others. Thus, we see that the ranking exercise leads the student to simultaneously decide on several variables or considerations of the ethical case. Therefore, it is an analysis that could be considered global or holistic. On the other hand, we see that if *rank_diff* is in the range of 1 to 2, the most frequent observation, the student's response changes with a probability in the range of 30 to 50%, which shows that differences with peers can indeed be considered a "social influence" on what the student finally responds.

Regarding the sentiment analysis (Fig. 6), we see that in the case of Ana, the case's main character, rankings in the last positions decreased, and consistently, negativity in the students' justifications decreased, while positivity increased. In the case of the Bank, the students tended to lower it in the ranking, but the neutrality of the justifications for this actor increased. In Pedro's case, response changes were infrequent, so it was expected that there would be no change in sentiment, and this finally happened. Lastly, Carolina was the worst-rated actor by students in both phases. In the second phase, her rankings worsened even more. There was no significant change in sentiment, meaning that the tendencies in phase 1, where negativity was high (the distribution median was around 0.75/1.00), remained, which is consistent with her being the worst-rated character in both phases.

The analyses carried out in this study should be taken with caution since, on the one hand, the sample size is small, which affects the reliability of Bayesian model parameter estimations for values of variables *rank_diff* and *rank_delta* for cases observed less frequently. On the other hand, about the sentiment analysis, there was no control in the activity regarding the minimum and maximum word length of comments. This means that long responses can have higher positive or negative sentiment than short ones.

Notwithstanding the above, we see that both hypotheses have been validated, since in relation to H_1, it is effective that the rank that a student assigns to an actor in phase 2 of the activity varies compared to phase 1 when the differences that the student has with their peers in the rank of that actor in phase 1 are greater. On the other hand, the sentiment in the students' responses in phase 2 varies significantly depending on the actor in question.

8 Conclusions and Future Work

In this study, we implemented an environment for the analysis and discussion of ethical cases, where students were required to rank case actors according to a specific criterion in two phases: an initial individual phase and a subsequent collaborative phase. In the collaborative phase the students were shown the responses of their peers from the individual phase and were allowed to chat anonymously.

The results indicate that social influence leads students to modify their decisions when deliberating on an ethical case. The greater the differences between students and their peers, the more likely it is that students will change their responses. In general, in the observed case where students had to rank four actors, if there was a change in the ranking of an actor, it was limited to one or at most two positions. When ranking difference among a student and their peers was 2 or 3, the probability of changing was approximately 40%. We observed that justifications with negative sentiment were more associated with actors who were rated worse according to the question's criteria. Therefore, sentiment analysis can be considered a good complement to the quantitative ranking information in responses.

In the context of analyzing ethical cases with multiple alternatives that require ranking, peer influence can play an important role in decision-making and evaluating the available ethical options. Participants can learn from their peers how to approach and analyze ethical dilemmas, as well as which criteria to use to evaluate different alternatives. If negative justifications about alternatives have solid and well-founded approaches, this can impact the ethical decision-making of their peers.

In the future, we plan to perform topic analyses of student responses, complementing what was developed in this study, with the aim of developing content analysis tools that facilitate the teacher's monitoring of the activity and feedback to the students. Additionally, we plan to conduct a more granular analysis of the probability distribution of ranking changes by actor, using a dataset with a greater number of observations.

References

1. Kolodner, J.L., et al.: Theory and practice of case-based learning aids. In: Theoretical Foundations of Learning Environments, pp. 142–170. Routledge (2012)
2. Merseth, K.K.: Cases for decision making in teacher education. In: Case Methods in Teacher Education, pp. 50–63 (1992)
3. Kolodner, J.L., Owensby, J.N., Guzdial, M.: Case-based learning aids. In: Handbook of Research on Educational Communications and Technology, pp. 820–852. Routledge (2013)
4. Angeli*, C.: The effects of case-based learning on early childhood pre-service teachers' beliefs about the pedagogical uses of ICT. J. Educ. Media 29(2), 139–151 (2004)
5. Choi, I., Lee, K.: Designing and implementing a case-based learning environment for enhancing ill-structured problem solving: classroom management problems for prospective teachers. Educ. Tech. Res. Dev. 57, 99–129 (2009)
6. Shulman, J., Case Methods in Teacher Education.: Teachers College Press. Columbia University, Teachers College (1992)
7. Zeng, R., Blasi, L.: Learning through web-based multistoryline case studies: a design-based research. Q. Rev. Distance Educ. 11(3), 175 (2010)
8. Wang, H., Tlili, A., Lehman, J.D., Lu, H., Huang, R.: Investigating feedback implemented by instructors to support online competency-based learning (CBL): a multiple case study. Int. J. Educ. Technol. High. Educ. 18(1), 1–21 (2021). https://doi.org/10.1186/s41239-021-002 41-6
9. Li, S., Ye, X., Chen, W.: Practice and effectiveness of "nursing case-based learning" course on nursing student's critical thinking ability: a comparative study. Nurse Educ. Pract. 36, 91–96 (2019)
10. The, B., Yang, L., Wang, Q.: What's on your mind? promoting cognitive engagement using utterance annotations in online collaborative learning. In: ICIS (2019)
11. Sharipova, M.: Supporting Students in the Analysis of Case Studies for Professional Ethics Education. University of Saskatchewan (2015)
12. Searing, D.R.: Harps Ethical Analysis Methodology: Method Description. Taknosys Software Corporation (1998)
13. Goldin, I.M., Ashley, K.D., Pinkus, R.L.: Introducing PETE: computer support for teaching ethics. In: Proceedings of the 8th International Conference on Artificial Intelligence and Law (2001)
14. Van der Burg, S., Van de Poel, I.: Teaching ethics and technology with Agora, an electronic tool. Sci. Eng. Ethics 11, 277–297 (2005)
15. Scheuer, O., et al.: Automated analysis and feedback techniques to support and teach argumentation: a survey. In: Educational Technologies for Teaching Argumentation Skills, pp. 71–124 (2012)
16. McKenzie, A., McCalla, G.: Serious games for professional ethics: an architecture to support personalization. In: AIED 2009: 14th International Conference on Artificial Intelligence in Education Workshops Proceedings (2009). Citeseer
17. Hodhod, R., Kudenko, D., Cairns, P.: AEINS: adaptive educational interactive narrative system to teach ethics. In: AIED 2009: 14th International Conference on Artificial Intelligence in Education Workshops Proceedings (2009)
18. Weinberger, A., et al.: Epistemic and social scripts in computer–supported collaborative learning. Instr. Sci. 33, 1–30 (2005)
19. Weinberger, A.: Principles of transactive computer-supported collaboration scripts. Nordic J. Digit. Lit. 6(3), 189–202 (2011)
20. Goldin, I.M., Ashley, K.D., Pinkus, R.L.: Teaching case analysis through framing: prospects for an ITS in an ill-defined domain. In: Proceedings of the ITS 2006 Workshop on ITS for Ill-Defined Domains, Jhongli, Taiwan (2006)

21. Hoffmann, M., Borenstein, J.: Understanding ill-structured engineering ethics problems through a collaborative learning and argument visualization approach. Sci. Eng. Ethics **20**, 261–276 (2014)
22. Lees, A.B.: Learning about ethical decision making in health care using web-based technology: a case study. Auckland University of Technology (2011)
23. Álvarez, C., et al.: Scaffolding of intuitionist ethical reasoning with groupware: do students' stances change in different countries?. In: Wong, LH., Hayashi, Y., Collazos, C.A., Alvarez, C., Zurita, G., Baloian, N. (eds.) Collaboration Technologies and Social Computing. CollabTech 2022. Lecture Notes in Computer Science, vol. 13632. Springer, Cham (2022). https://doi.org/10.1007/978-3-031-20218-6_18
24. Barbieri, F., Anke, L.E., Camacho-Collados, J.: Xlm-t: multilingual language models in twitter for sentiment analysis and beyond. In: Proceedings of the Thirteenth Language Resources and Evaluation Conference (2022)
25. Mohit, B.: Named entity recognition. Nat. Lang. Process. Semitic Lang. 221–245 (2014)
26. Allam, A.M.N., Haggag, M.H.: The question answering systems: a survey. Int. J. Res. Rev. Inf. Sci. (IJRRIS) **2**(3) (2012)
27. Çeliktuğ, M.F.: Twitter sentiment analysis, 3-way classification: positive, negative or neutral? In: 2018 IEEE International Conference on Big Data (Big Data). IEEE (2018)
28. Agarwal, A., et al.: Sentiment analysis of twitter data. In: Proceedings of the Workshop on Language in Social Media (LSM 2011) (2011)
29. Hasan, M.R., Maliha, M., Arifuzzaman, M.: Sentiment analysis with NLP on Twitter data. In: 2019 International Conference on Computer, Communication, Chemical, Materials and Electronic Engineering (IC4ME2). IEEE (2019)
30. Cañete, J., et al.: Spanish pre-trained bert model and evaluation data. Pml4dc at ICLR 2020, pp. 1–10 (2020)
31. Cañete, J., et al.: Albeto and distilbeto: Lightweight spanish language models. arXiv preprint arXiv:2204.09145 (2022)
32. Pérez, J.M., Giudici, J.C., Luque, F.: Pysentimiento: a python toolkit for sentiment analysis and socialnlp tasks. arXiv preprint arXiv:2106.09462 (2021)
33. Araujo, V., et al.: Evaluation Benchmarks for Spanish Sentence Representations. arXiv preprint arXiv:2204.07571 (2022)
34. Kruschke, J.: Doing Bayesian data analysis: a tutorial with R, JAGS, and Stan (2014)
35. Beraha, M., Falco, D., Guglielmi, A.: JAGS, NIMBLE, Stan: a detailed comparison among Bayesian MCMC software. arXiv preprint arXiv:2107.09357 (2021)

Exploring the Reciprocal Emotional Interaction Between Humans and Affective Technology Through Design Fictions and "Speculative Entanglement"

Hong Yang[1], Ching-Yang Lin[2], Chung-Ching Huang[3], and Ying-Yu Chen[1]([✉])

[1] Department of Communication and Technology, National Yang-Ming Chiao Tung University,
Hsinchu, Taiwan
yungyu18@gmail.com
[2] Graduate Program in Digital Content and Technologies, National Chengchi University, Taipei,
Taiwan
109462012@g.nccu.edu.tw
[3] College of Planning and Design, National Cheng Kung University, Tainan, Taiwan
10808037@gs.ncku.edu.tw

Abstract. This paper explores how emotion recognition technology is perceived, understood, felt, and reimagined through a set of design fiction processes by making and re-making arrangements of complex relationships between technologies, practices, emotions, and everyday lives. Emotion plays a crucial part in how we interact with the world: it is ephemeral, contingent, and contextual. Technologies capturing human emotions trace how we feel from almost all perspectives of our lives. To start with our explorations, we first write design fiction and take them to workshops as a probe into complex relationships between emotion recognition and our everyday lives. Participants work in teams to create design fiction prototypes that expand and respond to the fictional worldbuilding. By analyzing how the entanglements of emotion recognition technology in human lives are carried through and transformed among multiple design fiction processes, we contribute to a set of design processes that uses design fiction as a probe for the next speculation, in this case, reconfigure emotional recognition among humans and technology in design fiction workshops.

Keywords: Design Fiction · Emotion Recognition · Artificial Intelligence · Intelligent Systems · Design Workshop

1 Introduction

Emotional recognition (ER) technology has been everywhere and ubiquitous in our lives and almost omnipresent in our daily encounters with technology [15]. ER technology uses algorithms capable of comprehending, predicting, and influencing human behaviors in almost all human activities, from shopping behaviors, academic achievement, health conditions, political opinions, employee recruitment or assessment, and family lives [7].

© The Author(s), under exclusive license to Springer Nature Switzerland AG 2023
H. Takada et al. (Eds.): CollabTech 2023, LNCS 14199, pp. 36–51, 2023.
https://doi.org/10.1007/978-3-031-42141-9_3

While ER technology is increasingly capable of measuring and inferring human emotions, how humans perceive or might be influenced by such an intelligent system is underexplored [1]. Andalibi and Buss looked into people's attitudes towards emotional recognition technology on social media and the benefits and harms they associate with it [1]. They argue that Developing emotion recognition is a social-technical issue, thus crucial to account for the needs of people who provide data to make ER technology possible. Along the same line of this work, Roemmich and Andalibi use speculative scenarios to understand data subjects' attitudes and values toward ER technology on social media. They found that in some cases, participants' attitudes toward ER change when they contend with ER-enabled well-being interventions for others instead of themselves. The paper concludes that ER development should center data subjects' considerations on "ethical and trustworthy" applications [20]. Their result indicates how humans perceive ER technology as tangential to people around us.

In response to the rapid advances in Artificial Intelligent (AI) applications that lack clarity and transparency on the social and ethical implications, HCI scholars have called for careful consideration of how the systems are designed and developed [12]. However, AI systems are inheritably complex for HCI professionals to design due to challenges in iterative prototyping, crafting thoughtful interactions, understanding AI capacities, etc. [29]. HCI researchers have used design fiction to speculate near-future scenarios of emerging technology, including privacy and sensing, virtual reality, and AI systems. Design fiction is presented in HCI research with forms including design workbooks, prototypes, catalogs, imaginative abstracts, and more [8, 16, 22]. There are also multiple ways that design fiction is used to elicit user enactments and reactions in real-world practices [9, 24]. Given the above considerations, our goal in this study is to use design fiction as a probe to elicit people's perspectives and imaginations towards ER technology and further reimagine and remake ER technology through these configurations of design fiction.

We propose to provide a set of original design fiction that emerges from the Taiwanese situations, which gives contexts to perceptions of emotional recognition technology use that might be closer to the lived experience of workshop participants. In addition, we present a case study probing into possibilities of how future ER technology is considered, configured, and reconfigured by collaboratively situating design fiction in workshops.

2   Related Work

2.1   Design Fiction and Intelligent Systems

Design fiction reconstructs futuristic or contemporary objects in order to stimulate discussion and explore possibilities. Literacy and design processes have been entangled in design fiction [10]. Blythe et al. state that fiction seminars are anti-solutionist and encourage the imagination of the future [4]. In recent years, design fiction, as is more frequently associated with the speculative design [8], has been shown to be a valuable resource for collaboratively conveying design concepts [6, 26] and inspiring the design of future technologies [21]. Through speculation, narration, and prototyping, design fiction investigates advanced human augmentation that integrates human technology and human intelligence [8]. Science fiction prototypes can be utilized to illustrate how future co-creative intelligence will integrate human technology with human intelligence [8, 13].

AI technology has given computers new functions in human-machine systems due to its independence [16]. AI technology has caused a paradigm shift in HCI design, as well as the emergence of new challenges and opportunities. For instance, AI technologies can assist humans to make more effective decisions in certain operational scenarios. However, ethical and safety failures are under disguise since there is no guarantee that humans will have the final decision-making authority of the systems in unpredictable situations [16, 17].

The future of intelligent systems requires interdisciplinary collaboration [9], and design fiction can contribute to the advancement of AI technology in a number of ways. Firstly, it can be used to investigate the future potential of human-assisted intelligence and to develop imaginative scenarios that can help academics and designers better comprehend user experience in the future [6, 14]. Secondly, as a core competence of AI literacy, design fiction encourages imagination of future technological designs and applications [15]. AI assistance in the creation of design fiction can be used to boost creativity and promote technology-related critical thinking [14]. Besides, design fiction can be used to foresee the ethical implications of AI technology by evaluating the implications and unintended consequences of introducing new technologies, processes, and behaviors before they become a reality [2]. Design fiction can be utilized to raise ethical questions or ethical concerns about AI technology by involving value-sensitive and contextual designs to investigate the technology from a variety of perspectives and uncover ethical problems [2]. Through the use of design fiction to anticipate the ethical implications of AI technology, researchers and designers can create engaging and imaginative scenarios that help them better understand user experience in new contexts, explore the future possibilities of human augmented intelligence, and develop AI that avoids causing societal harm [7].

2.2 Emotion Recognition Technology Embedded in Social Context

Automatic emotional recognition (ER) technology is a type of artificial intelligence that uses algorithms to detect, analyze and predict human emotions via the surveillance of an individual's everyday use of internet-enabled devices, collecting cues like facial expressions and tones of voice [1], and responding in a personalized way [15, 28]. As a rapidly expanding area that has received considerable attention in recent years, emotional recognition technology is enhanced rapidly and highly contested [3, 5, 11]. In terms of the key application domain for ER technology, Andalibi has employed blended methods and social media behavior theory to develop ER models, contributing to the investigation of people's attitudes and conceptions regarding the application of ER inferences to develop automatic ER-enabled wellness interventions [12]. The use of ER technology in the workplace is studied, with an emphasis on the input data and the ethical consequences of such devices [5].

In recent years, the negative effects of emotional AI systems on society have been accorded increasing importance, like the enlarged bias, invasion of privacy, conflicts of private and public interests, etc. [11, 14, 23]. Prior researches claim that ethical and socially responsible AI applications are incompatible with current ER-enabled automated wellness interventions, emphasizing the significance of cultural and linguistic differences in ER research. The negative concerns emerging among social media users also indicate the imperativeness of ethical considerations when implementing ER technologies [20]. As ER technologies continue to advance and become more pervasive, it is essential to consider their potential repercussions and ensure that they are used under control and ethically.

ER technology is not merely a neutral tool used by individuals to recognize and express emotions. Instead, it becomes embedded within social contexts and practices, influencing how emotions are recognized, expressed, and perceived [20]. Orlikowski proposes the concept of "constitutive entanglement" to suggest that technology and social structures are not separate entities but are deeply interconnected and co-constitutive [17]. In other words, technologies entangle in the very fabric of social practices, and their development and usage are influenced by social and contextual factors. Since emotions are socially constructed and cannot be studied independently [3], emotional AI is also embedded within social contexts and practices. What people and society believe about inferences and predictions of the "interiority, judgments, and potential future actions of humans" should be considered to comprehend the ethical and social implications of ER [25]. In this paper, we thereby explore the entanglement between ER technology and our emotional experiences in an iterative design fiction approach to probe into the potential future of emotional AI.

3   Method

3.1   Making (Writing) Design Fiction

When writing design fiction, our goal is to understand the role emotional recognition plays in our daily experiences and make our own "possible worlds" [13]. Markussen and Knutz recommend employing "possible world theory" when writing design fiction. They see strong connections between literary practices and design fiction, denying a contribution hierarchy between a physicist (scientist) and a writer of design fiction. The research team and a group of graduate students interested in Human-Computer Interaction (HCI) from multiple disciplines, including computer science, electrical engineering, communication, business, and Chinese literature, created stories relevant to Taiwanese daily life.

We convene weekly and generate nine independent design fiction. These novels focus on the relationship with families, and we explore how the situation might look like with novel technology solutions through world-making. The writing process allows the writers to contemplate "possible worlds that can be easy or difficult to access" [5]. We were inspired by research works that write design fiction to explore alternative expressions of reality and create various forms of the artifact as a reflective process to rethink social-technical arrangements [13], so we decided to make design fiction relevant to the social arrangements and cultural norms of Taiwan, where we live. The authors wrote about family/home freely. The theme helps authors focus on an emotionally charged topic, and there are no other writing constraints. Design fiction writers choose their most passionate topics. We didn't review each other's writing. After all writing is done, we had a group member who was a Chinese major proofread the stories and post them on Medium [31]. Each design fiction explores how ER-enabled technology affects our daily lives:

1. *Family Message board* records the mental status of each family member, visualizes the emotional data, and shares it among families to facilitate the parent-child relationship.
2. *Mind Watch* collects people's emotions and suggests what to say. The watch eliminates barriers to communication between people and improves interpersonal relationships.
3. *Monitoring Bracelet* detects wearers' physiological signals to learn about their mental status, assembling the emotional data for laboratory use manipulated by the nation, accompanied by an electric shock to control the wearers.
4. *Perfect Study Plan* is an application that detects the utmost studying mode and schedules for students taking college entrance exams by gathering their past academic behaviors and detecting their emotional and mental status.
5. *Parenting Guide* collects users' emotions and records interactions between parents and children. The mobile and wearable applications provide real-time advice to parents to raise emotionally and academically intelligent children.
6. *Arkangel* is an intelligent system that collects users' daily activities, body information, and emotions to boost their academic performance. The system helps users predict the probability of admission to the ideal college.
7. *Moderator Mirror* is an intelligent mirror that enables users to transfer knowledge, messages, and emotions into the brain. The mirror saves time and effort in preparing for exams and communicating with others.
8. *Contact Lens* detects users' fear and uses their emotional weakness to represent a pandemic virus in a horrific way to reduce the chance of contracting it.
9. *Dreamland* is a game console that controls the user's brain and detects players' subconscious emotions to create dreams.

3.2 Speculative Design Workshops

After publishing a set of design fiction on Medium, we held two design workshops applying the fiction as a probe to stimulate new speculations (see Fig. 1). The workshops were advertised mainly to students and people interested in HCI topics and methods as a venue to learn, experience, and produce speculative prototypes. From design fiction to creative lo-fi prototypes, the goal of workshops was not to presume or speculate on the future of ER technology, but rather on how emotions are embedded in and recognized by technology, and how they are transferred and transformed from different contexts across a broader definition of design-fiction-making processes.

Both workshops are one-day events, and the collaborative design process was recorded by photos and field notes. Before attending these workshops, we asked participants to read the design fiction published on Medium. The workshops begin with a thirty-minute presentation on what design fiction is and what it can do. We asked the participants to take as many sticky notes as they could during the fiction storytelling. We asked the participants to post their sticky notes on the wall, read them, move them, group them, and write more sticky notes as they went. We went through all of the notes as a group and asked participants to elaborate on the grouping and descriptions of the notes using the *Affinity Diagram* [30].

After the lunch break, participants started to work in teams to develop the prototypes. We provided each group with assorted materials and let them know they could use any form to present their speculative prototypes. After the two-hour working session, each group presented the designs they created, and we concluded with two prototypes in the first workshop and three more in the second round.

Fig. 1. Discussion during the design fiction workshops.

4 Findings

4.1 ER Technology in Design Fiction

How ER Technology Captures Emotions. In design fiction, there are two main ways to use ER technology to detect users' emotions: collecting physiological signals and recording personal activities. Physiological signals can be measured to monitor physical processes and extract features for various applications, such as pain detection, heart rate variability analysis, and emotion recognition [27]. Collecting physiological signals is carried out through the built-in sensors of the products, which are presented in all fiction. Besides, personal activities are recorded through external cameras in four fictions by hidden cameras gathering photos or videos of personal actions and feelings (Table 1).

Users' Attitudes to ER Technology. The user in the story experiences several changes in attitude toward emotion recognition technology, including hope, trust, doubt, or aversion (see Fig. 2). Initially, the user has a positive attitude toward achieving goals when purchasing or subscribing to related services. In the early stages of use, the user develops strong trust in the technology because it meets some expectations. In the later stages of use, the user becomes skeptical of the emotion recognition technology due to adverse effects such as privacy invasion.

Characters in fictions often hold "hope" about the future potential of ER technology before its integration into daily life. In Arkangel, a student purchases ER technology with the hope of passing medical school and trusts its advice wholeheartedly. Similarly, in Moderator Mirror, the student initially doubts the technology, but their parents buy it with the expectation of getting their child into a good university.

The characters in Contact Lens demonstrate a "trust" attitude toward technology, as they believe in the effectiveness of wearing contact lenses to prevent epidemics. However, when the technology is later shown to be used maliciously, society begins to doubt its use. Moreover, the protagonists' prolonged exposure to technology leads to a change in attitude characterized by "doubt" and "aversion". In Arkangel, a student begins to doubt the efficacy of the technology's recommendations and demands more reliable information about the ER technology's accuracy in predicting exam outcomes.

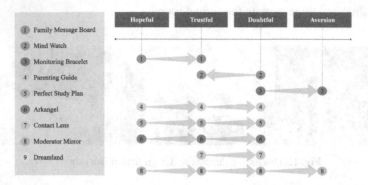

Fig. 2. Users' attitudes to ER technology change during the usage period.

Expected and Unintended Effects of ER Technology. All fiction features a background of ER technology being popular in the market, with four of them envisioning an ideal future that solves practical problems through the use of ER technology. The effectiveness of ER technology often satisfies users' needs. However, six of the fiction explicitly reveal that ER technology can also have some unintended side effects, such as causing interpersonal alienation, erasing human differences, and being used by those in power to monitor the people.

Expected Effectiveness of Use. ER technology solves complicated problems and improves user experience through data visualization and other approaches. Four fictions show how ER technology may aid with interpersonal emotional exchanges, parenting, and health education. ER technology improves parent-child relationships and family problems by displaying emotional data. ER technology's accurate emotion recognition can optimize user attention advantages, boosting work, learning, and quality of life. *Contact Lens* can identify viruses and warn users, improving epidemic response. ER technology can also improve parents and children. The *Parenting Guide* has helped young children become polite, emotionally secure, and patient. ER technology can improve our lives and change how we handle complex challenges.

Unintended Side Effects. ER technology's flaws, uneven access to developing technical channels, and authoritarian governments' and others' exploitation have unknowingly caused harmful society and individual effects across six fictions, which depict how ER technology can promote emotional apathy and social isolation. AI interventions in three fictions improve academic performance swiftly, but overreliance on technology isolates parents and children emotionally. For instance, *Arkangel's* intentionally poor assessment scores motivate kids to learn under AI algorithms, whereas *Moderator Mirror's* compulsory use of ER technology breaks up parent-child relationships. Fictions demonstrate how technology is used in Taiwanese students' education and enlarges inequality.

The misuse can also lead to children's homogeneous behavior and features. Besides, all fiction mentions collecting and analyzing physiological data including facial expressions, heartbeats, sweating, and muscular contractions, which might lead to negative sentiments and exploitation by authoritarian governments or other evil actors.

4.2 Introducing Design Fictions into Speculative Design Workshops

Two design workshops on two university campuses followed the nine design fictions, which were used to investigate how emotion recognition technologies can be redesigned. Participants raised concerns regarding ER technology and reconfigured it from design fiction to speculative design prototypes.

First Speculative Design Workshop. At the first workshop, 11 participants were split into two groups for novel reading and debate at a national university in northern Taiwan. Five concepts "Technology analyzes emotions and provides feedback" (23 notes), "Technology affects autonomy" (20 notes), "Technology monitors people" (19 notes), "Technology regulates relationships" (18 notes), and "real-time and historical data" (19 notes) were derived from 99 sticky notes. The first two ideas generalize the fiction, while the latter three expand it. The new concepts inspired new design prototypes in each group.

Technology Monitors People. The design workshop sticky notes show ER technology product monitoring concerns. "Machines control behavior" and "Machines control children's lives" argue that such items undermine privacy. This problem stems from the conflict between parents' desire to use technology to better understand and care for their children and its tendency to constantly monitor them, putting them under strain. Transmitting sensitive bodily and emotional data raises privacy concerns, compounding this worry.

Technology Regulates Relationships. Workshop participants were supportive of the role ER technology plays in mediating interpersonal relationships, especially within families. Five sticky notes mentioned concepts related to family, such as "not afraid to communicate with elders" and "family accepting system suggestions." Participants also discussed how technology could intervene, such as through an AI assistant that provides tailored suggestions. The use of technology to coordinate family interactions and make more appropriate decisions was also discussed.

Real-Time and Historical Data. The workshop looked into ER technologies that collect longitudinal data. With bracelets in design fiction, ER technology monitors pulse rate, dilated pupils, perspiration, anger, and muscle contraction. *Mind Watch* and *Monitoring Bracelet* use "pinhole cameras" to record users' real-time data for third-party use, allowing caregivers or monitors to assess the user's condition remotely. Participants suggested "digital trace" and "digital memory" as longitudinal data. Participants also regarded "expired" traces for ER technology evaluation and feedback as valuable. Participants suggested using parents' mobile devices to monitor children's behavior, location, and well-being.

Affinity diagrams inspire the development of speculative prototypes. The participants designed the *"Emotional Cup"* and *"Home Theater"* (Table 2). Emotions are communicated by analog prototypes through sensory experiences. During the ideation process, "Technology Intervention Regulating Family Relationships" was proposed. *Emotional Cups* assisted parents in understanding and managing their children's anxieties, whereas the *Home Theater* utilized furniture to monitor and manage family members' emotions, thereby preventing conflicts. These prototypes dealt with emotion.

Second Speculative Design Workshop. The second workshop held at a university in South Taiwan included 15 participants in four groups. The narrative inspired new speculative ER technology design suggestions. In 210 sticky notes, participants discussed "Technology analyses and provides emotional feedback" (29 notes), "User attitudes toward emotion recognition technology" (31 notes), "Technology affects education and competition" (39 notes), and "Technology affects autonomy" (32 notes). They also added "Emotions as tradable entities" (24 notes), "Technology undertakes emotional labor" (32 notes), and "Emotionalizing technology" (23 notes).

Emotions as Tradable Entities. The concept as a new application of ER technology, derived from the externalization of knowledge, considers emotions an asset with tradable value and feasibility. Since assets have long-term stability, this perspective is similar to the concept of the *"temporality of emotional data"* presented in the first workshop. 24 sticky notes explored this topic, and participants believed that humans could exchange emotions as assets through the exchange (*"knowledge exchange," "consciousness exchange,"* etc.), backup/storage (*"backup restoration,"* etc.), and inheritance (*"perfect inheritance of ancient memories,"* etc.).

Technology Undertakes Emotional Labor. Emotional work was originally applied to industries that required observable facial and bodily expressions [10]. Since human organizations already have emotional expression rules [2, 18], emotional labor can be broadly defined as the emotional burden imposed by societal expectations [19]. Despite lacking emotions or consciousness, ER technology collects and processes users' physiological and psychological data in the novel. In novels, ER technology detected users' emotional stress and bore their emotional work, prompting participants to examine the ramifications of transferring this responsibility. Sticky notes like "All behavior is data-driven" and "An entire day's behavior is handed over to the system" were critical of technology's overuse to solve emotional labor.

Emotionalizing Technology. This topic elicited a total of 23 sticky notes, which can be divided into two categories: anthropomorphizing animals and plants (8 notes) and endowing machines with human consciousness and emotions (15 notes). These technological objects were viewed as meaningful actors in the ideation process by participants. With the help of ER technology, these objects can no longer merely assist humans, but can even displace them, posing a threat to human subjectivity. The anthropomorphizing of animals, plants, and machines also involves the objectification of humans, putting objects and humans under the same scrutiny and resulting in a power structure reversal, such as "humans becoming robots' pets" and "from assistance to domination."

Table 1. Emotions recognized in design fiction.

Design fiction Title	Description of Fiction	Data Detected
Family Message Board	The smart device monitors the mental state of users, visualizes their emotional data, and communicates it with other family members	Collect physiological data from multiple users via cell phones
Mind Watch	To improve communication between linked people, a smartwatch gathers emotions and suggestions what to say	Take videos of daily life
Monitoring Bracelet	The monitoring bracelet detects physiological signals from the wearer to better understand their mental state	Collect users' physiological data. Take videos from the pinhole camera
Parenting Guide	Parenting Guide is an App that chronicles family activities and feelings, providing parenting tips	Take videos and audios of a person's daily life
Perfect Study Plan	An app can recommend study styles and timetables based on academic success and mental health	Assess users' abilities with online tests. Take videos of daily life
Arkangel	AI tracks users' daily activities, bodily data, and moods. The education system predicts college admissions for users	Take videos of daily life. Capture physiological data through wearable devices
Contact Lens	The Contact Lens detects the user's inner dread and displays the catastrophic infection to scare them away	Detect users' inner fear via the contact lens
Moderator Mirror	The intelligent mirror lets users share thoughts and feelings. The Mirror streamlines studying and socializing	Capture users' physiological data by touching the mirror
Dreamland	The Dreamland interface game console manipulates the user's brain to generate any lucid dream desired	Detect users' brain waves during sleep

Participants returned to their groups after the affinity diagramming and created three speculative design prototypes (see Table 3). Storyboards, drawings, paper artifacts, and other formats were used to present these prototypes.

Table 2. Prototypes in the 1st workshops.

Prototype	Description	Draft
Home Theater	The Home Theater uses cameras and sensors to monitor family members' emotional state and to give soothing sensory experiences. To console family members, the projection museum recites poems based on emotional data.	
Emotional Cup	Emotional Cups evaluate children's anxiety. As intensity increases, it becomes heavier, giving parents a subtle tactile hint when toddlers don't express themselves, which helps parents understand kids' stress.	

Table 3. Prototypes in the 2nd workshops.

Prototype	Description	Scenario & Prototype
Memory Fluid	The Memory Fluid stores one's feelings and information, which can be passed on to others. The transmission is accomplished by a watch that distills the fluid to reach the skin.	
Rhino Cat	Rhino Cat is a robotic pet that offers the company. It senses emotions and tells the user's mental state via cameras (the pet's eyes). After a period of time with the user, the pet develops its own emotions and features.	
Emotion Watch	Brain waves determine the Emotion Watch's emotional state. The watch helps the wearer's buddies communicate when they're distressed. The watch can also convey a masterwork's emotions and theme to the observer.	

4.3 From Design Fiction to Prototypes

The workshop participants not only expanded and supplemented the novelist's imagination of the possible future but also speculated on various aspects of ER technology. The prototypes produced at the end of the speculative design workshops provided insights into how ER technology recognizes emotions, utilizes emotion data, and impacts human society, both intended and unintended. Furthermore, the participants examined the issues surrounding ER technology highlighted in the novel's contextual story and revised the role of ER technology in everyday life, as depicted in new prototypes (see Table 4).

Table 4. Transitions from Design Fiction to Prototypes.

Codes from Design Fiction	Concepts from Workshops	Prototypes
• How ER technology captures emotions (2 codes)	• Real-Time and Historical Data (1st Workshop)	Home Theater Emotional Cups
• Emotions recognized by ER technology (4 codes) • Users' Attitudes to ER Technology (3 codes)	• Emotions can be stored and exchanged (2nd Workshop) • Emotional labor (2st Workshop)	Memory Fluid Mind Watch
	• Giving object emotions (2nd Workshop)	Rhino cat
• Influence of ER technology: Expected effectiveness of use (4 codes)	• ER technology improve the relationship (1st Workshop)	Home Theater Emotional Cups Mind Watch
• Influence of ER technology: Unintended side effects (6 codes)	• ER Technology Trade-off (1st & 2nd Workshop) • Technology monitoring of people (1st Workshop)	Home Theater Emotional Cups Rhino cat

5 Discussion

5.1 Reopening Dystopia Spaces as Imaginative Playgrounds for Crafting Design Fiction Narratives

The concept of "reopening dystopia spaces as imaginative playgrounds for crafting design fiction narratives" involves taking imagined or real dystopian spaces and using them as a creative inspiration to craft fictional narratives through design [13]. In this context, a "dystopia space" refers to any environment that is characterized by oppressive or dystopian conditions. This is evident in the nine design fictions our participants generated. The attitude towards ER technology in the stories often ended with doubt or aversion. However, such narratives highlight practical issues commonly seen in ER technology today, such as concerns over privacy, technology regulating human beings rather than supporting them, etc. We saw that participants critically reflected on these issues in the affinity diagram process and later intended to address them in their speculative prototypes.

Risk is frequently viewed as an essential element of innovation. Despite the fact that the concept of risk may be associated with negative outcomes, uncertainty, and potential loss, embracing risk and admitting the possibility of failure is essential for advancing novel solutions to complex problems. By using dystopian narratives to highlight the risk of using ER technology, we can conjecture, learn from the consequences, and develop innovative ideas that move further away from them.

5.2 Designing Empathetic Systems Through "Speculative Entanglement"

Exploring the potential of *"speculative entanglement"* as a design approach to create intelligent systems that can recognize, respond, and suggest human emotions. By materializing the capabilities of affective technology and exploring its capacity in intimate family contexts through design fiction, we can better understand the reciprocal emotional interaction between humans and machines. This approach takes into account the socially constructed nature of emotions and emphasizes the importance of contextual and cultural factors in shaping emotional expression and perception. By considering these factors in the design process using design fiction as a probe to co-constructive speculative futures, we might create more effective and empathetic intelligent systems that better reflect the complexity of human emotions.

We were inspired by the concept of *"Constitutive entanglement"* proposed by Orlikowski [17] in her work on the relationship between humans and technology. It refers to the idea that humans and machines are not separate entities, but rather are mutually constitutive of each other in their interactions. According to Orlikowski, humans and machines become entangled with each other in a way that shapes their respective identities and capacities. For example, in a workplace setting, employees may rely on technologies such as computers and software to perform their jobs. However, the organizational context and the social and cultural norms that affect their use influence the design and implementation of these technologies. At the same time, the employees' use of the technologies shapes the technologies themselves, as they develop workarounds and alternative practices to make the technologies more useful for their purposes. She further argues that this entanglement between humans and machines is an ongoing and dynamic process, and that it is important to study and understand this relationship in order to design technologies that are more responsive to the needs and practices of the people who use them.

The writing of the nine design fictions is how we might generally think about the relationship between emotion recognition and our cultural imagination. By materializing the capabilities of affective technology in intimate family contexts, we can better understand the reciprocal emotional interaction between humans and ER technology. Such intimate capacities between humans and machines were brought to the speculative design workshops by fiction writers to help participants envision the intimate capacities of such technology. As Barrett claims, emotions, which are highly contagious, are socially constructed and contextually formed, and their expression and perception depend on cultural and social roles and situations [4]. Since how we express and perceive certain emotions depends on local situations and contexts, studying emotions in isolation can result in an inaccurate understanding of how they work together to construct our emotional experiences. Through the emotional AI design fiction probe case study, we can develop a better understanding of how to design intelligent systems that recognize, respond to, and even suggest human emotions, while taking into account the complex and socially constructed nature of emotions.

6 Conclusion and Future Work

We conducted a design fiction investigation to determine how individuals perceive the capabilities and possibilities of ER-enabled technology. Living with technologies that monitor and sense the emotional life of every aspect of human activity, our emotions are social, contextual, and contagious, posing a significant challenge when designing ER systems. Initially, we wrote a collection of design fictions featuring emotionally-enabled AI systems. Then, we brought the design fictions to workshops to elicit the perspectives and imaginations of participants regarding the emotional capacity of ER technology. Through the configuration and entanglement of emotions, technologies and situations, we hope to contribute to the application of ER and provide a method for using design fiction probes as "speculative entanglement" to envision our interaction with emotional AI. By acknowledging the constitutive connection between ER technology and cultural imagination, we obtain a more nuanced interpretation of how these technologies affect our everyday lives.

There are several limitations to this study. The small number of participants in each workshop may have affected the representativeness of the ER technology perspectives that emerged. Yet as an exploratory study, we did not attempt to generalize participants' attitudes toward ER techniques, but rather to construct a new way of facilitating design fiction workshops through individualized, diverse, and contextualized affective experiences, as well as a shift in perspective from authors to readers. In the future, designs and implementations of ER technologies are supposed to take into account the intricate interplay between technological capabilities, cultural contexts, and social practices to avoid reinforcing or perpetuating existing biases or power imbalances.

References

1. Abaskohi, A., et al.: Persian Emotion Detection using ParsBERT and Imbalanced Data Handling Approaches (2022). http://arxiv.org/abs/2211.08029
2. Ashforth, B.E., Humphrey, R.H.: Emotional labor in service roles: the influence of identity. Acad. Manage. Rev. 18(1), 88–115 (1993). https://doi.org/10.2307/258824
3. Barrett, L.F., et al.: Emotional expressions reconsidered: challenges to inferring emotion from human facial movements. Psychol. Sci. Public Interest. 20(1), 1–68 (2019). https://doi.org/10.1177/1529100619832930
4. Barrett, L.F.: How Emotions are Made: The Secret Life of the Brain. Houghton Mifflin Harcourt, Boston, MA (2017)
5. Blythe, M.: Research fiction: storytelling, plot and design. In: Proceedings of the 2017 CHI Conference on Human Factors in Computing Systems, pp. 5400–5411 Association for Computing Machinery, New York, NY, USA (2017). https://doi.org/10.1145/3025453.3026023
6. Cheon, E., et al.: I beg to differ: soft conflicts in collaborative design using design fictions. In: Proceedings of the 2019 on Designing Interactive Systems Conference, pp. 201–214 Association for Computing Machinery, New York, NY, USA (2019). https://doi.org/10.1145/3322276.3322350

7. Cowie, R., et al.: Emotion recognition in human-computer interaction. IEEE Signal Process. Mag. **18**(1), 32–80 (2001). https://doi.org/10.1109/79.911197

8. Dunne, A., Raby, F.: Speculative Everything: Design, Fiction, and Social Dreaming. The MIT Press (2013)

9. Elsden, C., et al.: On speculative enactments. In: Proceedings of the 2017 CHI Conference on Human Factors in Computing Systems, pp. 5386–5399 Association for Computing Machinery, New York, NY, USA (2017). https://doi.org/10.1145/3025453.3025503

10. Hochschild, A.R.: The Managed Heart: Commercialization of Human Feeling. University of California Press (2012)

11. Lee, M., et al.: Where is Vincent? Expanding our emotional selves with AI. In: 4th Conference Conversational User Interfaces, pp. 1–11 (2022). https://doi.org/10.1145/3543829.3543835

12. Loi, D., et al.: Co-designing AI futures: integrating AI ethics, social computing, and design. In: Companion Publication of the 2019 on Designing Interactive Systems Conference 2019 Companion, pp. 381–384 Association for Computing Machinery, New York, NY, USA (2019). https://doi.org/10.1145/3301019.3320000

13. Markussen, T., Knutz, E.: The poetics of design fiction. In: Proceedings of the 6th International Conference on Designing Pleasurable Products and Interfaces, pp. 231–240 Association for Computing Machinery, New York, NY, USA (2013). https://doi.org/10.1145/2513506.251 3531

14. McStay, A.: Emotional AI and EdTech: serving the public good? Learn. Media Technol. **45**(3), 270–283 (2020). https://doi.org/10.1080/17439884.2020.1686016

15. McStay, A.: Emotional AI: The Rise of Empathic Media (2018). https://doi.org/10.4135/978 1526451293

16. Noortman, R., et al.: HawkEye - deploying a design fiction probe. In: Proceedings of the 2019 CHI Conference on Human Factors in Computing Systems, pp. 1–14 Association for Computing Machinery, New York, NY, USA (2019). https://doi.org/10.1145/3290605.330 0652

17. Orlikowski, W.J.: Sociomaterial practices: exploring technology at work. Organ. Stud. **28**(9), 1435–1448 (2007). https://doi.org/10.1177/0170840607081138

18. Parkinson, B.: Emotional stylists: strategies of expressive management among trainee hairdressers. Cogn. Emot. (2008). https://doi.org/10.1080/02699939108411051

19. Raval, N., Dourish, P.: Standing out from the crowd: emotional labor, body labor, and temporal labor in ridesharing. In: Proceedings of the 19th ACM Conference on Computer-Supported Cooperative Work & Social Computing, pp. 97–107 ACM, San Francisco California USA (2016). https://doi.org/10.1145/2818048.2820026

20. Roemmich, K., Andalibi, N.: Data subjects' conceptualizations of and attitudes toward automatic emotion recognition-enabled wellbeing interventions on social media. In: Proceedings of the ACM Human-Computer Interaction, vol. 5, CSCW2, 308:1–308:34 (2021). https://doi. org/10.1145/3476049

21. Schulte, B.F., et al.: Homes for life: a design fiction probe. In: Proceedings of the 9th Nordic Conference on Human-Computer Interaction, pp. 1–10 Association for Computing Machinery, New York, NY, USA (2016). https://doi.org/10.1145/2971485.2993925

22. Sharma, S., et al.: From mild to wild: reimagining friendships and romance in the time of pandemic using design fiction. In: Designing Interactive Systems Conference 2021, pp. 64–77 Association for Computing Machinery, New York, NY, USA (2021). https://doi.org/10.1145/ 3461778.3462110

23. Shimo, S.: Risks of bias in AI-based emotional analysis technology from diversity perspectives. In: 2020 IEEE International Symposium on Technology and Society ISTAS, pp. 66–68 (2020). https://doi.org/10.1109/ISTAS50296.2020.9462168

24. Simeone, A.L., et al.: Immersive speculative enactments: bringing future scenarios and technology to life using virtual reality. In: Proceedings of the 2022 CHI Conference on Human Factors in Computing Systems, pp. 1–20 Association for Computing Machinery, New York, NY, USA (2022). https://doi.org/10.1145/3491102.3517492

25. Stark, L., Hoey, J.: The ethics of emotion in artificial intelligence systems. In: Proceedings of the 2021 ACM Conference on Fairness, Accountability, and Transparency, pp. 782–793 Association for Computing Machinery, New York, NY, USA (2021). https://doi.org/10.1145/3442188.3445939

26. Tanenbaum, T.J.: Design fictional interactions: why HCI should care about stories. Interactions 21(5), 22–23 (2014). https://doi.org/10.1145/2648414

27. Wei, W., et al.: Emotion recognition based on weighted fusion strategy of multichannel physiological signals. Comput. Intell. Neurosci. **2018**, 5296523 (2018). https://doi.org/10.1155/2018/5296523

28. Yan, H., et al.: Automatic detection of eating disorder-related social media posts that could benefit from a mental health intervention. Int. J. Eat. Disord. **52**(10), 1150–1156 (2019). https://doi.org/10.1002/eat.23148

29. Yang, Q., et al.: Re-examining whether, why, and how human-ai interaction is uniquely difficult to design. In: Proceedings of the 2020 CHI Conference on Human Factors in Computing Systems, pp. 1–13 Association for Computing Machinery, New York, NY, USA (2020). https://doi.org/10.1145/3313831.3376301

30. Constructing Grounded Theory: A practical guide through qualitative analysis Kathy Charmaz Constructing Grounded Theory: A practical guide through qualitative analysis Sage 224 £19.99 0761973532 0761973532 [Formula: see text]. Nurse Res. **13**, 4, 84 (2006). https://doi.org/10.7748/nr.13.4.84.s4

31. Into the Unknown: Speculating the Future of AI – Medium. https://medium.com/into-the-unknown-speculate-the-future-of-ai. Accessed 17 April 2023

Citation Recommendation Chatbot
for Professional Communities

Alexander Tobias Neumann(✉) ⓘ, Michal Slupczynski(✉) ⓘ, Yue Yin,
Chenyang Li ⓘ, and Stefan Decker ⓘ

RWTH Aachen University, Aachen, Germany
{Neumann,Slupczynski,Yin,Li,Decker}@dbis.rwth-aachen.de

Abstract. In recent years, the proliferation of academic literature has made it increasingly challenging for researchers and professionals to discover relevant citations for their work. To address this issue, this paper presents CitBot, a novel Citation Recommendation Chatbot designed specifically for professional communities. We describe the design, development, and evaluation of CitBot focusing on its performance and usefulness. CitBot combines the citation context with document-level embeddings utilizing SPECTER to generate personalized citation recommendations based on the community's research interests. The system is designed to seamlessly integrate with online professional platforms, providing users with citation suggestions in response to their queries. A user study was conducted to assess the chatbot's performance, comparing it to other citation recommendation tools. The findings of the study, along with a discussion of CitBot's benefits and limitations, are presented. By enhancing the citation discovery process, CitBot has the potential to improve the productivity of professional communities and transform the way researchers and practitioners access and engage with scientific knowledge.

Keywords: Citation Recommendation · Chatbots · Community of Practice · Recommender Systems

1 Introduction

In today's fast-paced academic world, researchers are constantly striving to stay ahead of the curve by discovering new knowledge and contributing to their respective fields. The exponential growth of scholarly publications has led to a significant increase in the number of citations that researchers must navigate and manage to produce high-quality research [1]. Citation is an important aspect of academic writing, as it allows authors to acknowledge the contributions of others and to provide a clear and transparent record of the sources used in their research [8]. As a novice researcher or student, it can be challenging to locate relevant literature due to a lack of expertise or familiarity with the field [32]. This can make it difficult to identify the most influential papers and determine which

© The Author(s), under exclusive license to Springer Nature Switzerland AG 2023
H. Takada et al. (Eds.): CollabTech 2023, LNCS 14199, pp. 52–67, 2023.
https://doi.org/10.1007/978-3-031-42141-9_4

resources will be most useful for your research. Citation management tools, such as Citavi, Mendeley or Zotero, allow authors to store and organize their citations, and to generate bibliographies and in-text citations in the required style [30]. These tools are useful for helping authors to keep track of their citations and to ensure that their bibliographies are complete and accurately formatted. However, relying on individual citation management tools may not fully capture the breadth of relevant literature in a particular field, which can be especially problematic for authors who are seeking to establish themselves as experts in their area of research [22]. One way to overcome this challenge is by joining a Community of Practice (CoP), a group of individuals who share a common profession or discipline and engage in regular, ongoing discussions and activities related to their field [37]. By participating in a CoP, community members can gain access to the collective knowledge and expertise of more experienced members, as well as share insights and perspectives. Collaborating with more experienced researchers and peers within a CoP can be an effective strategy for building a more comprehensive understanding of the literature in the relevant field. By sharing knowledge and expertise and requesting recommendations from others, peers can contribute to a more comprehensive understanding of the literature in their field. We hypothesize that a community-oriented citation recommender can be a valuable resource for young researchers and students, helping to accelerate the pace of research and to facilitate the discovery of new ideas and insights. Therefore, we developed a citation recommendation chatbot, which uses machine learning algorithms to recommend relevant citations to authors based on the content of their manuscripts and their community. The chatbot can understand the context and meaning of the text and suggest citations that are relevant to the topic and arguments being presented. Researchers can simply type their requests into a chat with the bot, and the chatbot uses natural language processing to understand their requests and provide relevant recommendations. To address the mentioned problems we formulated the following research questions in this paper:

RQ1: *How demanding is using a chatbot interface to request citation recommendations in comparison with traditional citation search engines?* To address RQ1, we designed and tested the chatbot interface and other citation recommendation systems. We utilized selected questions from the NASA Task Load Index (NASA TLX) questionnaire to measure the workload.

RQ2: *How does the design of a chatbot interface impact the usability of recommending citations for researchers?* Assuming that the chatbot offers better usability than traditional citation search engines, we conducted a comparative study using the System Usability Scale (SUS) questionnaire.

In this paper, we present the design, development and evaluation of a citation recommendation chatbot, and discuss the results of a user study that was conducted to assess the chatbot's performance and usefulness. We also compare the chatbot to other citation recommendation tools and discuss its potential benefits and limitations. The primary objective of this research is to provide a comprehensive examination of the chatbot and to contribute to the understanding of the application of machine learning in supporting authors in the citation process, including identifying potential benefits and limitations.

2   Related Work

In this chapter, we present background knowledge and related work in the field of citation recommendation and chatbots.

2.1   Fundamentals of Citation Recommendation

Citation recommendation involves suggesting appropriate citations for a given text. For instance, given the sentence "BERT is a model based on Attention Mechanism" within a document, it may be necessary to include two citations: "BERT [9] is a model based on Attention Mechanism [34]". Following the opinion of Färber et al., state of art citation recommendation approaches are based on supervised learning, and content-based filtering techniques [11], except for a few models based on collaborative filtering techniques [23,31]. Citation recommendation systems often utilize metadata (such as author and venue information) and citation relationships (e.g., when paper A cites paper B) to improve performance. Some previous studies have assumed that papers with similar metadata, such as those written by the same author, may have similar content [5,10,27]. Our approach utilizes both global citation recommendation and local recommendation [11]. In contrast to local citation recommendations, which only use a portion of the input text document as citation context, global citation recommendations use the full input text document or the publication's abstract for citation suggestion.

Global Citation Recommendation. Bhagavatula et al. utilized a vector space representation of the query document and its nearest neighbors as candidates for citation recommendations [5]. They found that the metadata introduces bias even though it can help improve performance. Their method consists of two phases: a recall-oriented candidate selection phase and a precision-oriented reranking phase. Nogueira et al. evaluated some pre-trained transformer models for citation recommendation [27]. Their work shows the possibility of using BERT for citation recommendation [9]. They also proposed a global citation recommendation method that follows the iterative strategy commonly employed by researchers when searching for relevant literature [27]. First, the initial candidate papers are found by searching the query using a keyword search engine. They reranked these candidates by calculating the probability of a query citing this document using a BERT rerank model based on the relevance between the query and candidates [26]. However, performance was insufficient when the term overlap between the query document and candidate documents was low, indicating the importance of exact match signals for this model. In contrast to other methods, their approach used results from keyword-based searches as initial papers and achieved excellent performance when keywords were well-matched.

SciBERT [4] is a BERT model that is trained using scientific corpus and was fine-tuned to SPECTER model [7] for comparing scientific documents. As BERT has an encoder-decoder structure, it can encode the inputs to embeddings. As the BERT-based model also extract the semantics of the input sentences, and the semantics of the sentences are not relevant to their length, this method could also be used for local citation recommendation. Guo et al. proposed a content-sensitive citation representation approach for citation recommendation that considers both citation relationships and relevance without citation relationships [15]. They used the Doc2Vec model to generate paper content embedding vectors based on titles and abstracts and calculated the cosine similarities between each pair of paper content embedding vectors [20]. Paper embeddings were then represented using DeepWalk methods based on a new network that includes both citation and relevance information [28]. Their study utilized graph embedding methods to present candidate papers, preserving both citation and relevance relationships.

Local Citation Recommendation. As each composer of literature has their writing style, Ebesu et al. adopted an author network in their end-to-end model Neural Citation Network [10] for local citation recommendation. Its input is citation context and its author, then the cited paper's title will be generated as output. The problem with this method under our scenario is that the author's information may not be in our training dataset, which would significantly influence the performance. Yang et al. proposed an Long Short-Term Memory (LSTM)-based model for local citation recommendation that takes into account both the semantic similarity between the citation context and candidate papers and the authors and venues of the candidate papers [39]. Venues are considered because similar scientific papers may be published by the same venue [29,39]. Their study only utilized author and venue metadata, resulting in a bias toward recommending papers by certain authors or from specific venues. Jeong et al. followed the basic idea of Yang et al. and proposed a new model with BERT and Variational Graph AutoEncoder (VGAE) based on Graph Convolutional Network (GCN) [16,18,19,39]. This approach places greater emphasis on citation relationships and has been shown to provide more accurate recommendations compared to the model proposed by Yang et al., which only utilized metadata [16,39]. This suggests that citation relationships are more critical than metadata. Wang et al. hypothesized that a researcher is likely to cite papers that they have cited previously and incorporated this concept, known as the author-paper relation, into their deep memory network with Bi-LSTM for local citation recommendation [35]. However, this approach assumes that the model is aware of which papers the user has previously cited, which is not feasible in our study. Additionally, users may expect the citation recommendation to suggest new papers, as recommending previously known papers may not be meaningful. There is also an alternative method for local citation recommendation, proposed by Wang et al., which involves text evidence mining through spherical heterogeneous information network embedding [36]. The authors seek to identify textual evidence sentences in the scientific literature that support a given scientific hypothesis query triplet (<*head entity, relation, tail entity*>). Their study constructs a large heterogeneous information network linking the user-input query and candidate evidence sentences to determine if the entities and relationships in the query match those in the candidate sentences. However, this method has high requirements for the dataset and only handles explicit evidence within a single sentence, without considering implicit evidence spanning multiple sentences. It also requires a well-prepared dataset, which is not feasible in our scenario.

2.2   Chatbots

A social bot, as defined by Ferrara et al., is a computer algorithm that generates the content and interacts with humans on social media platforms [12]. Chatbots, a specific type of social bot, are capable of conversing with humans on chat platforms through text or voice and are widespread examples of intelligent human-computer interaction [3,17]. A chatbot must not only inform the user of available content and functionality and guide them through achieving their desired goal but also understand the user's needs and determine the most effective means of assisting them [13]. Chatbots can be classified into two categories: retrieval-based chatbots and generative chatbots [2]. Retrieval-based chatbots use predefined rules to respond to specific tasks and queries from users, while generative chatbots can understand and interpret natural language and perform corresponding tasks based on the text received from users [2]. We focus on a retrieval-based chatbot, as it only requires the execution of a few specific tasks and does not need to comprehend natural language. Additionally, the design of a generative chatbot may introduce complexity to the system. Chatbots can be utilized in a variety of domains and serve various purposes, including facilitating social connections, providing customer support, engaging in marketing and e-commerce, entertaining, delivering news and factual content, and acting as personal assistants [14]. In pedagogical settings they can be summarized as learning, assisting, and mentoring, meaning they can act as educational tools to teach content or skills, take on tasks for the student to varying degrees, and support the student's development [24,38]. Chatbots can support students in three ways: scaffolding, recommending and informing. Scaffolding refers to the provision of direct assistance in learning new skills, particularly activities that benefit beginners. Recommending involves providing supportive information, tools, or other materials for specific learning tasks. Informing involves encouraging and supporting students in developing skills such as self-regulation [38]. This paper presents the implementation of an assisting chatbot that primarily assists students or researchers in searching for literature by recommending papers for a given input sentence.

3   Design and Realization of CitBot

The Citation Recommendation Bot (CitBot) is intended to assist students and researchers with academic paper authorship and literature research. The bot's citation recommendations can help users properly credit the work of others, ensuring that all sources of information are properly acknowledged and respected. Interaction via chat allows for collaborative group work among researchers, as well as individual use supporting members of CoPs in their academic work. Users can request citation recommendations using either keywords or full sentences. The search results are then compiled and presented in a paginated list of the most relevant publications. Additionally, the chatbot can export the obtained results in the BibTeX format, which is a widely accepted standard for bibliographic references and is compatible with various text editors commonly used in academic settings. This feature makes it easier for users to add citations to their documents without having to manually format them, saving time and effort in the process. Moreover, the bot can be used in conjunction with other tools, such as citation managers, to further streamline the research process.

3.1 Datasets

The CitBot is designed to personalize its suggestions to the research interests of the target CoP. As the target CoP is focused on computer science research, the CitBot is trained by taking into account three data collections: an academic corpus of computer science related publications based on DBLP[1] [21] (*DS_DBLP*) and AMiner[2] [33] (*DS_AMiner*), and the citations accumulated by the CoP (*DS_CoP*). By making use of these three collections, the bot can provide tailored citations that are highly relevant to the CoP's research interests, while also avoiding the risk of being limited by the scope of the CoP's corpus of citations. *DS_AMiner* is based on the AMiner database, which is a yearly updating dataset of publications in the Computer Science domain containing the abstracts and citation relations of more than 5 million papers. *DS_DBLP* represents the DBLP database, which is updated more often, so even if it has no abstract or citation relation in the dataset, it can be used to complete the AMiner dataset. To provide up-to-date recommendations, only items in *DS_AMiner* and *DS_DBLP* after a certain date (in this case 2018 and 2021, respectively) are used in the recommendation. *DS_CoP* is based on the Citavi database (containing around 25,000 items) collected by the CoP. This dataset is used to cater and tune the recommendations to the CoP academic interests and make the citation recommendations more relevant to the research field of the target CoP.

3.2 Architecture and Used Technologies

The CitBot is created using our Bot Framework and is composed of two main components (see Fig. 1): the CitBotRec Web service (see Sect. 3.4), and the CitBot Training Module (see Sect. 3.3). While the Training module manages the input datasets and generates paper embeddings, the CitBotRec service is responsible for providing the chatbot interface and finding relevant papers in the dataset.

---

[1] https://dblp.org.
[2] https://www.aminer.org.

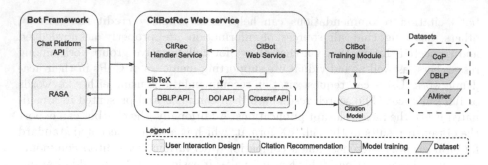

Fig. 1. Overview of the constituent elements comprising the CitBot architecture.

Bot Framework. The Bot Framework[3] [25] is a Web-based platform that enables users to create, train and deploy bots for self-hosted environments. It supports both retrieval-based bots that react to predefined events, as well as generative bots that use open-source deep learning technologies. Utilizing OpenAPI specifications and REST APIs, the Bot Framework provides a model-driven framework for creating bots that can interact with multiple social media platforms.

Chat Platforms. In this research project, we chose to deploy our investigation on two distinct chat platforms: Slack and Rocket.Chat. Slack and Rocket.Chat, although both highly popular, offer different levels of chatbot interactivity. Slack features a rich user interface that includes interactive buttons, enabling a more engaging and interactive user experience. In contrast, Rocket.Chat restricts chatbot communication to purely text-based messages, thereby setting a limit on the level of interactivity possible. This limitation is a valuable facet of our research because it allows us to study the impact of reduced interactivity on user engagement. By comparing the two environments, we can draw inferences about the relationship between interactivity and engagement. Additionally, the two platforms differ significantly in terms of their deployment models. Rocket.Chat is open-source, granting developers significant control over their data, which is particularly important in the context of data privacy and control. On the other hand, Slack adopts a freemium model that does not support self-hosting, thereby creating a reliance on Slack's security measures to protect user data.

3.3   Training—CitBot Training Module

The CitBot Training Module contains the training process of the citation recommendation algorithm (see Fig. 2), which consists of the following stages: Dataset selection, dataset manipulation and paper embedding generation.

---

[3] https://github.com/rwth-acis/Social-Bot-Framework.

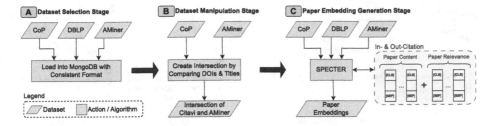

Fig. 2. The training process of the citation recommendation algorithm.

Dataset Selection Stage. During the dataset selection stage, the core datasets (DS_AMiner, DS_DBLP and DS_CoP) (c.f. Sect. 3.1) are transformed into a consistent format and loaded into a MongoDB database. The combined dataset is obtained by merging the records from multiple sources, ensuring that metadata such as titles, authors, and publication venues are consistently formatted and deduplicated.

Dataset Manipulation Stage. The main goal of this stage is a comparison of DOIs and titles between the Citavi and AMiner datasets to create an intersection. This intersection is a subset of DS_CoP as AMiner only contains information about publications but not on conferences or books. To generate relevant recommendations, only items in DS_AMiner that have similar topics to the works in DS_CoP are considered as candidate papers for the recommendation. This increases the quality of items selected from DS_AMiner and accelerates the computation.

Paper Embedding Generation Stage. The paper embedding generation stage of the citation recommendation algorithm uses SPECTER to generate document-level embeddings of scientific documents from the AMiner, DBLP and Citavi datasets. This algorithm is based on the Transformer language model architecture and relies on pre-trained models to generate document-level embeddings of scientific documents. It uses a combination of in- and out-citations to generate the embeddings for each paper. In-citations are used to incorporate the content of the paper itself, while out-citations are used to incorporate information about the paper's relevance in the field.

3.4 Recommendation—CitBotRec Web Service

The CitBotRec Web service (see Fig. 1) is comprised of two main components: the *CitRec Handler* service and the *CitBot Web* service.

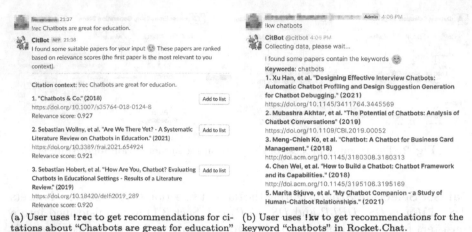

(a) User uses **!rec** to get recommendations for citations about "Chatbots are great for education" in Slack.

(b) User uses **!kw** to get recommendations for the keyword "chatbots" in Rocket.Chat.

Fig. 3. Usage of CitBot for (a) context recommendation in Slack and (b) recommendation based on keywords in Rocket.Chat.

CitRec Handler Service. The *CitRec Handler* acts as an interface between the citation recommendation and the API of the target chat platform. The user interaction design of the CitBot is based on a chat interface, which is available in Slack[4] and Rocket.Chat[5]. Chat was selected as the interaction medium for several reasons. First, it provides intuitive usage for CoP members, making it easy for users to quickly understand how to use the interface. Second, it is well-suited for use on the go, where access to a desktop interface of a citation tool may be limited. Finally, chat enables collaborative use, allowing multiple users to work together on a citation project. Chat is also highly accessible, allowing users to access it from a variety of devices, such as laptops, tablets, and smartphones. The system has been designed to provide an intuitive and user-friendly interface. It provides visual cues to indicate when it is processing a request and when it is finished. CitBot can be interacted with via direct messages, or it can be added to a channel to interact with users in a collaborative setting. Users of CitBot can request citation recommendations using either keywords or full sentences (see Fig. 3). Based on the user's input, CitBot will generate a list of relevant papers with their associated relevance score, authors, URL and publication year.

Citation Recommendation — CitBot Web Service. The *CitBot Web* service is the core of the application, which makes use of the recommendation algorithm to provide relevant papers for the input context. It also polls DBLP and Crossref APIs[6] to generate BibTeX information for the requested publications.

---

[4] https://slack.com.
[5] https://www.rocket.chat.
[6] https://www.crossref.org/documentation/retrieve-metadata/rest-api/.

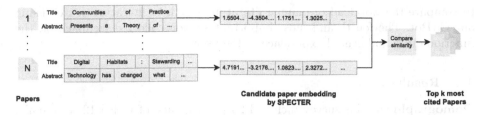

Fig. 4. The application process of the citation recommendation algorithm.

To achieve effective citation recommendations, the CitBot citation recommendation algorithm (see Fig. 4) employs state-of-the-art pre-trained embeddings such as SPECTER and SciBERT (c.f. Sect. 2.1). This is accomplished by first generating candidate paper embeddings, which represent the content of the paper in a vector format. This means that for each publication in the database, a vector representation is generated which can then be used to compare their similarity. The embeddings are generated using unsupervised learning algorithms that capture semantic relationships between publications. The embedding generation is fine-tuned on the combined dataset from DBLP, AMiner, and the CoP's citations (c.f. Sect. 3.1) to create a dense vector representation of the documents. To recommend a publication to a given input context, the embeddings generated by SPECTER are then used to find the most similar papers given the provided citation context. Finally, out of the most similar articles, the most cited candidates are selected for further consideration. By combining the citation context with the document-level embeddings, the algorithm can identify the most relevant and highly-cited papers in the field.

4 Evaluation

This contribution presents a community-oriented citation recommendation chatbot using an existing recommendation approach instead of implementing a new recommendation algorithm. The purpose of the evaluation was to gather end-user feedback regarding the interactions with CitBot. The evaluation focused on collecting information about the usability of the system and the overall user experience. However, we did not evaluate the quality of recommendations in this study. This is because our primary goal was to provide a useful and accessible chatbot for the community rather than focus on developing a new recommendation algorithm. Future studies may explore the integration of new recommendation algorithms to improve the quality of recommendations, but for this research, we prioritized providing a chatbot that was convenient and user-friendly.

4.1 Design, Procedure and Tasks

The user evaluation consisted of four sections. The first section inquired about the demographics of the users. The second section included a SUS questionnaire [6]. The third section modified the NASA Task Load Index (NASA-TLX) to compare the workload of manual literature search to literature search using our CitBot. The fourth and most important section collected feedback on the functionalities and overall experience of the users.

4.2　Results

Demographics. This survey included 24 participants, of which 12 were male, nine were female, and three did not disclose their gender. All participants were students, with 10 identifying as computer science students. One participant specifically mentioned their focus on computer vision, machine learning, and computer graphics. The age range of the participants was 18–24 for 14 participants and 25–34 for 10 participants. CitBot was designed specifically for computer science students, making the sample population highly representative of the intended user base and increasing the reliability of the survey results. The participants used a variety of devices, with all but three using computers, one using a tablet, and the remaining two using mobile phones. Only one participant had used a citation recommendation application similar to CitBot, though they did not specify which one. 19 out of the 24 participants had interacted with chatbots before.

SUS. Table 1 shows the detailed SUS results for each statement. The resulting SUS score was calculated according to Brooke [6]. As the two implemented chat interfaces provide different functionality (most notably, Slack allows developers to use buttons for user interaction, which is not available in Rocket.Chat, c.f. Sect. 3.2), the SUS scores for the different platforms were calculated separately. For Slack, this resulted in a SUS score of 81.3 ($n = 18$), whereas the Rocket.Chat interface scored 82.9 ($n = 6$). The final SUS score of CitBot is 81.7 ($n = 24$).

NASA-TLX. In this question group, we selected some relevant questions from the NASA-TLX to compare the workload of literature searches using CitBot and other search engines. Table 2 shows the results of this question group and compares the mental and physical demands and the difficulty of using CitBot and other search engines.

Additional Feedback. We also solicited feedback and suggestions from the participants. One suggestion was to provide a filter function that allows users to search for papers that meet certain criteria. Further, participants requested the ability to customize the ranking order of the recommended papers. Another suggestion was to include a feature that allows users to take quick notes when adding papers to their marking list, to prevent forgetting the reason for adding the paper. Another feature request was that the bot provides keywords based on the recommendation results, as this could be helpful when searching for papers on a specific topic without knowing the exact wording. Finally, a participant mentioned the use of logical operators, such as OR and AND, in most search

Table 1. Results of the SUS questionnaire. Score is an ordinal scale where 1 ≅ "strongly disagree" and 5 ≅ "strongly agree" (n=24).

Question	Rocket.Chat (n=6) $\bar{X}(\sigma_X)$	Slack (n=18) $\bar{X}(\sigma_X)$	Total (n=24) $\bar{X}(\sigma_X)$
I think that I would like to use CitBot frequently	4.5 (±0.84)	4.28 (±0.83)	4.33 (±0.82)
I found CitBot unnecessarily complex	1.67 (±1.63)	2.28 (±1.27)	2.13 (±1.36)
I thought CitBot was easy to use	4.50 (±0.55)	4.39 (±0.78)	4.42 (±0.72)
I think that I would need the support of a technical person to be able to use CitBot	1.67 (±1.63)	1.89 (±1.13)	1.83 (±1.24)
I found the various functions in CitBot were well integrated	4.00 (±0.89)	3.89 (±1.02)	3.92 (±0.97)
I thought there was too much inconsistency in Cit-Bot	2.33 (±1.37)	1.94 (±0.87)	2.04 (±1.00)
I would imagine that most people would learn to use CitBot very quickly	5.00 (±0.00)	4.56 (±0.62)	4.67 (±0.56)
I found CitBot very cumbersome to use	1.67 (±1.63)	1.44 (±0.70)	1.50 (±0.98)
I felt very confident using CitBot	4.50 (±0.55)	4.17 (±0.92)	4.25 (±0.85)
I needed to learn a lot of things before I could get going with CitBot	2.00 (±1.55)	1.22 (±0.55)	1.42 (±0.93)

Table 2. Results of relevant NASA-TLX questions. Score is an ordinal scale where 1 ≅ "very low/easy" and 5 ≅ "very hard/difficult" (n = 24).

Question	CitBot $\bar{X}(\sigma_X)$	Others $\bar{X}(\sigma_X)$
How mentally demanding was using the system to find citations?	2.21 (±1.14)	2.88 (±1.19)
How physically demanding was using the system to find citations?	2.00 (±1.29)	2.5 (±1.29)
How hard was using the system to find suitable papers?	2.17 (±1.13)	2.71 (±1.00)

engines, which allow users to filter results based on logical conditions and potentially find more relevant papers.

4.3 Discussion

The majority is using computers is expected, as students are likely to prefer using computers for literature searches in a production environment. The small sample size of mobile users did not allow for a thorough evaluation of mobile usability, which may be addressed in future evaluations. This may indicate that the majority of participants had not previously used such applications, and their comparison of CitBot with other paper search engines in the survey may have primarily been with Google Scholar, IEEE Xplore, Web of Science and others. The fact that most participants have interacted with a chatbot before might influence their comparison of CitBot's usability and computer-human interaction with other chatbots. While all SUS scores are "excellent", the slightly higher score of Rocket.Chat can be explained by a smaller functionality set and thus a simpler interface. During the experiments, we observed that the bot was able to provide relevant citations for sentences that summarized the main points of a paper but struggled to give suitable recommendations for sentences that contained excessive detail. This suggests that the bot is more effective at providing global rather than local citation recommendations. Additionally, the citation recommendation algorithm relies on extracting the semantics of sentences, which means it is unable to recommend papers based on proper nouns.

5   Conclusion and Future Work

This research investigated the impact of our chatbot CitBot on literature search and management, with a focus on the usability of the interface and the impact of the interface design on the usability of recommending citations for researchers. Regarding RQ1, the evaluation results suggest that using a chatbot interface like CitBot for requesting citation recommendations is not significantly more demanding than using traditional citation search engines. Participants found CitBot to be more convenient than traditional search engines because the bot can recommend papers for the input text. Concerning RQ2, the feedback and suggestions from the participants highlight the importance of the interface design in the usability of recommending citations for researchers. The SUS score of 81.7 confirms the usability of CitBot as a chatbot interface for literature search and management. Participants requested additional features to enhance the usability of CitBot, such as a filter function, customizable ranking order, note-taking, keyword suggestions, and logical operators. The observation that the bot is more effective at providing global rather than local citation recommendations suggests that the design of the citation recommendation algorithm could be improved to better handle detailed sentences. The main strength of CitBot is its user-friendly interaction, which enables users to easily search for and manage their literature. The evaluation results indicate that CitBot is a welcome addition to students' tools, and they find its convenience and efficiency to be superior to traditional paper search engines. Furthermore, the potential for future development and integration with new technologies, such as MLOps and large language models, further strengthens the benefits of this work. For instance, CitBot can be trained on feedback to improve the accuracy and relevance of the citation recommendations. Additionally, expanding CitBot to other chat systems like Telegram could enhance its reach and accessibility, making it available to a wider range of users. Moreover, in the context of large language models and knowledge graphs, it would be illuminating to position CitBot in a comparative context with established chat systems like ChatGPT. A comprehensive comparative analysis could facilitate a deeper understanding of the chatbot's performance and effectiveness, spotlighting the unique characteristics, benefits, and limitations of CitBot. By evaluating CitBot alongside ChatGPT, we can accentuate its distinct contributions to the field, demonstrating its particular strengths and areas for improvement more explicitly. Overall, this research contributes to the field of literature search and management by providing a novel approach to citation recommendation through the implementation of the CitBot chatbot. The CitBot has the potential to significantly improve the efficiency and effectiveness of literature search and management, particularly in academic and research settings. Its user-friendly interface, efficient citation recommendation algorithm, and potential for future development make it a valuable tool for students, researchers, and academics alike.

Acknowledgements. The research leading to these results has been financially supported by the German Federal Ministry of Education and Research (BMBF) through the project "Personalisierte Kompetenzentwicklung und hybrides KI-Mentoring" (tech4compKI) with grant no. 16DHB2213.

References

1. Aksnes, D.W., Langfeldt, L., Wouters, P.: Citations, citation indicators, and research quality: an overview of basic concepts and theories. SAGE Open **9**(1), 215824401982957 (2019)
2. Babar, Z., Lapouchnian, A., Siu-Kwong Yu, E.: Chatbot Design - Towards a Social Analysis Using i* and process architecture. In: iStar Workshop, pp. 73–78 (2017)
3. Bansal, H., Khan, R.: A review paper on human computer interaction. Int. J. Adv. Res. Comput. Sci. Softw. Eng. **8**(4), 53 (2018)
4. Beltagy, I., Lo, K., Cohan, A.: SciBERT: a pretrained language model for scientific text. In: Inui, K., Jiang, J., Ng, V., Wan, X. (eds.) Proceedings of the 2019 Conference on Empirical Methods in Natural Language Processing and the 9th International Joint Conference on Natural Language Processing (EMNLP-IJCNLP), pp. 3613–3618. Association for Computational Linguistics, Stroudsburg (2019)
5. Bhagavatula, C., Feldman, S., Power, R., Ammar, W.: Content-based citation recommendation. In: Walker, M., Ji, H., Stent, A. (eds.) Proceedings of the 2018 Conference of the North American Chapter of, pp. 238–251. Association for Computational Linguistics, Stroudsburg (2018)
6. Brooke, J.: SUS: a quick and dirty usability scale. In: Jordan, P.W., Thomas, B., Weerdmeester, B.A., McClelland, I.L. (eds.) Usability Evaluation in Industry, pp. 189–194. Taylor & Francis (1996)
7. Cohan, A., Feldman, S., Beltagy, I., Downey, D., Weld, D.: SPECTER: document-level representation learning using citation-informed transformers. In: Jurafsky, D., Chai, J., Schluter, N., Tetreault, J. (eds.) Proceedings of the 58th Annual Meeting of the Association for Computational Linguistics, pp. 2270–2282. Association for Computational Linguistics, Stroudsburg (2020)
8. Derntl, M.: Basics of research paper writing and publishing. Int. J. Technol. Enhanced Learn. **6**(2), 105–123 (2014)
9. Devlin, J., Chang, M.W., Lee, K., Toutanova, K.: BERT: pre-training of deep bidirectional transformers for language understanding. In: Burstein, J., Doran, C., Solorio, T. (eds.) Proceedings of the 2019 Conference of the North, pp. 4171–4186. Association for Computational Linguistics, Stroudsburg (2019)
10. Ebesu, T., Fang, Y.: Neural citation network for context-aware citation recommendation. In: Kando, N., Sakai, T., Joho, H., Li, H., de Vries, A.P., White, R.W. (eds.) Proceedings of the 40th International ACM SIGIR Conference on Research and Development in Information Retrieval, pp. 1093–1096. ACM, New York (2018)
11. Färber, M., Jatowt, A.: Citation recommendation: approaches and datasets. Int. J. Digit. Libr. **21**(4), 375–405 (2020)
12. Ferrara, E., Varol, O., Davis, C., Menczer, F., Flammini, A.: The rise of social bots. Commun. ACM **59**(7), 96–104 (2016)

13. Følstad, A., Brandtzæg, P.B.: Chatbots and the new world of HCI. Interactions **24**(4), 38–42 (2017)
14. Følstad, A., Skjuve, M., Brandtzaeg, P.B.: Different chatbots for different purposes: towards a typology of chatbots to understand interaction design. In: Bodrunova, S.S., Koltsova, O., Følstad, A., Halpin, H., Kolozaridi, P., Yuldashev, L., Smoliarova, A., Niedermayer, H. (eds.) INSCI 2018. LNCS, vol. 11551, pp. 145–156. Springer, Cham (2019). https://doi.org/10.1007/978-3-030-17705-8_13
15. Guo, L., Cai, X., Qin, H., Hao, F., Guo, S.: A content-sensitive citation representation approach for citation recommendation. J. Ambient Intell. Humanized Comput. (2021)
16. Jeong, C., Jang, S., Park, E., Choi, S.: A context-aware citation recommendation model with BERT and graph convolutional networks. Scientometrics **124**(3), 1907–1922 (2020)
17. Khanna, A., Pandey, B., Vashishta, K., Kalia, K., Pradeepkumar, B., Das, T.: A Study of Today's A.I. through chatbots and rediscovery of machine intelligence. Int. J. u- and e-Service. Sci. Technol. **8**(7), 277–284 (2015)
18. Kipf, T.N., Welling, M.: Variational Graph Auto-Encoders. NIPS Workshop on Bayesian Deep Learning (2016)
19. Kipf, T.N., Welling, M.: Semi-supervised classification with graph convolutional networks. In: Proceedings of the 5th International Conference on Learning Representations, ICLR 2017 (2017)
20. Le, Q., Mikolov, T.: Distributed representations of sentences and documents. In: Proceedings of the 31st International Conference on International Conference on Machine Learning - Volume 32, ICML 2014, pp. II-1188–II-1196. JMLR.org (2014)
21. Ley, M.: The DBLP computer science bibliography: evolution, research issues, perspectives. In: Laender, A.H.F., Oliveira, A.L. (eds.) SPIRE 2002. LNCS, vol. 2476, pp. 1–10. Springer, Heidelberg (2002). https://doi.org/10.1007/3-540-45735-6_1
22. Li, J., Burnham, J.F., Lemley, T., Britton, R.M.: Citation analysis: comparison of web of science®, Scopus™, SciFinder®, and Google Scholar. J. Electron. Resources Med. Libraries **7**(3), 196–217 (2010)
23. Liu, H., Kong, X., Bai, X., Wang, W., Bekele, T.M., Xia, F.: Context-based collaborative filtering for citation recommendation. IEEE Access **3**, 1695–1703 (2015)
24. Neumann, A.T., Arndt, T., Köbis, L., Meissner, R., Martin, A., de Lange, P., Pengel, N., Klamma, R., Wollersheim, H.W.: Chatbots as a tool to scale mentoring processes: individually supporting self-study in higher education. Front. Artif. Intell. **4**, 64–71 (2021). https://doi.org/10.3389/frai.2021.668220
25. Neumann, A.T., de Lange, P., Klamma, R.: Collaborative creation and training of social bots in learning communities. In: 2019 IEEE 5th International Conference on Collaboration and Internet Computing (CIC), pp. 11–19. IEEE (2019)
26. Nogueira, R., Cho, K.: Passage Re-ranking with BERT
27. Nogueira, R., Jiang, Z., Cho, K., Lin, J.: Navigation-based candidate expansion and pretrained language models for citation recommendation. Scientometrics **125**(3), 3001–3016 (2020)
28. Perozzi, B., Al-Rfou, R., Skiena, S.: DeepWalk. In: Proceedings of the 20th ACM SIGKDD International Conference on Knowledge Discovery and Data Mining, pp. 701–710. ACM, New York (2014)
29. Pham, M.C., Cao, Y., Klamma, R.: Clustering technique for collaborative filtering and the application to venue recommendation. In: Proceedings of I-KNOW '10 : 10th International Conference on Knowledge Management and Knowledge Technologies; Graz, Austria, September 1–3, 2010, pp. 343–354 (2010)

30. S. Kaur, K. S. Dhindsa: comparative study of citation and reference management tools: Mendeley, Zotero and ReadCube. In: 2016 International Conference on ICT in Business Industry & Government (ICTBIG), pp. 1–5 (2016)
31. Sakib, N., Ahmad, R.B., Haruna, K.: A collaborative approach toward scientific paper recommendation using citation context. IEEE Access **8**, 51246–51255 (2020)
32. Sibanda, J.: Citation mania in academic theses writing: a case study. Acad. J. Interdisciplinary Stud. **9**(4), 219 (2020)
33. Tang, J., Zhang, J., Yao, L., Li, J., Zhang, L., Su, Z.: ArnetMiner. In: Li, Y., Liu, B., Sarawagi, S. (eds.) The 14th ACM SIGKDD International Conference, p. 990 (2008)
34. Vaswani, A., et al.: Attention Is All You Need
35. Wang, J., Zhu, L., Dai, T., Wang, Y.: Deep memory network with Bi-LSTM for personalized context-aware citation recommendation. Neurocomputing **410**, 103–113 (2020)
36. Wang, X., Zhang, Y., Chauhan, A., Li, Q., Han, J.: Textual evidence mining via spherical heterogeneous information network embedding. In: 2020 IEEE International Conference on Big Data (Big Data), pp. 828–837. IEEE (2020)
37. Wenger, E.: Communities of Practice: Learning, Meaning, and Identity. Learning in doing, Cambridge University Press, Cambridge (1998)
38. Wollny, S., Schneider, J., Di Mitri, D., Weidlich, J., Rittberger, M., Drachsler, H.: Are we there yet? - a systematic literature review on chatbots in education. Front. Artif. Intell. **4** (2021)
39. Yang, L., et al.: A LSTM based model for personalized context-aware citation recommendation. IEEE Access **6**, 59618–59627 (2018)

Differential Characteristics and Collaborative Interactions of Institutional and Personal Twitter Accounts in a Citizen Science Context

Simon Krukowski[1,3](✉) ⓘ, Fernando Martínez-Martínez[2] ⓘ,
and H. Ulrich Hoppe[3] ⓘ

[1] University of Duisburg-Essen, Duisburg, Germany
simon.krukowski@uni-due.de
[2] Universidad Rey Juan Carlos, Móstoles, Spain
fernando.martinezm@urjc.es
[3] RIAS Institute, Duisburg, Germany
{sk,uh}@rias-institute.de

Abstract. The analysis of Twitter data can help to better understand the interplay between scientific institutions, volunteers and other actors in a Citizen Science (CS) context. A first essential distinction has to be made between different user types such as organizations and individuals. We have applied and evaluated different machine learning approaches for this purpose. On this basis, we have analyzed networks based on different Twitter relations to characterize roles and interactions between different user types. Relations based on retweets, quotes, and replies capture the short term dynamics of on-going discussions. Our findings indicate that institutions are the main information sources, whereas personal users have an important role in active information spreading and dissemination through retweeting and quoting. Projecting the dynamic interactions onto a static network based on the follower relationship shows that pathways of dynamic information diffusion are largely determined by the static follower topology. These findings provide strategic information for managing CS-related discussions.

Keywords: Twitter · user classification · Citizen Science · participation profiles · network measures of collaboration

1 Introduction

In recent years, Citizen Science (CS) has become a significant source of contributions to the democratization of knowledge production and scientific collaboration. The current practice of CS relies to a large extent on web and social media platforms supporting internal collaboration as well public outreach [14,15,18]. In this context, Twitter facilitates communication and collaboration between individuals and organizations within the CS community and beyond, which makes

H. Takada et al. (Eds.): CollabTech 2023, LNCS 14199, pp. 68–83, 2023.
https://doi.org/10.1007/978-3-031-42141-9_5

it an important source of empirical evidence for analyzing the communication within and around the CS community.

In a critical analysis and reflection of the achievements and benefits of CS, one focal point is the role of the actual "citizens", namely the non-professional volunteers engaging in CS activities. Is their role more subordinate and instrumental, or are they bringing in their own interests and dynamics in a way that shapes the process of joint knowledge creation? This question has been addressed in studies of project-specific internal collaborations manifested in forum activities (e.g., [10]). By analyzing the Twitter communication from within and around the CS community, we shift the attention to a more macroscopic perspective addressing the interaction between projects and with entities outside the CS community.

As exemplified by several studies [12,19], standard techniques of data and network analysis can yield basic insights about the overall structure and characteristic of Twitter communications in a CS context. Twitter data allows for differentiating between more stable or "static" relations based on the follower relation and time-dependent and content-driven "dynamic" interactions based on *retweets*, *replies* or *quotes*. However, when trying to interpret these interactions, we are confronted with different types of actors with potentially different participation profiles [13]. In this context, we need to distinguish between two basic types of actors: personal and institutional users, which can both appear as nodes in Twitter-based actor-actor social networks. Personal and institutional actors differ in terms of available resources, expertise, and objectives. In the context of CS, researchers are interested in spreading the word about their projects and attracting volunteers to join scientific discussions around CS-related topics, whereas institutional actors represent the perspective of "official" science and research, while volunteers will come in as personal actors. Recent research has brought forth methods for classifying institutional and personal accounts on Twitter in other contexts [13,16], providing a solid foundation for our analyses in and around the CS community. These approaches make use of machine learning algorithms in combination with natural language processing and network analysis techniques.

The work reported here extends and specializes these approaches in the application context of CS. In our approach, the classification of user/actor types as personal or institutional acts as a preliminary step that allows for a first characterization of different profiles and types of participation. We are particularly interested in studying the collaborative dynamics and potential synergies between institutional and personal Twitter accounts as they emerge in the context of CS. By conducting a comprehensive analysis of the interactions between these user groups, we aim to provide valuable insights and recommendations for researchers, practitioners, and policy-makers involved in the development and implementation of Citizen Science initiatives, and for the wider Citizen Science community. Thus, we pursue four central research questions:

RQ1: Which features (user/network attributes) are particularly relevant and contribute to a good classification?

RQ2: How can we adequately represent the relevant dynamic relations in a multi-relational network model?

RQ3: How can we characterise the different roles and behavior of individuals and institutions in the discussions around CS?

RQ4: In how far are the dynamic interactions reflected by static relations between actors?

2 Background and Related Work

2.1 Participation and Roles in CS Projects

Citizen Science activities, particularly in their online manifestations, have themselves become a subject of scientific investigation (cf. [22]). An important aspect of such scientific reflections is the characterization of roles and types of contribution and interaction between participating citizens ("volunteers") and professional scientists who represent established scientific institutions [20]. Such relations have already been studied based on the analysis of micro-level interactions in forum pages of specific projects [10]. These data reflect the local, internal characteristics of underlying cooperative relations and can shed light on the question in how far volunteers take initiative in shaping project activities. Still within the realm of available online information associated to CS, Twitter communication can reveal characteristics of the interactions between projects, individuals and public institutions. From this end, it is again possible to gain insight into the interplay between individual and institutional roles and their respective contributions.

The distinction between different types of users behind Twitter accounts is of particular importance for the analysis and interpretation of CS-related interactions on Twitter. For example, Mazumdar et al. [12], who examined Twitter discussions with regard to content, structure and behavior, found that CS-discussions specifically evolve around certain centralised clusters of highly active organizations who act as broadcasters. Thus, being able to automatically distinguish these two user types in the context of CS (**RQ1**) and subsequently examine their respective behavior (**RQ2-4**) allows for highly-desired insights that are of interest to different stakeholders. Accordingly, there is a need to look into existing approaches for the classification of different types of Twitter users.

2.2 Classifying Institutional and Personal Twitter Accounts

The analysis of different user types on Twitter (e.g., [9,16]) is a common approach to better understand interaction dynamics as well as their ramifications regarding a myriad of research questions. A basic but particularly important distinction to be made is that between personal users (e.g., individuals) and institutions (e.g., governmental entities, companies etc.). Between these user types, behavior might substantially differ and introduce bias when it is not properly addressed during analyses [16]. For example, governmental entities might follow entirely different motifs when participating in Twitter, likely trying to disseminate information, while personal users might primarily consume information and engage with other personal users. To this end, there are several approaches to classify Twitter users based on such a binary distinction. For example, McCorristin et al. [13] created a support-vector based classification algorithm that takes post content, stylistic and structural features into account. By combining features such as words used in tweets and average word length, they were able to correctly classify 95.5% of the users correctly. Similarly, by using gradient boosting, Oentaryo et al. [16] showed that content, social and temporal features (e.g., tweets, social metrics and behavior such as tweeting times) can be used as features to accurately predict whether an account is an institution or a personal account. Textual features such as the content of the user biography can also be encoded and the resulting embeddings can be used as features to train a classifier, like in Kreutz et al. [9]. However, most approaches use a complex and rich set of features that might be non-trivial to retrieve (e.g., past tweets of a user), thus posing the question whether a classification is also possible by merely using the features present in the users public Twitter profile. Additionally, user characteristics might differ in the context of CS, where different stakeholders might act differently. Thus, to approach **RQ1**, we try to extend these findings and examine features that contribute to a good prediction.

2.3   Network Models Based on Twitter Data

A large body of research on user behavior in Twitter exists, ranging from content analyses (e.g., sentiment) to studies on information dissemination. The inherent social structure of the network allows for a particularly insightful combination of topological features (e.g., *relations* such as retweeting) with content-level information such as the tweets (*content*), which can then be used to infer opinions, political orientations or stock prices [3].

However, many studies resort to single types of interactions between users (e.g., based on retweets), although multiple additional ways of interacting exist, such as quoting or replying. Such multiple dimensions of interaction can be operationalized by representing them in the form of a multi-relational network, which in turn allows for a richer and more fine-grained analysis [21]. Specifically in the context of CS, it can yield more insights relevant for different stakeholders, such as the appropriate way to disseminate information. Another way of using SNA to analyze Twitter discussions is to consider the following relation, i.e., connect users to each other based on whether they follow each other or not. Complementary to *dynamic* relations such as retweeting or quoting), these *static* connections based on the "following" relation enable us to check if dynamic interactions follow already existing static pathways. The multi-relational approach allows us to determine potential incongruences between different dynamic relations (**RQ2**), including also the differentiation between different user types (**RQ3**). Mapping these interactions onto the underlying static follow-relations, we can furthermore examine **RQ4** how *potential* interactions (static) relate to *actual* interactions (dynamically enacted). This mapping of multiple types of dynamic interactions onto static "pathways" for information diffusion has rarely been done so far, and presents a novelty of the SNA approach used in this study.

3 Method

3.1 Data Collection and Sampling

The initial basis for our sample is a set of CS-related tweets that was collected over a time span of almost two years (09/30/2020 - 07/26/2022) based on the occurrence of certain keywords such as "citsci" or "Citizen Science". The sample includes 448,247 tweets from 151,718 unique users. To facilitate homogeneous automatic processing, we limited our sample to users with biographies in English, as determined by a language-detection API[1], which resulted in a set of 352,683 English tweets from 114,488 users. For each tweet, we have data fields such as *username, text, contained entities* (e.g., hashtags etc.) or *public metrics* (received retweets etc.) and similarly, for each user we have information such as their *name, profile picture* and *biography*.

3.2 Classifying Users

To infer whether a user is an institution or a personal account, we used manual labelling and machine learning algorithms. Although recent advances in machine learning such as deep learning allow for the autonomous learning of features, due to the structured (tabular) nature of our data, we chose to manually engineer the features, and then train several classifiers on them [7].

Annotation. We manually labelled a subset of 2,448 randomly chosen users based on their biography, profile picture or username as either "personal" or "institution". The task was conducted by a single annotator and resulted in a set of 1,779 personal accounts and 665 institutions. We decided to work with this unbalanced distribution, as it depicts the distribution of user types in Twitter more accurately, where we also expect that the majority of accounts are personal users [24].

Feature Engineering. Based on related literature (e.g., [13,24]) and the experience gained from the labelling, we then decided to use the following features for the classification: *protected, verified* (is a user protected/ verified?), *followers_count* (how many followers does a user have?), *following_count* (how many other users does the user follow?), *listed_count* (in how many lists is the user?), *tweet_count* (how many tweets did the user make?) and the *number of entities* present in the biography (e.g., number of hashtags). Additionally, we used a Python package for face detection [6] to create the *face* feature (i.e., whether a

---

[1] https://detectlanguage.com.

face is in the profile picture), and a large database of international names[2] to infer whether the name of the user corresponds to a proper name (*nameslist*). We introduced the two latter features because we expect most personal accounts to have a profile picture with a face and a proper name.

Related literature on the classification of Twitter users (e.g., [9]) also points to the user biographies as another valuable feature. To examine this, we included them in another model by using the state-of-the-art language model sentence-BERT [17] with a pre-trained model (*all-MiniLM-L12-v2*) to create text embeddings. This yielded an additional 384 features that were added along the other features. All numerical features were standardized individually. The categorical features (which are all binary) were labelled with 1 and 0.

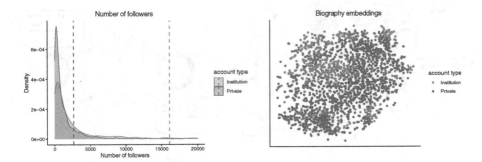

Fig. 1. Features used for classification. Left: Difference in followers between account types. Right: t-SNE plot of Sentence-BERT embeddings of the user biographies per account type

A descriptive analysis revealed significant differences between the two account types in the features chosen for our models. This can be seen exemplary in Fig. 1, where we see an expected tendency of institutional accounts to have a higher number of followers (as indicated by the dotted vertical line) on the left. Similarly, the t-SNE plot showing the biography embeddings coloured by account type reveals certain clusters, differentiating personal users from institutions. A similar picture emerges for the other features and as such, they show inferential value in differentiating between institutional and personal user accounts.

Classification. We chose to train four different classification algorithms and then use the one performing the best to predict the values for our sample. We used *Logistic Regression, Random Forests, TabNet* and *XGBoost* [1,4,5] in Python, based on their applicability and accuracy for data that is structured like the one in our sample. The labelled sample was split 70/30 into train- and test sets. All algorithms were trained with the default parameters from the implementations in their respective publications. To assess accuracy, we use *accuracy* (percentage of correctly classified users), *precision, recall* and *F1* (see [11])

---

[2] https://damegender.davidam.com.

3.3   Network Extraction

Dynamic Networks. To assess collaborative interactions between the account types, we used the tweets in our sample to construct a dynamic, multirelational network. Using the networkX Python package [8], we extracted a directed Multigraph (parallel edges for multiple interactions) from the set of tweets described above, where users in our sample who created a tweet containing relational information (e.g., *retweeting*) appear as unique nodes {u, $u1$, $u2$ ...} in the constructed network. For the edges, there are three different kinds of interactions that we use to create an edge (u, v): *Retweeting, replying* and *quoting.*

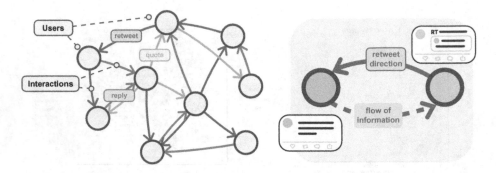

Fig. 2. Multidimensional network structure and flow of information for retweeting

We then save this information as an edge attribute. Thus, if user u quotes user v, we create a directed edge (u, v). The result is a heterogeneous, multidimensional network with 107,413 nodes and 258,704 edges corresponding to the different types of interactions between users. For the construction, we used the filtered set of English users. Figure 2 illustrates this, showing the different types of interactions. For the retweet relation, the directionality has to be explicitly taken into account: If node u retweets node v (thereby establishing a directed edge (u,v), the actual flow of information goes from the creator of the tweet (v) to the retweeter u.

Evaluating Dynamic Interactions in Static Networks. As the network described above only captures *dynamic* interactions between users, we were also interested in how such interactions are reflected by the more stable and static "pathways" that are the follow-relationships between users. However, due to limitations in the Twitter API, retrieving such information is not easily possible for the large number of users in our sample. A common approach to deal with this limitation is to extract ego-networks for given users. Such an ego-network contains all nodes linked to the central node ("ego"), also including the links between the neighbors, also called a 1.5-neighborhood. To distinguish the interaction behavior between personal and institutional users, a natural choice for an ego-network was to start from an organizational account with sufficient followers, allowing for the construction of such an ego-network. Thus, we chose the *SciStarter* account, as it appears to be a central actor in the CS discussions on Twitter. The static network was created using the networkX Python package with the users mentioned before (friends and followers) and the follow relation as edges. The Twitter API was used to retrieve the followers and followees of *SciStarter* (i.e., user that SciStarter follows). Similarly, we retrieved these users' followers and followees, resulting in a network for which we know the relation between all the users present in it. This network then involves all users who are directly connected to *SciStarter* (i.e., by following or being followed), and their respective connections to each other, and contains 17,694 nodes and 2,004,840 edges. This so-called "1.5-neighbourhood" is a typical approach when constructing ego-networks.

The static ego network serves as a reference model that allows us to examine, to which extent the dynamic interactions coincide with static connections (**RQ4**), thereby generating insights regarding paths of information flow (e.g., whether retweets occur between users who follow each other or not). We can interpret user u following user v (thereby creating a directed edge (u,v)) as u "watching" v. Accordingly, a congruent retweet action (i.e., dynamic edge) would be u retweeting v, and not the other way around. However, the information itself flows from v to u. This is exemplified in Fig. 2.

For our approach, we filtered the interactions from the dynamic network and the nodes that form it to retain only those from the *SciStarter* ego-network. Once we isolated these interactions and the nodes, we used the edges of the ego-network (follow relation) to create a list of tuples containing the source account and the account they follow (source, target) in order to iterate the rows of the interactions. Iterating over these rows if the pair (source, target) was present in the tuple list it got labelled as *Follower*, if not it got labelled as *Not follower*. Here, we also used the networkX Python package to create the network, and the filter left 44,229 unique interactions for the *SciStarter* ego-network.

3.4 Measuring Interactions

To approach **RQ3** and **RQ4** in characterizing the different roles of individuals and organizations, we examined their interaction behavior by deploying several measures from SNA. To this end, we examined the degree (i.e., degree centrality) of the users, indicating the number of users [23] adjacent to them. Multiple interactions between users are represented by the degree accordingly. As the constructed network is directed, we can also examine the in- and out-degree, representing incoming and outgoing interactions. We can consider nodes with higher degrees as more influential and prominent. Thus, the degree allows us to examine interaction behavior on the node-level. Additionally, we can examine interactions on the edge-level, by counting the general occurrences of interactions as well as their directionality.

4   Results

4.1   Classification

To approach **RQ1**, we examined the classification performance for our different model types. For this, we defined two models: one including the sentence-BERT biography embeddings, and one without. We assessed model performance by using the metrics (accuracy, precision/recall) described above. As can be seen in Table 1, both models achieve good (> .80) accuracy for all classifiers and particularly, high F1 values.

Table 1. Results of the classification algorithms for the two different models.

Algorithm	Embeddings	Accuracy (train)	Accuracy (test)	Precision	Recall	F1
Random Forest	False	0.906	0.894	0.901	0.956	0.928
Log. Regr.		0.854	0.871	0.928	0.887	0.907
tabNet		0.881	0.894	0.942	0.906	0.924
XGBoost		0.965	0.903	0.928	0.937	0.932
Random Forest	True	0.948	0.838	0.821	0.989	0.897
Log. Regr.		**0.939**	**0.925**	**0.938**	**0.958**	**0.948**
tabNet		0.945	0.918	0.922	0.967	0.944
XGBoost		1.000	0.924	0.930	0.966	0.947

Adding the biography embeddings as features significantly improves model performance by increasing the accuracy and leading to the highest F1 score. The respective model was able to correctly classify 92.5% of the users in our test set. Thus, our chosen features as described in Sect. 3.2 allow for a good distinction between personal and organizational Twitter users. Furthermore, the addition of the user's biography embeddings leads to an increase in model performance. Thus, we can extend this model to our larger sample of unseen users.

The classification results in a distribution of 30,214 (26.4%) institutions and 84,264 (73.6%) personal accounts for the whole sample, and 27,124 (25.3%) institutions as well as 80,289 (74.7%) personal accounts for our slightly smaller set of nodes in the dynamic interaction network, and finally, 5,596 (39.0%) institutions and 8,769 (61.0%) personal accounts in our static network, the direct neighborhood of *SciStarter*.

4.2   Social Network Analysis

To examine the applicability of modeling interaction behavior by using multiple relation types, we first examined the distribution of degrees across our network. The average degree (involving all dynamic interaction types) is at 4.87 and ranges from 1 to 7,567, with a high standard deviation of 49.14. Visually, the degree distribution appears to be heavy-tailed, although comparing a fitted power-law distribution to it leads to a Kolmogorov-Smirnov test with $K = 0.011$ and p

<.001, showing that the degrees do not follow a power-law distribution. However, the high variance and visual evaluation indicate that the majority of users shows little interactions, while there are few, highly active users (i.e. "hubs", see [2]). The network thus shows indications for a scale-free social network, signaling that our multi-relational approach appears to be adequately representing the multirelational interactions between Twitter users (**RQ2**).

When differentiating further per user type, we observe that *institutions* have a significantly higher degree with ($M = 9.09$, $SD = 89.65$) than *personal* users ($M = 3.45$, $SD = 22.50$), with a small effect size (Wilcoxon rank sum, $p < .001$, $r = 0.17$), hinting at their possible role as hubs.

Table 2. Degrees per user and interaction type

User type	Interaction	total degree	in-degree	out-degree
		M (*SD*)	M (*SD*)	M (*SD*)
institution	quoting	1.19** (8.43)	0.75** (5.69)	0.44** (3.56)
	replying	0.48* (7.35)	0.24** (2.12)	0.24** (6.09)
	retweeting	7.37** (80.62)	4.60** (62.42)	2.77** (37.04)
personal	quoting	0.43** (2.98)	0.16** (2.14)	0.27** (1.53)
	replying	0.25* (2.22)	0.13** (1.00)	0.13** (1.31)
	retweeting	2.70** (19.08)	1.04** (14.76)	1.66** (9.45)

* sign. difference between user types with $p < .001$ (**) or $p < .05$ (*)

In a next step, we compared the average degrees per interaction type for the two user types. As expected, institutions have a significantly higher degree for all types of interactions, and especially for retweeting (see Table 2). A closer look reveals a significantly higher in-degree for *institutions* than for *personal* users, meaning that institutions get retweeted significantly more often than personal users, which points to their function as information sources. Personal users, on the other hand, show smaller average in-degrees overall, yet relatively higher out-degree values as compared to their in-degrees. The excess of out-degree over in-degree is particularly high for retweets, which are by far the most frequent dynamic interactions. This compensates for the inverse pattern with institutions, considering also that the number of personal nodes is almost three times higher as compared to institutions. However, the high standard deviation for institutions also indicates that not all institutions are similarly involved in information spreading through retweets, possibly based on different strategic approaches to handling social media presence. At this point, we can state that institutional nodes are the main information sources in terms of retweets and quotes (by in-degree) whereas personal users have an important role in active information spreading and dissemination (**RQ3**).

To further investigate this, we examined the difference in interaction behavior between these two user types from another perspective: While the above analyses are related to the node-level (i.e., individual degrees), we can also consider the differences on the edge-level (i.e., interactions). To this end, we compared the number of interactions for the different interaction- and user types by looking at the target (incoming interactions) and the source (outgoing interactions). The results are represented in Table 3.

Table 3. Direction of interactions per user and interaction type

User type			Interaction type		
Source	Target	Total	Retweeting	Quoting	Replying
institution	institution	65,358 (25%)	51,661 (79%)	8,527 (13%)	5,170 (8%)
institution	personal	28,314 (11%)	23,527 (83%)	3,396 (12%)	1,391 (5%)
personal	institution	86,236 (33%)	73,109 (85%)	11,856 (14%)	1,271 (1%)
personal	personal	78,779 (31%)	60,261 (77%)	9,749 (12%)	8,769 (11%)

Apparently, most interactions occur between personal users and institutions (33%) with institutions being the target of the interaction. In the vast majority of such cases, users interact by retweeting (85%) or quoting (14%). Another significant source of interactions are those between personal users (31% of all interactions). For these, retweeting is again the most common type of interaction, and replying happens to a larger degree than for other interactions, which is consistent with a more personal type of interaction. Interestingly, we see comparatively little interaction from institutions targeting personal accounts (only 11%), corroborating the point that information primarily flows from institutions to individuals or between individuals. Additionally, it is worth noting that interactions between institutions make up 25% of the total interactions, again with retweets being the dominating type of interaction, i.e., institutions also appear to retweet each other, thereby helping in the spreading of information.

4.3 Static and Dynamic Interactions

To approach **RQ4**, we examined how the dynamic interactions are related to static connections as indicated by the follow-relationship, again using the ego-network around *SciStarter*. As reported above, *retweeting* appeared to be the major mode of interaction, thus we focused our analyses on this. In a first step, we filtered for interactions made by the users inside the ego-network, from which 2,751 users actively participated by retweeting. We then calculated the in- and out-degree of retweet interactions for the users, that is, how many times they retweeted others/got retweeted and set this in relation to their in- and out-degrees of the follow-relation (potential paths for interactions) (see Fig. 3).

As expected, institutions generally have higher numbers of followers. More precisely, we found that the in-degree values for institutional nodes were almost exactly three times higher than those for personal accounts regarding both following (i.e., being followed) as well as dynamic interactions (esp. being retweeted). As we have already seen, there is a substantial difference between in- and out-degrees for institutions, showing that they receive more retweet interactions than they give (i.e., other users retweet them and they act as information

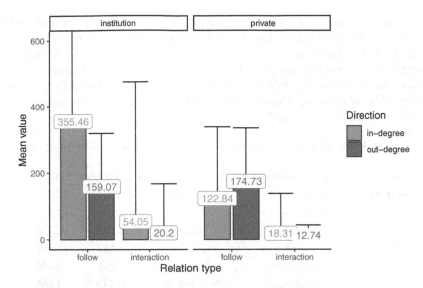

Fig. 3. In- and out-degrees for both user- and relation types (follow/retweet) in the ego-network around *SciStarter*

spreaders). This difference is not observable for personal users, where it appears to be more balanced.

To address **RQ4**, we analyzed the interactions (retweeting, quoting & replying) according to whether or not the passive node (source of information) was followed by the active node who initiated the interaction. The results show that most of the interactions coincide with static follow relations, accounting for 35,033 interactions (79.2%) out of 44,227. The total amount of static follow relations in the ego-network amounts to 1,725,960, so the dynamic interactions only go along the static edges in 2% of cases.

To investigate if this differs per interaction type, we checked whether it changed depending on the user type that interacted (personal or institution). What we found is that there were 35,629 (80.5%) retweets, 5,453 (12.3%) quotes and 3,145 (7.1%) replies. Considering the user type, 64% of the retweets are given by institutions, while 36% are given by personal users. For the replies, 64% of the replies were done by institutions and 36% by personal users, while 53% of the quotations were done by institutions and 46% by personal users. When we checked the target of the interactions, we discovered that the 77% of the times the retweeted account was an institutional account, 73% of the times the quoted account was an institutional one and 65% the times the reply was done to an institutional account.

We further examined to which extent the dynamics of interaction project onto the static following relation. Thus, we checked the distribution of the different types of interactions in relation to whether the source of the interaction follows the user, or not. The results are shown in Table 4, in which we can see that the most common interaction is retweeting as we previously stated and further, retweets by users that follow institutional accounts. Retweeting an account that they do not follow is the second most common interaction. According to the numbers, institutions are slightly more active in retweeting inside this ego-network. As an interesting finding, we see that replying is the only interaction in which this dynamic is altered, both institutions and personal users tend to reply to accounts they do not follow.

Table 4. Distribution of interactions per user type and follow relation

User type	Type of interaction	Follow relation	Count	Proportion
institution	retweeted_by	Follower	19,246	43.5%
	retweeted_by	Non follower	3,398	7.7%
	quoted_by	Follower	2,266	5.1%
	quoted_by	Non follower	659	1.5%
	replied_to	Follower	253	0.6%
	replied_to	Non follower	1,749	4.0%
personal	retweeted_by	Follower	10,984	24.8%
	retweeted_by	Non follower	2,001	4.5%
	quoted_by	Follower	1,975	4.5%
	quoted_by	Non follower	553	1.3%
	replied_to	Follower	309	0.7%
	replied_to	Non follower	834	1.9%

5 Discussion

We approached CS-related discourse on Twitter by examining interactions between institutional and personal users. For this, we first explored features that can accurately predict such user types (**RQ1**). We found that using features that only stem from the users' public profiles enriched with additional information (i.e., face detection, biography embeddings) can lead to a highly accurate prediction, extending earlier findings in other domains [13,16] by providing an easily applicable method for user classification on Twitter. We addressed **RQ2** by capturing different types of interactions (retweeting, quoting & replying) in a multi-relational model as a rich basis for an accurate assessment using SNA techniques. This, in turn, revealed significant differences between the user types (**RQ3**): Most of the dynamic interactions are retweets, and institutions are primarily being retweeted by personal users, who share information with other personal users, thereby acting as "information spreaders". Our results regarding the distinction of user types and the general distribution of activities are consistent with related research [13] in characterizing institutions as information providers and active personal users as information spreaders. We have corroborated this for the case of CS and we have refined the picture looking at the distribution of link types, which accentuates the imbalance between institutional and personal nodes.

An additional aspect addressed in our work is the relation of dynamic interactions and the static follower topology of the Twitter network. Using a 1.5-neighborhood around a prominent CS organization as a sample, we found that institutions receive higher numbers of retweets, of which the majority stems from followers. This is in line with institutions acting as information providers. Further dissemination through retweets and quotations is rather driven by followers, which could be facilitated by the fact that users follow the accounts with shared interests and therefore find their content more trustworthy. An exception to this is the opposite tendency for replying, although this can be attributed to the inverse information flow in replies, as tweets that the users reply to primarily stem from non-followers, yet we did not consider whether they themselves follow the source of the tweet that was replied to. However, the high values for retweeting are opposed to significantly smaller values for the other interaction types. An explanation for this is that retweets are more likely to happen although the users are not connected via the follow relation, while interactions such as quoting seem to be more likely when the account is followed closely.

Our findings can help researchers to better distinguish different user types, as well as project-owners and other stakeholders to have a better idea of the information uptake and dissemination that occurs within and beyond the CS community. The high variance in the in- and out-degrees in retweeting for both types of accounts suggests that it might be beneficial to particularly look into the "long tail" of the degree distribution and identify the most active "hubs". For the out-degree, we would expect to find the most proficient disseminators, and among these many personal users. In a way, these are potential "influencers" that could be particularly helpful in supporting science communication in a CS perspective.

However, our findings come with certain limitations. We had decided on beforehand to focus on network analysis and not on the content of Twitter messages (as, e.g., done in [12]). We used a limited follower network in terms of the 1.5 neighbourhood around *SciStarter*. This obviously limits the space of interactions, although still giving > 1.5 million edges. Scraping the follow-relation for all users in our sample would have been more desirable but computationally very costly, also considering the restrictions of the Twitter API. Regarding our focus of interest in the role of volunteers in CS discussions and interactions, there is another caveat: While the distinction of personal vs. institutional users correctly classifies volunteers as personal users, there may be personal accounts of users who are officially affiliated to institutions as researchers or administrators. We plan to address and overcome these limitations in our future studies.

6   Conclusions and Future Work

In this study, we introduced a novel and simple, yet highly accurate method to classify Twitter users, and built on these results to model and examine their interaction behavior in multiple dimensions. This combination of machine learning and SNA methods, especially with the projection onto static pathways in the context of CS really sets this study apart from other related studies. Future studies should extend the user categorization beyond a binary classification, allowing for a more fine-grained analysis of user types and their respective behavior. While the mapping onto static connections rather serves as a case study, it provides a foundation for the extension onto other ego-networks, or even a full sample of CS-related discussions for a given time-frame. Such an analysis might be valuable information for multiple stakeholders, providing the basis to foster more engagement on the side of personal users and volunteers, and information dissemination on the side of institutions and professional scientists. Content analysis could be an interesting technique to be used in the future to combine it with the interactions and the static structure in order to gain a more thorough knowledge of what makes information interesting to be disseminated on Twitter.

Acknowledgments. This work was partially funded by the European Union (EU) in the context of the CS Track project (Grant Agreement no. 872522) under the Horizon 2020 program. This document does not represent the opinion of the EU, and the EU is not responsible for any use that might be made of its content. We thank all CS Track team members for the good collaboration.

References

1. Arik, S.O., Pfister, T.: Tabnet: attentive interpretable tabular learning (2020)
2. Barabasi, A.L.: Network Science, 1st edn. Cambridge University Press, Cambridge (2016)
3. Batrinca, B., Treleaven, P.C.: Social media analytics: a survey of techniques, tools and platforms. Ai Soc. **30**, 89–116 (2015)
4. Breiman, L.: Random forests. Mach. Learn. **45**(1), 5–32 (2001). https://doi.org/10.1023/A:1010933404324
5. Chen, T., Guestrin, C.: XGBoost: a scalable tree boosting system. In: Proceedings of the 22nd ACM SIGKDD International Conference on Knowledge Discovery and Data Mining, KDD 2016, pp. 785–794. ACM, New York (2016). https://doi.org/10.1145/2939672.2939785
6. Geitgey, A.: face-recognition 1.3.0, https://pypi.org/project/face-recognition/
7. Grinsztajn, L., Oyallon, E., Varoquaux, G.: Why do tree-based models still outperform deep learning on tabular data? (2022)
8. Hagberg, A., Swart, P., S Chult, D.: Exploring network structure, dynamics, and function using networkx. Technical report, Los Alamos National Lab. (LANL), Los Alamos, NM (United States) (2008)
9. Kreutz, T., Daelemans, W.: Detecting vaccine skepticism on twitter using heterogeneous information networks. In: Rosso, P., Basile, V., Martínez, R., Métais, E., Meziane, F. (eds.) NLDB 2022. LNCS, vol. 13286, pp. 370–381. Springer, Cham (2022). https://doi.org/10.1007/978-3-031-08473-7_34
10. Krukowski, S., Amarasinghe, I., Gutiérrez-Páez, N.F., Hoppe, H.U.: Does volunteer engagement pay off? an analysis of user participation in online citizen science projects. In: Wong, L.H., Hayashi, Y., Collazos, C.A., Alvarez, C., Zurita, G., Baloian, N. (eds.) CollabTech 2022, vol. 13632, pp. 67–82. Springer, Cham (2022). https://doi.org/10.1007/978-3-031-20218-6_5

11. Manning, C.D., Raghavan, P., Schütze, H.: Introduction to Information Retrieval. Cambridge University Press (2008)
12. Mazumdar, S., Thakker, D.: Citizen Science on Twitter: using data analytics to understand conversations and networks. Future Internet **12**(12), 1–22 (2020). https://ideas.repec.org/a/gam/jftint/v12y2020i12p210-d451652.html
13. McCorriston, J., Jurgens, D., Ruths, D.: Organizations are users too: characterizing and detecting the presence of organizations on Twitter. In: Proceedings of the International AAAI Conference on Web and Social Media **9**(1), 650–653 (2021) https://ojs.aaai.org/index.php/ICWSM/article/view/14672
14. Newman, G., Wiggins, A., Crall, A., Graham, E., Newman, S., Crowston, K.: The future of citizen science: emerging technologies and shifting paradigms. Front. Ecol. Environ. **10**(6), 298–304 (2012). https://doi.org/10.1890/110294
15. Nov, O., Arazy, O., Anderson, D.: Scientists@ home: what drives the quantity and quality of online citizen science participation? PLoS ONE **9**(4), e90375 (2014)
16. Oentaryo, R.J., Low, J.-W., Lim, E.-P.: Chalk and Cheese in Twitter: discriminating personal and organization accounts. In: Hanbury, A., Kazai, G., Rauber, A., Fuhr, N. (eds.) ECIR 2015. LNCS, vol. 9022, pp. 465–476. Springer, Cham (2015). https://doi.org/10.1007/978-3-319-16354-3_51
17. Reimers, N., Gurevych, I.: Sentence-BERT: sentence embeddings using siamese bert-networks (2019)
18. Robson, C., Hearst, M., Kau, C., Pierce, J.: Comparing the use of social networking and traditional media channels for promoting citizen science. In: Proceedings of the 2013 Conference on Computer Supported Cooperative Work, pp. 1463–1468 (2013)
19. Roldán-álvarez, D., Martínez-Martínez, F., Martín, E.: Citizen science and open learning: a twitter perspective. In: 2021 International Conference on Advanced Learning Technologies (ICALT), pp. 6–8 (2021)
20. Senabre Hidalgo, E., Perelló, J., Becker, F., Bonhoure, I., Legris, M., Cigarini, A.: Participation and Co-creation in Citizen Science, pp. 199–218. Springer, Cham (2021). https://doi.org/10.1007/978-3-030-58278-4_11
21. Tang, L., Liu, H.: Community Detection and Mining in Social Media, 1st edn. Morgan and Claypool Publishers (2010)
22. Vohland, K., et al.: The science of citizen science. Springer Nature (2021)
23. Wasserman, S., Faust, K.: Social Network Analysis: Methods and Applications. Cambridge University Press, New York (1994)
24. Yan, L., Ma, Q., Yoshikawa, M.: Classifying Twitter users based on user profile and followers distribution. In: Decker, H., Lhotská, L., Link, S., Basl, J., Tjoa, A.M. (eds.) DEXA 2013. LNCS, vol. 8055, pp. 396–403. Springer, Heidelberg (2013). https://doi.org/10.1007/978-3-642-40285-2_34

Fairness in Socio-Technical Systems: A Case Study of Wikipedia

Mir Saeed Damadi[✉] and Alan Davoust

Université du Québec en Outaouais, Gatineau, Québec, Canada
{damm15,alan.davoust}@uqo.ca

Abstract. Wikipedia content is produced by a complex socio-technical systems (STS), and exhibits numerous biases, such as gender and cultural biases. We investigate how these biases relate to the concepts of algorithmic bias and fairness defined in the context of algorithmic systems. We systematically review 75 papers describing different types of bias in Wikipedia, which we classify and relate to established notions of harm and normative expectations of fairness as defined for machine learning-driven algorithmic systems. In addition, by analysing causal relationships between the observed phenomena, we demonstrate the complexity of the socio-technical processes causing harm.

Keywords: Fairness · Socio-technical system · Bias · Wikipedia

1 Introduction

Wikipedia is arguably the greatest success of large-scale collaboration on the Web: with over 60 million articles across more than 300 language editions, Wikipedia has become one of the most visited Web sites in the world, with additional impact through search results and other channels [39].

Wikipedia content is produced through a complex collaborative process involving humans, bots and semi-automated tools, with a large number of rules, protocols and procedures [18,26]. This process is designed to support the production of quality encyclopedic content, aiming in particular for *neutrality* and *verifiability*. Wikipedia's neutrality principle (*neutral point of view*, NPOV) is formulated as "representing fairly, proportionately, and, as far as possible, *without editorial bias*, all the significant views that have been published by reliable sources on a topic." [41] (emphasis added).

However, many studies have identified biases in Wikipedia content, including gender bias [38,40,44,48], political bias [15,43], cultural bias [2,7], and others. These biases, affecting one of the most influential information sources in the world, can be compared to the systematic biases, broadly known as *algorithmic biases*, that affect web search results and advertisements [17,36], machine translation services [29], and other automated services powered by machine learning algorithms. Such biases have recently become an important focus of research:

H. Takada et al. (Eds.): CollabTech 2023, LNCS 14199, pp. 84–100, 2023.
https://doi.org/10.1007/978-3-031-42141-9_6

many normative fairness concepts have been proposed [4,22] along with testing procedures [8] and corrective measures [47].

In the case of Wikipedia, the biased output is not produced by a single automated system: it is produced by a *social machine* [33], i.e., a network of people interacting over a large-scale digital infrastructure, including various automated and semi-automated components. These automated components include thousands of bots [12,49] responsible for 20% of edits [20], as well as many other automated or semi-automated tools routinely used by experienced editors.

Despite this internal difference, we believe that the fairness and bias concepts defined for algorithmic systems are also applicable to social machines.

In this paper, we examine the biases reported about Wikipedia in a new light, relating them to the fairness-related concepts defined in the algorithmic fairness literature. We proceed in two steps. First, we systematically review the academic literature describing "bias" in Wikipedia, identifying and categorizing the problematic phenomena discussed in the papers. We then analyze these bias concepts in relation to established notions of *harm* and *fairness* defined for algorithmic systems, and analyze the causal relationships between these phenomena.

Our systematic review covers 75 papers investigating bias in Wikipedia, and our analysis addresses the following research questions:

- **(RQ1)** What specific phenomena, occurring in Wikipedia, are described as *bias*, and which groups are affected by these biases?
- **(RQ2)** In what sense are these biases considered harmful, and can we relate them back to normative expectations expressed as technical fairness criteria?
- **(RQ3)** What are the causal relationships between these bias phenomena?

Our analysis first demonstrates that the term *bias* in the literature refers to several distinct phenomena, and that similar phenomena have been reported for different social groups: difference in participation, under-representation, biased representation. Secondly, these phenomena can be related in meaningful ways to the fairness concepts defined for algorithmic systems. Finally, the complexity of the causal relationships between different bias phenomena justifies having a holistic view of the social machines, because interventions on any bias phenomena are likely to have consequences on multiple others.

In the rest of the paper, we present our systematic review of bias in Wikipedia in Sect. 2, identifying and categorizing the bias phenomena, then in Sect. 2.6 we analyze these phenomena in terms of harm and fairness, before analyzing the causal relationships between them in Sect. 4.

2   Fairness Issues in Wikipedia

We now turn to our first research question:

(**RQ1**) What specific phenomena, occurring in Wikipedia, are described as *bias*, and which groups are affected by these biases?

2.1   Methodology

In order to answer this question, we conducted a systematic review of papers reporting *bias* (and other fairness-related concepts) in Wikipedia. In order to identify relevant papers, we searched the Scopus database and Google Scholar using the keywords "bias", "fairness", "discrimination", "fair" and "unfair" in conjunction with "Wikipedia", and collected papers published up to December 2022. In Scopus we limited the scope of the search to titles, abstracts and introductions. In addition, we also collected more general surveys of scholarly research about Wikipedia – using the keywords "review" or "survey" and "Wikipedia" in Google Scholar – and searched these surveys for other relevant papers and terms to describe fairness-related issues. The terms "disparity" and "inequality" were identified in this manner. We obtained 161 papers altogether.

The most common fairness-related keyword in the surveyed papers is "bias", and we retained all the papers where the term referred to a lack of fairness towards specific groups. In particular, we eliminated papers referring to statistical or cognitive biases, and papers where "bias" was used to describe a violation of Wikipedia's NPOV policy, but did not describe editorial bias against particular people or social groups, for example papers presenting techniques to identify "biased" text in general.

We ended up with 75 papers, which almost all described biases against identifiable social groups. One paper discussed the unfair treatment of a single person, in the sense of individual fairness.

For each paper, we identified the phenomena described as problematic and the social groups that they affect. In the following, we list these phenomena, categorized according the groups that they affect: we first list phenomena described as *gender bias*, then phenomena of *cultural, geographical and racial bias*, and finally phenomena affecting *anonymous Wikipedia contributors*.

2.2   Gender Bias

Among the papers that we reviewed, most described forms of *gender bias*: phrases such as "gender gap", "gender biases" or "gender disparities" refer to several phenomena where women are disadvantaged compared to men. We note that we did not find any research discussing biases affecting other gender identities (e.g., non-binary, or cis- vs. transgender people).

Under-Participation of Women. In many papers, the terms *gender bias/gender gap* refer to the disparity between the number of men and women participating in Wikipedia, as readers, writers, and editors [13,27,28,30,44,46]. According to surveys by the Wikimedia Foundation and others, the proportion of women participating in Wikipedia in 2013 was between 13% and 22% [48].

Number of Women's Biographies. Many papers compare the number of biographies of men and women [38,40,42,45,46,48], and find that women are significantly under-represented: in July 2019, only 17.9% of biographies in Wikipedia were women's biographies [38]. In addition, two studies compare the number of male/female biographies with Wikipedia's criterion for inclusion, i.e. the concept of *notability*. The question is, are *notable* men and women equally represented in Wikipedia? Wagner et al. [40] study the phenomenon using external databases of "notable" people, and find that women listed in these databases are not under-represented in Wikipedia. On the other hand, Adams et al. [1] study Wikipedia biographies of American Sociologists, and using bibliometric definitions of notability, they find that for similar notability levels, men are at least twice as likely to have a Wikipedia biography. In other words, there is a clear under-representation of women when compared with the approximate ratio of women to men in the world population in general, but the results are less conclusive when we attempt to control for the (ill-defined) notion of "notability".

Deletion of Women's Biographies. A related but separate phenomenon is the disparate rate of deletion for biographies of men and women: for one of Wikipedia's page deletion processes (Article for deletion, AFD), a study found that 25% of the biographies being deleted were women's biographies [38]: since there are only around 18% of women's biographies, women are *over-represented* in the biographies deletion process.

Structural Bias in Women's Biographies. In a few papers, a disparity is reported regarding the number of links between biographies of people of different genders [40,48], called *structural bias*: according to this analysis, there are statistically more links from women's biographies to men's biographies than from men's biographies to women's biographies, even when controlling for group sizes.

Lexical Bias in Biographies. The lexical content of articles in general, including the particular case of biographies, is the primary mechanism of biased representation of women [23,24,30,31,40,42,44,48]. This *lexical bias* [40], is visible when the content of men and women's biographies differs following stereotypical patterns: women's biographies contain more information related to their families, their spouse and children, whereas men's biographies contain more information about their activities and achievements [35,40,48].

Categorization Bias. Yanisky-Ravid et al. [44] describe a bias in Wikipedia's page category structure, where the minority group (or, in this case, women) are treated as an exception within the majority group (or men). For example, in 2013 the category of "American novelists" contained a sub-category of "American female novelists", where the main category contained only men.

Under-Representation of Women's Interests. A small number of studies have explored whether Wikipedia contains more articles on topics of interest to men than articles on topics of interest to women [30,42,44]. Different experiments assigned topics to men and women either using "well known" stereotypical associations, or by extracting these topics from corpora of magazines intended for male/female audiences. Analysis by Worku et al. [42] also shows that articles of presumed interest to women were nominated for deletion at slightly higher rates than articles presumed to be of interest to men.

2.3   Cultural and Geographical Bias

After gender bias, a large number of papers report different forms of bias affecting members of cultural groups – primarily defined by their country of citizenship or the languages that they speak, and therefore the Wikipedia language editions that they contribute to: we group here phenomena described by terms such as "cultural bias", "geographical bias", "language-specific bias", "local bias", "ingroup bias", the "colonization of Wikipedia" or "political bias".

Wikipedia Contributors by Countries. A similar phenomenon to the under-participation of women can be described here, as a *geographical bias*: a Wikimedia Foundation report [14] notes that 45% of Wikipedia contributors are from only five countries (Italy, France, Great Britain, Germany and the United States). If a single language edition of Wikipedia is considered, a similar situation will occur: the contributors of that edition will be predominantly from the country or countries where the language is spoken. In addition, the demographic make-up of Wikipedia contributors within a given country may not reflect the overall demographic distribution of the country, meaning that there are potentially other ways of defining under-participating groups (e.g., along racial lines).

Biographies and Countries. Beytáa [3] evaluates the over-representation of the "Global North" in Wikipedia biographies, considering the same five dominant countries. He finds that among biographies available in at least 25 language editions, 50% are from those five countries, and considering their importance weighted by an index calculated by the Pagerank algorithm, they account for 62% of the global weight index.

Cultural Biases. An important aspect of cultural bias is the under-representation of certain cultural groups' perspectives in Wikipedia articles. For example, Young et al. [46] evoke the *colonization of Wikipedia*, meaning the dominance of western perspectives, even on topics primarily associated with other cultures. They point to an example of an article describing a plant used in Chinese traditional medicine, where all mentions of its traditional medicinal uses were removed, along with all references except a western scientific article. Several authors have also studied *linguistic points of view* [2,7,21,32], i.e., differences in how a topic is described in different Wikipedia language editions. A striking example is how historical international conflicts are portrayed by groups representing the two sides of the conflict, and editing different Wikipedia language editions [2, 32].

2.4 Racial Bias

Only one paper was found explicitly reporting racial bias in Wikipedia, describing the under-representation of non-white academics in Wikipedia biographies: in their study focusing on American sociologists, Adams et al. [1] found that non-white scholars were under-represented in Wikipedia, compared to their white counterparts of similar notability (as measured by bibliometrics). While no other types of racial bias have been reported, it should be noted that the under-representation of the "Global South" in Wikipedia (which is also described as "geographical bias") also implies some level of racial bias.

2.5 Anonymous Users

In addition to the demographic groups discussed previously, for which biases are commonly discussed in the context of algorithmic fairness, a small number of papers [9, 19, 37] have discussed biases affecting the social group of *anonymous editors*, i.e., editors of Wikipedia that did not register for an account. This group may have some overlap with the other categories, but this cannot be confirmed as we don't know the demographic make-up of anonymous users.

In this case the reported bias occurs within Wikipedia's editing process, and can be described as *over-policing*: TeBlunthuis et al. [37] found that the contributions of anonymous editors are more closely scrutinized than those of registered users, and more likely to be reverted. De Laat [19] attributes this to bots that use machine learning to detect potentially problematic edits, and flags them for review by "patrolling" editors. The software shows the users' registration status, which leads the editors reviewing the edits to "profile" these users and disproportionately revert their edits.

2.6 Summary

The biases identified in our systematic review are summarized in Table 1. In this classification, a type of bias is defined by the social group affected by the bias (column) and an abstract description of the phenomenon (line).

Taking a step back from the exact phenomenon reported in each academic paper, and grouping the bias phenomena in more abstract categories, we observe that similar biases have been reported as affecting women, and cultural groups outside of the cultural powers that are North America and Western Europe: depending on the analysis, these groups can be defined by a country of origin, a shared language (i.e. which language edition the members of the group contribute to), or cultural perspectives typical of a geographical region. We also note that given how the biases generally affect cultural groups of the "Global South", we include here biases that affect racial minorities within the "Global North".

Table 1. The number of papers describing the different types of bias. The total may exceed 75 as several papers discuss multiple bias issues.

	Gender	Culture and Geography	Anonymous Users
under-participation	17	5	-
under-representation	16	28	-
biased deletion processes	11	-	-
biased representation	27	6	-
over-policing	-	-	3

Here, *under-participation* refers to fewer contributors of Wikipedia belonging to the identified groups. *Under-representation* refers to quantitative biases about the group: fewer biographies, fewer links to those biographies, and fewer articles representing their interests and perspectives. *Biased deletion processes* refers to Wikipedia page deletion processes disproportionately affecting pages related to the group, and *biased representation* refers to qualitative biases about the group: lexical bias and categorization bias.

3   Bias Phenomena, Harm, and Fairness

We now analyze these biases and address our second research question:

(RQ2). In what sense are these biases considered harmful, and can we relate them back to normative expectations expressed as technical fairness criteria?

3.1   Bias and Harm

The first step in this analysis is to understand if and why each formulated bias is truly harmful, i.e., relate these biases to established definitions of *harm*. Here we adapt definitions by Shelby et al. [34] and Blodgett et al. [6], and include the following types of harm: *allocative harm*, *representational harm* and *quality-of-service harm*.

Allocative Harm occurs when a algorithmic system deprives the members of a disadvantaged group of information, opportunities or resources and allocates those resources to other dominant groups. Allocative harms typically occur in the context of *automated binary decision systems*, i.e., algorithmic systems where inputs are associated with people, and the outputs (outcome of the decision) include a more desirable outcome (e.g., the person obtains a loan from a bank) and a corresponding "negative outcome" (e.g., the loan is denied). In addition, it is usually assumed that there is a "correct" decision for each person, and that an algorithmic system's decisions are not always correct.

Among the biases identified for Wikipedia, the following fit the model of binary decisions:

Under-representation of a group in particular, we can model the process leading to biographies being written and added to Wikipedia as a binary decision process. A snapshot of Wikipedia represents a decision system: given a person, the social machine of Wikipedia may have given them a biography or not. Considering that the ideal situation would be if all *notable* people had Wikipedia biographies and *non-notable* people did not, there is also a *correct* decision for each person. Here, there is a form of allocative harm due to the fact that Wikipedia biographies increase people's reputation and online visibility: the (socio-technical) system deprives the affected group of this opportunity.

Biased Deletion Processes. As in the previous case, article deletions are also a binary process, with a reference *correct* decision: a biography should be deleted if the person is not notable. Allocative harm occurs for the same reason.

Over-policing over-policing also refers to a binary decision process, where a particular edit should be accepted (if it complies with Wikipedia rules), or reverted. A person (the editor) is also associated with each input of the decision, and will experience a negative outcome if the edit is reverted. As one group's contributions are more likely to receive the negative outcome, this phenomenon also matches the definition of allocative harm.

Representational Harm is caused by representations of a social group in a less favorable light than others, or that under-represent them or fail to recognize their existence altogether. In our context, the phenomena described as the *under-representation of a group*, the *under-representation of a group's interests and perspectives*, and the *biased representation of a group* all fit the definition of *representational harm.*

Quality-of-Service Harms are caused by algorithmic systems that do not provide the same service quality to different groups of people [5]. The problem of *over-policing*, in addition to causing allocative harm, can be seen as a process that verifies the quality of edits for different users. By disproportionately rejecting the edits by one group, it causes quality-of-service harm.

In addition to the identified harms above, the phenomenon of *under-participation of a group* does not correspond *per se* to any definition of harm. However, it may be a symptom of other problems (harmful phenomena which discourage members of the group from participating), and it may participate in causing other phenomena that do match definitions of harm.

3.2   Bias and Decision Fairness

The second step of our analysis is to identify the normative expectation of fairness corresponding to each bias phenomenon, from technical criteria defined for algorithmic systems.

We first consider the case of *binary decisions*, a relevant model for the under-representation of a group, for biased deletion processes and for over-policing. As we will see, the normative expectations underlying the analyses of these reported phenomena match the definitions of two well-known technical criteria, namely *demographic parity* and *equal opportunity*.

We describe them formally using the following notations: the membership of a person to a group is represented by a random variable $A \in \{0,1\}$, the "correct" decision for this person is represented by a random variable $Y \in \{0,1\}$, and the decision output by the system is $\hat{Y} \in \{0,1\}$.

Demographic Parity. One of the simplest fairness criteria, also called independence [47], demographic parity requires that a person's chance of obtaining the positive outcome from the decision system ($\hat{Y} = 1$) is independent of the group membership:

$$P[\hat{Y} = 1 | A = 0] = P[\hat{Y} = 1 | A = 1] \tag{1}$$

Demographic parity expresses that the members of the considered group (e.g., women) should receive a positive output at the same rate as those from the complement group (i.e., men). Using demographic parity as a reference fairness criterion means ignoring the "correctness" of decisions.

When the number of women's biographies is simply compared with the number of men's biographies (i.e., 18% vs. 82%), the implicit expectation is that both figures should be around 50%, i.e., similar to the proportions of women and men in the overall population. This implies that the expectation is that the *rates* at which women and women receive the positive outcome of having a Wikipedia biography should also be equal, i.e., the reference fairness criterion is demographic parity. The same analysis applies whenever the proportion of favourable outcomes for two groups are compared with the relative sizes of the groups (e.g., when it is reported that 50% of the biographies appearing in at least 25 language editions come from five countries, whereas those countries represent much less than 50% of the world population). In the case of biased deletion processes, the number of articles to be deleted are compared with the number of existing articles, i.e. the size of the input set: this also implies that the rates of positive outcomes are being compared, and thus the expectation is demographic parity.

Equal Opportunity. Also called Positive Rate Parity [16], this criterion defines fairness according to the probability of obtaining the favorable outcome from the decision system, conditional to this outcome being the correct decision:

$$P[\hat{Y} = 1 | Y = 1, A = 0] = P[\hat{Y} = 1 | Y = 1, A = 1] \tag{2}$$

Unlike demographic parity, equal opportunity considers the *correct* decision in determining whether decisions are fair towards a social group. In our context, if we consider the process of publishing Wikipedia biographies, applying equal opportunity means verifying whether *notable* women (or notable members of the considered group) obtain biographies at the same rate as *notable* men. This assessment of bias will differ from demographic parity if the proportion of notable people is different from one group to another. The analyses by Wagner et al. [40] and that of Adams et al. [1], which compare the probability of a person having a biography *conditional to some external definition of notability*, both implicitly define fairness as equality of opportunity. The case of *over-policing* is also one where equal opportunity is the implicit fairness expectation: in his analysis, De Laat [19] indicates that anonymous contributions to Wikipedia are more often problematic than those of registered editors, but indicates that the actual rejection rate of anonymous contributions is even higher than is warranted by this different base rate.

3.3 Bias and Fairness in Representation

The second relevant perspective on fairness in algorithmic systems relies on the concept of *representations*, without any particular model of the system behavior: in this perspective, fairness is defined over representations of social groups, output by or used in the system, where a fair representation is one where there is no *representational harm*.

This fairness concept is therefore relevant to the phenomena that cause representational harm: the *under-representation of a group*, the *under-representation of a group's interests and perspectives*, and the *biased representation of a group*. While the under-representation of a group or a group's perspectives can potentially be measured in a quantitative manner (using similar criteria to those for binary decisions), the more difficult case is for biased representations of a group, which mainly consist of *negative stereotypes and demeaning language*. Although there are no established definitions of fairness, from the techniques used to detect these biases we can infer the normative expectation of the system.

In the Wikipedia setting, representation biases as reported in the literature are typically measured by selecting words or concepts that represent a particular stereotype, and counting their occurrences across articles associated with the different groups (e.g., the biographies of men and women, or articles on the same topic in different language editions) [40]. The implicit normative expectation is that stereotypes affecting a given social group should not be detectable within articles describing people of this group, which is consistent with a kind of *counterfactual fairness*, similar to a concept defined for text classification [11]. In other words, given the description of a person or an event related to a disadvantaged social group, how would the description change if the person were a member of another social group, or if the event was associated with a different social group? Fairness would require that the changes should not be related to stereotypes about the social group.

4   Causality Relationships

We now turn to our third research question:

(RQ3). What are the causal relationships between these bias phenomena?

The purpose of answering this question is to identify the causal structure of the situation: how do the different problematic phenomena observed in the complex socio-technical system influence one-another? How might we affect the overall situation if we attempt to mitigate one of the phenomena?

For each of the abstract bias phenomena identified in Sect. 2.6, we discuss the main causes discussed across the literature.

4.1   Under-Participation of a Group

In the case of women, a fairly wide variety of causes has been invoked to explain their low participation in Wikipedia. In particular, Sue Gardner, a former executive director of Wikipedia, identified in 2011 nine reasons for this [10], most of which are also discussed by other papers reviewed for the present study. These reasons can be summarized by the following three general causes: (i) self-exclusion, (ii) the unwelcoming atmosphere of Wikipedia, and (iii) the poor design of Wikipedia's interface.

The first, self-exclusion, covers purely social causes why women cannot, or choose not to participate in Wikipedia. By "purely social" we mean that these causes are unrelated to the design or atmosphere of Wikipedia itself: women's lower of self-confidence compared to men and their already busy lives (jobs and a disproportionate share of house work).

The second general cause, which we refer to as the unwelcoming atmosphere of Wikipedia, refers to social factors specifically in how they occur within the community of editors: the conflictual culture [30], and a sometimes misogynist or "sexual" atmosphere [10], which may be perceived negatively by women.

Finally, the third cause is linked to the more technical aspects of Wikipedia, including its graphic user interface and the expected interaction protocols with other members of the community. This general cause is the only one that can be directly addressed by any technical changes to the Wikipedia infrastructure.

The causes of other groups' under-participation in Wikipedia have not been well studied. We conjecture that they are related to similar factors: self-exclusion factors (e.g., language barrier), unwelcoming atmosphere of Wikipedia (if the existing community of contributors is predominantly from a group with very different social norms from their own), and possibly user interface factors.

In addition to these factors, two additional causes should be added, related to other bias phenomena on Wikipedia. First, the problem of "over-policing" clearly leads to lower participation of members of a group affected by this phenomenon. As we do not know the demographic make-up of anonymous users (e.g., in terms of gender) we cannot infer how their over-policing may affect the participation of groups defined by other attributes (e.g., women or visible minorities), but there is a clear possibility that a causal relationship occurs here.

Secondly, we would conjecture that the under-representation of a group's interests in Wikipedia would also affect the group's participation in Wikipedia, by reinforcing the idea that Wikipedia is not "meant for them".

4.2 Under-Representation of Group Members

The under-representation of women in Wikipedia is related to three causes: one is their under-participation: assuming that women are more likely to be more interested than men in writing about other women, it stands to reason that a smaller community of women contributors will create fewer biographies of women or mentions of women in other articles. Similar phenomena most likely occur for other social groups, such as citizens of a given country or members of a tightly-knit cultural group: we would expect members of the group would be more likely than others to write about their fellow members. A second relevant reason is the influence of the *notability* rules on Wikipedia. As discussed previously, Wagner et al. [40] did not actually find that women were under-represented, in the sense that *notable* women – as defined by the external databases used in the study – were as likely as notable men of having a biography. This implies that to improve the representation of women in absolute terms, it may be necessary to change the existing notability rules.

Finally, another indirect causality relationship may exist between the under-participation of group members and their under-representation: the more active participants contribute to shape Wikipedia norms and policies, including notability rules. A group for whom existing notability criteria (e.g., references in print newspapers from a certain country) is biased may recognize that relying on the criteria is inadequate, and push for change. We therefore conjecture the existence of an additional causal connection between the under-participation of group members and the biases of notability rules towards that group.

4.3 Under-Representation of a Group's Interests and Perspectives

As for the previous case, the under-participation of a group also contributes to the under-representation of the group's interests and perspectives, simply because the members of a group are the most qualified and motivated to include their own perspectives and interests in Wikipedia. However, it is important to note that other groups, instead of merely failing to include the group's perspective in an article, may actively suppress it [25].

4.4 Biased Representation of a Group

In this case, the dominant reason for these biases is the societal biases present in the greater society: crowdsourced text naturally mirrors the biases in the minds of its authors. However, one may expect that members of the affected group would want to correct this situation, by editing the biased articles in order to reduce their bias; in this sense, the lack of participation from a group is also likely to contribute to biased representations of the group.

4.5 Over-Policing Bias

According to De Laat [19], this phenomenon occurs when editors patrol the new edits and misinterpret the interface of automated flagging tools: as they are aware the anonymous groups are more likely to vandalise articles or produce "bad" contributions (according to Wikipedia policies), they pay extra attention to edits produced by anonymous users, rather than simply relying on the flagging software, which already considers the anonymity of users as a risk factor.

4.6 Summary

The different causal relationships discussed in the previous subsections are illustrated in Fig. 1. The root causes are marked with blue rectangles: we distinguish causes related to Wikipedia as an institution – including the technical infrastructure as well as the rules and processes, and social causes, which are not affected by the technical definition of Wikipedia. In the top left, *unwelcoming atmosphere of Wikipedia* is depicted in both groups because it is directly caused by people's behaviour, but happens specifically within Wikipedia.

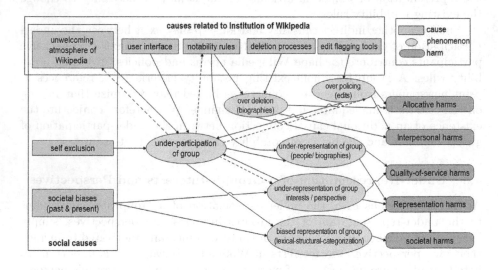

Fig. 1. Causality relationship network for Wikipedia's problematic phenomena.

Bias phenomena are shown with green ellipses, and harms as red rounded rectangles. Arrows indicate causal relationships documented in the literature; dashed arrows are additional causal relationships which we did not see explicitly formulated in the literature, but that we believe to be true.

5   Discussion and Conclusion

In the perspective of auditing social machines for fairness, we present a case study where we systematically review biases that have been reported in the academic literature about Wikipedia. We identify and categorize the different phenomena associated with bias, normatively framing them as harmful with specific meanings, and in reference to specific fairness concepts first defined for algorithmic systems. One of our key findings is that this STS exhibits many biases, but no strictly *algorithmic* biases (observable as the output of algorithms). There are several problematic processes, some of which are partially automated, for example through tools that automatically flag potential "bad edits".

The main bias phenomena that we identified can be described as under-participation, under-representation, and biased representations of disadvantaged groups. Similar phenomena occur for several disadvantaged groups, although they have been mostly analyzed with respect to the way they affect women. We conjecture that gender biases may be more widespread than other types of bias (e.g. racial bias), but more importantly they are probably easier to measure due to explicit gender indications in text (e.g. pronouns).

These biases are primarily instances of allocative harm – when they can be modeled as binary decision processes – and representational harm – when they amount to a group's perspectives being under-represented or represented in a stereotyped way. Allocative harms are described by implicitly invoking normative expectations of demographic parity or equal opportunity. To compare the two perspectives, under an expectation of *equal opportunity*, fairness is achieved if notability criteria are applied uniformly across groups, whereas under an expectation of *demographic parity* this will not be sufficient, because the ground truth criterion (Wikipedia's "notability" concept) is itself biased. In this view, fairness will require changing notability criteria.

Our analysis also demonstrates a complex network of causal interconnection between these phenomena. The identified relationships can help understand the effects of potential mitigation strategies. For example, if we take steps to reduce the under-participation of a group, this may help mitigate the *under-representation of the group* and the *biased representation of the group.*

Some of these issues can be addressed by social interventions including training workshops and edit-a-thons [10, 30]. The effects of deep-rooted social causes cannot easily be reduced in the short term, but media such as Wikipedia can be instrumental in gradually changing culture and removing historical beliefs and stereotypes. One clear opportunity is related to the technical infrastructure of Wikipedia: given the abundant presence of bots and semi-automated editing tools, if effective methods can be developed to identify localized biases (e.g. a specific biased article, as opposed to the overall corpus), they can be flagged automatically and be highly targeted for correction. This has proved effective for other problematic phenomena such as vandalism.

From a methodological perspective, the complexity of the causal relationships also demonstrates the need for more holistic auditing practices for STS: if there is any hope of mitigating biases in an STS such as Wikipedia – where there is no specifically harmful algorithm to fix – then we must focus on the socio-technical processes, which are algorithms in a "social computing" sense.

References

1. Adams, J., Brückner, H., Naslund, C.: Who counts as a notable sociologist on wikipedia? gender, race, and the "professor test". Socius 5 (2019)
2. Alvarez, G., Oeberst, A., Cress, U., Ferrari, L.: Linguistic evidence of in-group bias in English and Spanish Wikipedia articles about international conflicts. Discourse Context Media **35**, 100391 (2020)
3. Beytía, P.: The positioning matters: estimating geographical bias in the multilingual record of biographies on Wikipedia. In: Companion Proceedings of the Web Conference 2020, pp. 806–810 (2020)
4. Binns, R.: Fairness in machine learning: Lessons from political philosophy. In: Conference on Fairness, Accountability and Transparency, pp. 149–159. PMLR (2018)
5. Bird, S., et al.: Fairlearn: a toolkit for assessing and improving fairness in AI. Microsoft, Tech. Rep. MSR-TR-2020-32 (2020)
6. Blodgett, S.L., Barocas, S., Daumé III, H., Wallach, H.: Language (technology) is power: a critical survey of "bias" in NLP. arXiv preprint arXiv:2005.14050 (2020)
7. Callahan, E.S., Herring, S.C.: Cultural bias in Wikipedia content on famous persons. J. Am. Soc. Inf. Sci. Tech. **62**(10) (2011)
8. Chen, Z., Zhang, J.M., Hort, M., Sarro, F., Harman, M.: Fairness testing: A comprehensive survey and analysis of trends. arXiv preprint arXiv:2207.10223 (2022)
9. De Laat, P.B.: The use of software tools and autonomous bots against vandalism: eroding Wikipedia's moral order? Ethics and Information Technology 17
10. Gardner, S.: Nine reasons women don't edit Wikipedia (in their own words). Sue Gardner's blog (2011)
11. Garg, S., Perot, V., Limtiaco, N., Taly, A., Chi, E.H., Beutel, A.: Counterfactual fairness in text classification through robustness. In: Proceedings of AI, Ethics and Society Conference, pp. 219–226 (2019)
12. Geiger, R.S.: The lives of bots. arXiv preprint arXiv:1810.09590 (2018)
13. Glott, R., Ghosh, R.: Analysis of Wikipedia survey data. Topic: Age Gender Differences **14**, 2014 (2010)
14. Graham, M., Straumann, R.K., Hogan, B.: Digital divisions of labor and informational magnetism: mapping participation in Wikipedia. Ann. Assoc. Am. Geographers **105**(6), 1158–1178 (2015)
15. Greenstein, S., Zhu, F.: Do experts or crowd-based models produce more bias? evidence from encyclopedia Britannica and Wikipedia. Mis Quarterly **42**(3) (2018)
16. Hardt, M., Price, E., Srebro, N.: Equality of opportunity in supervised learning. Advances in neural information processing systems 29 (2016)
17. Kay, M., Matuszek, C., Munson, S.A.: Unequal representation and gender stereotypes in image search results for occupations. In: Proceedings of CHI (2015)
18. Kittur, A., Suh, B., Pendleton, B.A., Chi, E.H.: He says, she says: conflict and coordination in Wikipedia. In: Proceedings of ACM CHI (2007)
19. de Laat, P.B.: Profiling vandalism in Wikipedia: a schauerian approach to justification. Ethics Inf. Technol. **18**, 131–148 (2016)
20. Livingstone, R.M.: Population automation: An interview with wikipedia bot pioneer ram-man. First Monday (2016)

21. Massa, P., Scrinzi, F.: Manypedia: comparing language points of view of wikipedia communities. In: International Symposium on Wikis and Open Collaboration, pp. 1–9 (2012)
22. Mehrabi, N., Morstatter, F., Saxena, N., Lerman, K., Galstyan, A.: A survey on bias and fairness in machine learning. ACM Comput. Surv. **54**(6), 1–35 (2021)
23. Mesgari, M., Okoli, C., Mehdi, M., Nielsen, F.Å., Lanamäki, A.: "The sum of all human knowledge": a systematic review of scholarly research on the content of Wikipedia. J. Assoc. Inf. Sci. Tech. **66**(2), 219–245 (2015)
24. Mola-Velasco, S.M.: Wikipedia vandalism detection through machine learning: Feature review and new proposals. arXiv preprint arXiv:1210.5560 (2012)
25. Morris-O'Connor, D.A., Strotmann, A., Zhao, D.: The colonization of Wikipedia: evidence from characteristic editing behaviors of warring camps. J. Documentation (ahead-of-print) (2022)
26. Niederer, S., Van Dijck, J.: Wisdom of the crowd or technicity of content? Wikipedia as a sociotechnical system. New Media Soc. **12**(8), 1368–1387 (2010)
27. Nielsen, F.: Wikipedia research and tools: Review and comments. Technical University of Denmark, Working draft (2019)
28. Okoli, C., Mehdi, M., Mesgari, M., Nielsen, F.Å., Lanamäki, A.: Wikipedia in the eyes of its beholders: a systematic review of scholarly research on Wikipedia readers and readership. J. Assoc. Inf. Sci. Tech. **65**(12) (2014)
29. Prates, M.O., Avelar, P.H., Lamb, L.C.: Assessing gender bias in machine translation: a case study with google translate. Neural Comput. Appl. **32**, 6363–6381 (2020)
30. Ratković, N., Madžarević, I.: Women's participation in Wikipedia: cross-border balkan perspective. Área Abierta **21**(2), 237–253 (2021)
31. Rawat, C.: An ethical reflection on user privacy and transparency of algorithmic blocking systems in the Wikipedia community
32. Rogers, R., Sendijarevic, E., et al.: Neutral or national point of view? a comparison of Srebrenica articles across Wikipedia's language versions (2012)
33. Shadbolt, N., O'Hara, K., De Roure, D., Hall, W.: The theory and practice of social machines. Springer, Cham (2019)
34. Shelby, R., et al.: Sociotechnical harms: scoping a taxonomy for harm reduction. arXiv preprint arXiv:2210.05791 (2022)
35. Sun, J., Peng, N.: Men are elected, women are married: events gender bias on wikipedia. arXiv preprint arXiv:2106.01601 (2021)
36. Sweeney, L.: Discrimination in online ad delivery. Commun. ACM **56**(5), 44–54 (2013)
37. TeBlunthuis, N., Hill, B.M., Halfaker, A.: Effects of algorithmic flagging on fairness: Quasi-experimental evidence from Wikipedia. In: Proceedings of the ACM on Human-Computer Interaction 5(CSCW1), pp. 1–27 (2021)
38. Tripodi, F.: Ms. categorized: Gender, notability, and inequality on Wikipedia. New Media & Society, p. 14614448211023772 (2021)
39. Vincent, N., Hecht, B.: A deeper investigation of the importance of Wikipedia links to search engine results Proc. ACM Hum.-Comput. Interact. 5(CSCW1), April 2021. https://doi.org/10.1145/3449078
40. Wagner, C., Garcia, D., Jadidi, M., Strohmaier, M.: It's a man's Wikipedia? assessing gender inequality in an online encyclopedia. In: Proceedings of the international AAAI Conference on Web and Social media, vol. 9, pp. 454–463 (2015)
41. Wikipedia: Wikipedia: Neutral point of view. https://en.wikipedia.org/wiki/Wikipedia:Neutralpointofview (2023)

42. Worku, Z., Bipat, T., McDonald, D.W., Zachry, M.: Exploring systematic bias through article deletions on Wikipedia from a behavioral perspective. In: Proceedings of the 16th International Symposium on Open Collaboration, pp. 1–22 (2020)
43. Yang, P., Colavizza, G.: Polarization and reliability of news sources in Wikipedia. arXiv preprint arXiv:2210.16065 (2022)
44. Yanisky-Ravid, S., Mittelman, A.: Gender biases in cyberspace: a two-stage model, the new arena of Wikipedia and other websites. Fordham Intell. Prop. Media Ent. LJ **26**, 381 (2015)
45. Young, A., Wigdor, A.D., Kane, G.: It's not what you think: Gender bias in information about Fortune 1000 CEOs on Wikipedia (2016)
46. Young, A.G., Wigdor, A.D., Kane, G.C.: The gender bias tug-of-war in a co-creation community: core-periphery tension on Wikipedia. J. Manage. Inf. Syst. **37**(4), 1047–1072 (2020)
47. Zafar, B., Valera, I., Gomez-Rodriguez, M., Gummadi, K.P.: Training fair classifiers. In: International Conference on Artificial Intelligence and Statistics (2017)
48. Zandpour, M.: The gender gap on Wikipedia (2020)
49. Zheng, L., Albano, C.M., Vora, N.M., Mai, F., Nickerson, J.V.: The roles bots play in Wikipedia. Proc. ACM Hum.-Comput. Inter. **3**(CSCW), 1–20 (2019)

Students' Generated Text Quality in a Narrative-Centered Learning Environment: Effects of Pre-Collaboration, Individual, and Chat-Interface Submissions

Emily Theophilou$^{(\boxtimes)}$ ⓘ, René Lobo-Quintero ⓘ, Roberto Sánchez-Reina ⓘ,
and Davinia Hernández-Leo ⓘ

Universitat Pompeu Fabra, Barcelona, Spain
{emily.theophilou,renealejandro.lobo,
roberto.sanchez,davinia.hernandez-leo}@upf.edu

Abstract. Narrative-centered Learning Environments (NcLE) offer a powerful tool for enhancing students' learning through interactive experiences. The integration of open-ended questions in NcLEs encourages students to express their thoughts, opinions, and ideas without any restrictions. While different submission formats are implemented in NcLE, little research has argued the importance of assessing their potential effects. This study, therefore, investigates how the text quality in writing varies based on different submission formats for open-ended submissions in a NcLE. We proceed to analyze three types of submission formats within a narrative scripts platform: a) formal individual, b) pre-collaboration, and c) a chatbot interface. For this study, data was collected in a randomized controlled trial that involved 311 secondary school students participating in a social media literacy workshop. The quality of the submissions was assessed using an automated text cohesion and coherence analysis tool (Coh-Metrix). Our results show that having formal submission pages for open-ended questions has an effect in students' efforts to create submissions with higher writing quality, while submissions via chatbot interfaces tend to be brief and conversational in nature. The results presented in this study have practical implications for learning technology developers and educators, as they can guide decisions related to the creation, and integration of elements to promote writing quality in online learning environments.

Keywords: Narrative-centered Learning Environment · Computer Supported Collaborative Learning · Individual learning · Chat Interface · Writing Quality · Text Cohesion and Coherence

1 Theoretical Background

Narrative-centered Learning Environments (NcLE) in digital education have shown promising opportunities for engaging students with interactive practices.

H. Takada et al. (Eds.): CollabTech 2023, LNCS 14199, pp. 101–114, 2023.
https://doi.org/10.1007/978-3-031-42141-9_7

These platforms offer various benefits and support learning in different subjects [6,8,32]. Using NcLE not only empowers students' learning but also enhances their decision-making, perspective-taking, and critical thinking skills [8, 32,35]. NcLE's flexibility allows for different types of assignments, such as interactive story elements, chat interfaces, and open-ended questions [19,32]. This approach enables teachers to observe and capture learning qualitatively, highlighting the diversity and sensitivity of learning that may not be evident through traditional assessments [26].

The inclusion of qualitative questions in learning encourages students to express their thoughts and opinions effectively, enabling them to justify and explain their ideas using their own vocabulary in well-structured and coherent sentences [17]. By engaging in the process of explanation, students can achieve a more comprehensive understanding of the learning material, resulting in enhanced learning outcomes [3]. Moreover, self-explanation exercises activate cognitive processes, facilitating the connection of newly acquired knowledge with pre-existing understanding. This aids in enhancing comprehension, retention, and the ability to apply the information to draw further inferences [4]. To encourage this process, NcLE implement qualitative questions in the form of open-ended questions with the aim of triggering students' reflection from problem-based activities to situate learning scenarios [35]. While open-ended questions tend to generate more diverse answers, this format also presents certain drawbacks, such as a higher incidence of missing data and inadequate responses [31]. Moreover the evaluation of open-ended questions can be challenging and time consuming [28].

The evaluation of open-ended questions can be achieved by different methods. In the context of research this can be done through a thematic text analysis, with the help of coding systems [28]. Whereas, in educational settings this often sees the deployment of evaluation rubrics that provide teachers a scoring system based on a set of predetermined criteria [30]. When it comes to digital platforms, researchers have implemented diverse automated methods to evaluate and receive feedback of students' performance in online learning platforms [10,33]. Among these approaches, one method involves the automated analysis of linguistic features found in text. This method evaluates the quality of the text by analyzing its structure, with a particular emphasis on assessing its coherence and cohesion [11]. The analysis of coherence and cohesion is critical for evaluating whether a written text presents ideas in a clear and organized manner, with a logical progression of thoughts and a clear connection between concepts. In particular the analysis of text cohesion refers to how the various parts of the text are connected and flow together whilst text coherence, refers to how effectively the ideas and arguments presented in the text are logically connected and form a unified and understandable whole [24]. Both analyses ensure that the writing has a clear and logical progression of thoughts, with each idea building upon the previous one, leading to a comprehensive understanding of the topic or subject matter. The significance of text analysis centered on cohesion and coherence becomes evident through prior research indicating that texts with low cohesion can present challenges for students in analyzing text components and establishing connections [1]. Conversely, greater cohesion improves comprehension for diverse readers, particularly those with limited knowledge on the subject [9,22,25,27].

Even though cohesion indices have not been found to indicate higher quality text, studies have shown that higher text coherence is correlated with higher grades in essays [24] and is considered to be a critical element of writing quality [7]. The assessment of text quality, with attention to cohesion and coherence could provide valuable insights into students' information recall abilities by examining how well students structure and link their thoughts within written responses.

As coherence plays a vital role in ensuring writing quality, and the presence of cohesive features greatly contributes to the overall coherence of texts [21], the present study aims to analyze students' answers by focusing on text quality, specifically through a comprehensive analysis of coherence and cohesion. Considering that writing quality can be influenced by the type of activity students are asked to complete [5] and that it impacts the text cohesion [2], this study aims to compare the text quality of three different types of submissions in a NcLE.

1.1   The Present Study

There is a limited body of research that explores the variations in text quality, specifically in terms of cohesion and coherence, across different formats of open-ended submissions within a NcLE. Such research has the potential to offer valuable insights into the design principles for future developments of NcLE, guiding educators and developers towards more effective educational approaches. Therefore to close this gap, this paper compares the textual analysis of different types of open-ended submission available in a narrative script platform teaching about Social Media Risks and Threats [13,19]. The analyzed narrative scripts platform sees the incorporation of three different types of open-ended submissions to equally engage students in individual and collaborative learning during key points of the learning process. In particular, a generative open-ended question is used in the middle of each learning chapter of the narrative script platform. The primary objective of this approach is to actively stimulate students to recall information, as it plays a pivotal role in the encoding and retention of knowledge [14]. This process involves drawing connections between the authentic learning scenarios and the covered educational material, encouraging students to engage in reflective thinking.

By comparing how different formats of open-ended questions within the narrative scripts platform can affect students' writing quality, we aim to address their impact on student performance in both pre collaboration and individual submissions. In the context of the narrative scripts, the pre collaboration format refers to an individual submission made prior to collaboration. This type of submission differs from the typical individual submission as it is not only viewed by educators but also by fellow students for the purposes of discussion and collaborative knowledge building. These different scenarios might have an effect on the individual accountability of students when generating their answers [16]. Additionally, considering that the use of chat bots has shown the writing of higher-quality responses compared to traditional data collection methods [15, 36], there is a need to examine how the informal submissions within the chat interface of the platform differ from the other types of submissions. Therefore, the objective of this research is to determine whether and how different formats of open-ended submissions in a narrative-centered platform can differ in the quality of their textual properties. In particular, our study analyzes three open-ended submission formats within the narrative scripts platform; individual (formal), pre collaboration and chat-bot interface.

2   Methodology

2.1   Participants and Study Design

The study was carried out in three high schools across Barcelona, and involved a total of 311 students. The student ages ranged from 13 to 16. Our study design saw a randomized controlled trial where students were assigned to different conditions based on their classroom. The first condition saw students accessing the educational platform in an individual mode in which they did not engage into collaborative activities and instead completed equivalent individual tasks. In contrast, the second condition completed primarily collaborative activities.

To ensure ethical compliance, students and parents were briefed on the research objectives and the purpose of the workshop before its commencement. Both students and their families were required to provide electronic consent before participating in the study.

2.2   Procedure

The study was carried out as part of a social media literacy workshop that lasted four sessions. Data collection occurred during session 2 and session 4 when students were already familiar with the educational platform (see Fig. 1 for procedure). An open-ended task was added for each session to assess the learning material covered. In session 2, students explored topics about addictive social media features and completed an open-ended task that prompted them to reflect on the topic (task 1). In session 4, students explored social media scenarios related to wellbeing and completed a second open-ended task where they advised a young adolescent on how social media can impact their wellbeing (task 2). Students did not receive direct instruction on how to respond to these questions and were expected to formulate answers based on the situations they previously explored.

2.3   Instruments

The different instruments used in this study were implemented within a narrative scripted platform [13]. In the occasion of collaborative activities, the computer supported collaborative learning platform of PyramidApp was utilized [20].

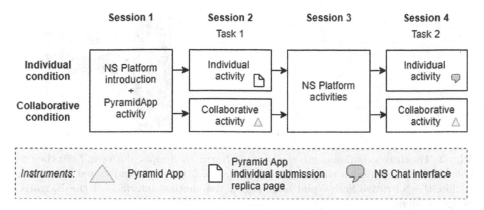

Fig. 1. The study utilized three main instruments: the PyramidApp CSCL tool, a replica page of the PyramidApp designed for individual submissions, and the chatbot interface within the Narrative Scripts platform. Both groups of students, under the individual and collaborative conditions, were provided with the same learning material. The key difference was their involvement in either individual or collaborative tasks during Session 2 and Session 4. Specifically, students in the individual condition completed the same activity as the collaborative condition but without the collaborative component. In Session 2, the individual activity was carried out using the replica page of the PyramidApp individual submission page. Meanwhile, in Session 4, the individual activity was conducted within the chatbot interface of the Narrative Scripts platform.

Overall, three different instruments were utilized to collect data within the narrative scripted platform (see Fig. 2). The first instrument of the PyramidApp allows students to individually prepare for collaboration by submitting an individual response to a task before initiating a collaborative activity. The second instrument was designed to replicate the individual preparation phase of the pyramid app without initiating collaboration. The third instrument was within the narrative scripts chat interface, where a chatbot asked students a question and students could reply in an open ended text format. Students in both the individual and collaborative conditions could access and interact with the chatbot interface and the learning material, however only the individual condition provided access to task 2 through the chatbot interface.

2.4   Measures and Data Analysis

To assess the quality of the students' submissions under each instrument, we used the Coh-Metrix tool [12]. The initial analysis focused on cohesion indices previously investigated by [2] and included the descriptive indices generated by the Coh-Metrix tool, along with the cohesion indices of: (a) Narrativity: whether a text resembles everyday conversations, with familiar characters, events, places, and things; (b) Syntactic Simplicity: text that contains fewer words and familiar structures; (c) Word Concreteness: the use of words that evoke mental images; (d) Referential Cohesion: the text with overlapping ideas and words across sen-

Fig. 2. The three submission interfaces of the Narrative Scripts platform. Left: the pre-collaboration submission within the PyramidApp. Middle: the individual submission within the Narrative Script platform. Right: the chatbot interface of the Narrative Script platform.

tences; (e) Deep Cohesion: how well a text uses causal and intentional connectives to explicitly show the causal relationships between ideas.

The second focus of the analysis focused on the coherence indices that were previously investigated by [24] and included the indices of: (a) Syntactic Complexity: the level of difficulty in the sentence structure and the organization of phrases and clauses in the text; (b) Lexical Diversity: the range of unique words in a text compared to the total number of words; (c) Word Frequency: refers to the average number of times that content or function words appear in the text.

To prevent abnormal submissions from affecting the findings, we proceed to manually remove submissions containing "I don't know" or gibberish inputs. After adding the data to Coh-Metrix, a normality test was conducted and found the data was not normally distributed, hence we utilized the Mann-Whitney test for statistical analysis.

3   Results

A total of 221 students' submissions were analyzed as part of the first task. (113 in the collaborative mode and 108 in the individual mode), whereas the second task involved the data of 244 students' submissions (119 from the collaborative mode and 125 from the narrative based platform).

3.1   Task 1: Pre-collaboration vs Individual Submissions

Descriptive Indices. The study did not reveal any significant differences between pre-collaboration and individual submissions. Specifically, the average word count was similar for both conditions, with pre-collaboration submissions having an average of 26.6 words and individual submissions having an average of 26.2 words. Moreover, students wrote an average of 1.4 sentences in both conditions, and sentences in the pre-collaboration condition were slightly longer on average (19.2) compared to those in the individual condition (17.9).

Text Cohesion Indices. As shown in Fig. 3, the study found no significant differences between pre-collaboration and individual submissions text easability indices. Although narrativity cohesion appeared higher under the individual condition, the difference was not statistically significant (preCollaboration mean = 28.65, individual mean = 36.8, $p < 0.05$). Similarly, no significant differences were found between the two conditions in terms of syntactic simplicity (preCollaboration mean = 39.1, individual mean = 41.9, $p < 0.05$), word concreteness (preCollaboration mean = 67.4, individual mean = 67.7, $p < 0.05$), and deep cohesion (preCollaboration mean = 38.9, individual mean = 38.4, $p < 0.05$). However, referential cohesion was found to be significantly different, with individual submissions having higher scores compared to pre-collaboration submissions (preCollaboration mean = 66.95, individual mean = 73.89, $p < 0.01$).

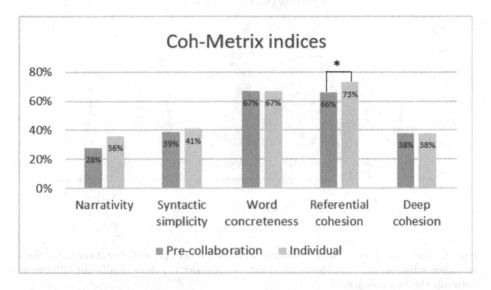

Fig. 3. The Coh-Metrix text cohesion indices of the pre-collaboration and individual submissions. Variables marked with an asterisk (*) show significant differences between the two conditions.

Text Coherence Indices. There were no significant differences between the syntactic complexity indices of the two conditions. The index of lexical diversity that showed a significant difference between the two conditions was the ratio of unique words in relation to the total number of words (preCollaboration mean = 0.93, individual mean = 0.94, $p < 0.01$). The word characteristic index that showed a significant difference between the two conditions was the word frequency for content words (preCollaboration mean = 2.26, individual mean = 2.39, $p < 0.03$).

3.2   Task 2: Pre-collaboration vs Chat Interface Submission

Descriptive Indices. According to the Coh-Metrix descriptive indices, submissions under the pre-collaborative individual mode had a significantly higher word count compared to those made in the chat interface submission (preCollaboration mean = 22.3, chatbot mean = 7.4, $p < 0.01$). Additionally, pre-collaborative individual submissions contained significantly more sentences (preCollaboration mean = 1.32, chatbot mean = 1, $p < 0.01$) and longer sentences (preCollaboration mean = 17.8, chatbot mean = 7.14, $p < 0.01$).

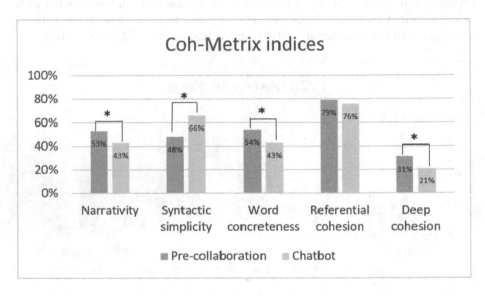

Fig. 4. The Coh-Metrix text cohesion indices of the pre-collaboration and chat-interface submissions. Variables marked with an asterisk (*) show significant differences between the two conditions.

Text Cohesion Indices. The Coh-Metrix text cohesion indices revealed significant differences between pre-collaboration and chat interface submissions in terms of text cohesion as seen in Fig. 4. Specifically, pre-collaboration submissions had significantly higher narrative cohesion than chat interface submissions (preCollaboration mean = 53.3, chatbot mean = 43.2, $p < 0.02$). In contrast, chat interface submissions had significantly higher syntactic simplicity compared to pre-collaboration submissions (preCollaboration mean = 48.5, chatbot mean = 66.3, $p < 0.01$). Pre-collaboration submissions also had significantly higher word concreteness compared to chat interface submissions (preCollaboration mean = 54.7, chatbot mean = 43.6, $p < 0.01$). No significant differences were found between the two conditions in terms of referential cohesion (preCollaboration mean = 79.3, chatbot mean = 76.8, $p < 0.05$), which may be due to the majority of submissions consisting of only one sentence. Finally, pre-collaboration submissions scored significantly higher in deep cohesion compared to chat interface submissions (preCollaboration mean = 31.9, chatbot mean = 21.6, $p < 0.01$).

Text Coherence Indices. The Coh-Metrix text coherence indices revealed significant differences between the two conditions. In syntactic complexity, the index that showed the largest difference between the two conditions was the words before the main verb index (preCollaboration mean = 1.85, chatbot mean = 0.63, $p < 0.01$). The index of lexical diversity that showed the largest difference between the two conditions was the ratio of unique words in relation to the total number of words (preCollaboration mean = 0.93, chatbot mean = 0.82, $p < 0.01$). The word characteristic index that showed the largest difference between the two conditions was the word frequency for all words (preCollaboration mean = 3.14, chatbot mean = 2.75, $p > 0.01$).

4 Discussion

This study aimed to examine the impact of different open-ended submission formats on the quality of writing generated by students as part of the learning activity in which open-ended submission is required. Specifically, we analyzed three types of submissions offered in the narrative scripts platform: formal individual, pre collaboration, and chatbot interface. The analysis involved examining the open-ended submissions using the descriptive, cohesion, and coherence indices of the Coh-Metrix tool. Our results provide a first look into how different types of open-ended submissions affect student-generated writing quality.

The first analysis saw a comparison of the formal individual and pre-collaborative type of submissions. Overall, the descriptive analysis did not reveal significant differences between the two conditions as students under both conditions performed similarly. A potential explanation for this observation is that the two submission types were closely comparable, thereby not significantly influencing students' level of formality. However, this finding contradicts previous research that demonstrated variations in student performance within peer assessment settings [2,5]. The analysis of cohesion between the individual and pre-collaborative submissions revealed that the individual submission had a higher referential cohesion, indicating that the sentences in this mode contained interconnected ideas and words that created a clear thread for the reader. One possible explanation for this finding is that students who submitted their work in the pre-collaborative mode were aware of the upcoming collaborative activity. Consequently, they may have opted to provide a brief description of one or a few ideas without delving into further detail, anticipating that they would collaborate with their peers to develop a collective answer.

The comparison of pre-collaboration submissions and chat interface submission saw notable differences in the descriptive and cohesion analysis. During the second task students who submitted through pre-collaboration wrote significantly more words and sentences compared to those who used the chat interface submission. We attribute this difference to the type of submission environment. The informal nature of the chatbot interface led to shorter and simpler responses from students. This is supported by the syntactic simplicity variable, which indicates a lower level of complexity in chatbot submissions. Additionally, the chatbot submissions scored lower in text narrativity, suggesting the use of less sophisticated vocabulary, lower word concreteness due to the presence of more abstract terms, and weaker deep cohesion, reflecting a lack of cohesion and connectedness in the submissions. Even though previous research has shown that the use of chatbots in place of open-ended questionnaires can help provide higher quality responses [15,36], this was not the case in our educational setting. Based on these findings, we believe that students perceive chatbot based educational settings as informal ways of assessment and do not produce high-quality responses when prompted by them. However, it is possible that the lack of AI-powered chatbot within the narrative scripts platform may have contributed to this outcome, and further research using more advanced chatbots is needed to provide more definitive conclusions.

A look into the coherence analysis to determine text quality [24], revealed that students using the individual submission format produced slightly higher quality text than those using the pre-collaboration mode. Since these two types of submissions share similarities in their design attributes, this finding shares an insight that social aspects that may encompass pre-collaborative activities do not surpass the writing quality of individual submissions. Notably, the chat interface submissions showed the lowest text quality among the three types of submissions. These results indicate a difference in the quality of text format between submission types, but do not necessarily reflect a difference in student performance in terms of accuracy. Further research needs to determine if there is a correlation between performance and accuracy.

As any study, we report a few limitations of our study that could have potentially influenced the findings. First and foremost, the study was conducted in Spanish schools and the collected submissions were in Spanish. However, as the Coh-Metrix tool is available only in English, we proceeded to translate the submissions using Google Translate. To ensure the accuracy of the answers, we carefully reviewed the translated text and removed any anomalies. In addition, our study only examined the text cohesion and coherence of the three interfaces. Other factors such as writing skills, prior subject knowledge, gender, socio-emotional skills, and motivation may also affect how students perform during learning activities [23,29,34]. Future work should take these variables into consideration when investigating the effects of different interfaces on student productivity. Furthermore, it is worth noting that the PyramidApp interface incorporates a diverse set of gamified elements designed to captivate students [18]. However, while these elements were present in the individual submission format, they were absent in the chatbot interface, which could have potentially influenced the outcomes of the study. Lastly, it is important to note that our analysis did not incorporate a qualitative analysis of students' performance by a teacher. Conducting a performance analysis would provide a more complete understanding of the strengths and weaknesses of the three interfaces and draw more nuanced conclusions.

In summary, our findings indicate that including formal pages for students to submit open-ended answers, whether by initiating individual preparation for collaboration or by formally requesting submissions in a separate interface, can be advantageous in narrative-based learning environments. While chat interfaces may appear to offer a more engaging approach to learning, our study found that student answers generated through such interfaces tend to be brief and conversational in nature.

5 Conclusion

The results presented in this study have practical implications for educators, as they can guide decisions related to the creation, and integration of elements to promote productivity and critical thinking in online learning environments. To enhance the quality of written responses in narrative-centered educational environments that use conversational chatbots for content delivery and self-explanations, our findings suggest that incorporating formal individual submissions or pre-collaboration phases can be more beneficial.

As chatbots become increasingly popular for educational purposes, it is crucial to explore how integrating such tools can impact student performance. In this study, we found that the use of chatbots to answer questions as part of a narrative learning activity leads students to generate answers with lower writing quality if compared with their answers when submitted to a devoted interface as part of an equivalent learning activity. While our analysis did not explore students' graded performance, the produced writing demonstrates students' effort in recall and the generation of self-explanations which eventually leads to learning [4,14]. Based on our findings, we recommend that developers and educators who are interested in integrating chat bots into educational settings should consider incorporating external interfaces for open-ended questions. This will lead students to devote more effort in producing higher quality written responses.

Acknowledgments. This work has been partially funded by the Volkswagen Foundation (COURAGE project, no. 95567). TIDE-UPF also acknowledges the support by FEDER, the National Research Agency of the Spanish Ministry, PID2020-112584RB-C33/MICIN/AEI/10.13039/501100011033, MDM-2015-0502 and by ICREA under the ICREA Academia programme (D. Hernández-Leo, Serra Hunter) and the Department of Research and Universities of the Government of Catalonia (SGR 00930).

References

1. Ainsworth, S., Burcham, S.: The impact of text coherence on learning by self-explanation. Learn. Instruct. **17**(3), 286–303 (2007). https://doi.org/10.1016/j.learninstruc.2007.02.004. https://www.sciencedirect.com/science/article/pii/S0959475207000308

2. Albó, L., Beardsley, M., Amarasinghe, I., Hernández-Leo, D.: Individual versus computer-supported collaborative self-explanations: how do their writing analytics differ? In: 2020 IEEE 20th International Conference on Advanced Learning Technologies (ICALT), pp. 132–134 (2020). https://doi.org/10.1109/ICALT49669.2020.00046

3. Aleven, V.A., Koedinger, K.R.: An effective metacognitive strategy: learning by doing and explaining with a computer-based cognitive tutor. Cogn. Sci. **26**(2), 147–179 (2002). https://doi.org/10.1016/S0364-0213(02)00061-7

4. Bisra, K., Liu, Q., Nesbit, J.C., Salimi, F., Winne, P.H.: Inducing self-explanation: a meta-analysis. Educ. Psychol. Rev. **30**, 703–725 (2018). https://doi.org/10.1007/s10648-018-9434-x

5. Cathey, C.: Power of peer review: an online collaborative learning assignment in social psychology. Teach. Psychol. **34**, 97–99 (2007). https://doi.org/10.1080/00986280701291325

6. Chen, Z.H., Chen, H.H.J., Dai, W.J.: Using narrative-based contextual games to enhance language learning: a case study. J. Educ. Technol. Soc. **21**(3), 186–198 (2018). http://www.jstor.org/stable/26458517

7. Crossley, S.A., Mcnamara, D.S.: Cohesion, coherence, and expert evaluations of writing proficiency. In: Proceedings of the 32nd Annual Conference of the Cognitive Science Society, pp. 984–989 (2010)

8. de dios, I.R., José Igartua, J., Leuven, K.: Narrative persuasion in a mobile environment: effectiveness of a mobile application for promoting digital skills and coping strategies in adolescents leen d'haenens. Int. J. Commun. **15**, 1637–1658 (2021)

9. Gernsbacher, M.A.: Language Comprehension as Structure Building, 1st edn. Psychology Press, Atlanta (1990). https://doi.org/10.4324/9780203772157

10. del Gobbo, E., Guarino, A., Cafarelli, B., Grilli, L., Limone, P.: Automatic evaluation of open-ended questions for online learning: a systematic mapping. Stud. Educ. Eval. **77**, 101258 (2023). https://doi.org/10.1016/J.STUEDUC.2023.101258

11. Graesser, A., McNamara, D., Kulikowich, J.: Coh-metrix. Educ. Res. **40**, 223–234 (2011). https://doi.org/10.3102/0013189X11413260

12. Graesser, A.C., McNamara, D.S., Louwerse, M.M., Cai, Z.: Coh-metrix: analysis of text on cohesion and language. Beh. Res. Meth. Instruments Comput. **36**, 193–202 (2004). https://doi.org/10.3758/BF03195564

13. Hernández-Leo, D., Theophilou, E., Lobo, R., Sánchez-Reina, R., Ognibene, D.: Narrative scripts embedded in social media towards empowering digital and self-protection skills. In: De Laet, T., Klemke, R., Alario-Hoyos, C., Hilliger, I., Ortega-Arranz, A. (eds.) EC-TEL 2021. LNCS, vol. 12884, pp. 394–398. Springer, Cham (2021). https://doi.org/10.1007/978-3-030-86436-1_42

14. Karpicke, J.D., Blunt, J.R.: Retrieval practice produces more learning than elaborative studying with concept mapping. Science **331**(6018), 772–775 (2011). https://doi.org/10.1126/science.1199327

15. Kim, S., Lee, J., Gweon, G.: Comparing data from chatbot and web surveys effects of platform and conversational style on survey response quality. In: Conference on Human Factors in Computing Systems - Proceedings (2019). https://doi.org/10.1145/3290605.3300316

16. Laal, M., Geranpaye, L., Daemi, M.: Individual accountability in collaborative learning. Procedia Soc. Beh. Sci. **93**, 286–289 (2013). https://doi.org/10.1016/j.sbspro.2013.09.191

17. Lee, Y., Kinzie, M.B., Whittaker, J.V.: Impact of online support for teachers open-ended questioning in pre-k science activities. Teach. Teach. Educ. **28**(4), 568–577 (2012). https://doi.org/10.1016/j.tate.2012.01.002. https://www.sciencedirect.com/science/article/pii/S0742051X12000042

18. Lobo-Quintero, R., Hernández-Leo, D.: An analysis of the game mechanics and learning analytics behind pyramid collaboration scripts. In: Companion Proceedings of the 10th International Learning Analytics and Knowledge Conference (LAK20) (2020)

19. Lobo-Quintero, R., Sánchez-Reina, R., Theophilou, E., Hernández-Leo, D.: Intrinsic motivation for social media literacy, a look into the narrative scripts. In: Fulantelli, G., Burgos, D., Casalino, G., Cimitile, M., Lo Bosco, G., Taibi, D. (eds.) HELMeTO 2022. CCIS, vol. 1779, pp. 419–432. Springer, Cham (2023). https://doi.org/10.1007/978-3-031-29800-4_32

20. Manathunga, K., Hernández-Leo, D.: Authoring and enactment of mobile pyramid-based collaborative learning activities. Br. J. Educ. Technol. **49**, 262–275 (2018). https://doi.org/10.1111/bjet.12588

21. McCulley, G.A.: Writing quality, coherence, and cohesion. Res. Teach. English **19**(3), 269–282 (1985)

22. McNamara, D.: Reading both high and low coherence texts: effects of text sequence and prior knowledge. Can. J. Exp. Psychol. = Revue canadienne de psychologie expérimentale **55**, 51–62 (2001). https://doi.org/10.1037/h0087352

23. McNamara, D.S.: Reading both high-coherence and low-coherence texts: effects of text sequence and prior knowledge. Can. J. Exp. Psychol. **55**, 51–62 (2001). https://doi.org/10.1037/H0087352

24. McNamara, D.S., Crossley, S.A., McCarthy, P.M.: Linguistic features of writing quality. Written Commun. **27**, 57–86 (2010). https://doi.org/10.1177/0741088309351547

25. McNamara, D.S., Kintsch, E., Songer, N.B., Kintsch, W.: Are good texts always better? interactions of text coherence, background knowledge, and levels of understanding in learning from text. Cogn. Instruct. **14**(1), 1–43 (1996). https://doi.org/10.1207/s1532690xci1401_1

26. Ndoye, F.: Using learning analytics to assess student learning in online courses. J. Univ. Teach. Learn. Pract. **13** (2016). https://doi.org/10.53761/1.13.3.7, https://ro.uow.edu.au/jutlp

27. Ozuru, Y., Dempsey, K., McNamara, D.S.: Prior knowledge, reading skill, and text cohesion in the comprehension of science texts. Learn. Instruct. **19**(3), 228–242 (2009). https://doi.org/10.1016/j.learninstruc.2008.04.003. https://www.sciencedirect.com/science/article/pii/S0959475208000534

28. Popping, R.: Analyzing open-ended questions by means of text analysis procedures. Bull. Sociol. Methodol. **128**, 23–39 (2015). https://doi.org/10.1177/0759106315597389

29. Portela-Pino, I., Alvariñas-Villaverde, M., Pino-Juste, M.: Socio-emotional skills as predictors of performance of students: differences by gender. Sustainability **13**(9) (2021). https://doi.org/10.3390/su13094807

30. Reddy, Y., Andrade, H.: A review of rubric use in higher education. Assess. Eval. Higher Educ.- ASSESS EVAL HIGH EDUC **35**, 435–448 (2010). https://doi.org/10.1080/02602930902862859

31. Reja, U., Manfreda, K., Hlebec, V., Vehovar, V.: Open-ended vs. close-ended questions in web questionnaires. Adv. Methodol. Stats. **19**, 159–177 (2003)

32. Rowe, J.P., Shores, L.R., Mott, B.W., Lester, J.C.: Integrating learning and engagement in narrative-centered learning environments. In: Aleven, V., Kay, J., Mostow, J. (eds.) ITS 2010. LNCS, vol. 6095, pp. 166–177. Springer, Heidelberg (2010). https://doi.org/10.1007/978-3-642-13437-1_17

33. Schonlau, M., Couper, M.: Semi-automated categorization of open-ended questions. Surv. Res. Methods **10**, 143–152 (2016). https://doi.org/10.18148/srm/2016. v10i2.6213

34. Tokan, M.K., Imakulata, M.M.: The effect of motivation and learning behaviour on student achievement. South African J. Educ. **39** (2019). https://doi.org/10.4314/saje.v39i1https://www.ajol.info/index.php/saje/article/view/184903

35. Vannini, N., et al.: "fearnot!": a computer-based anti-bullying-programme designed to foster peer intervention. Eur. J. Psychol. Educ. **26**, 21–44 (2011). https://doi.org/10.1007/s10212-010-0035-4

36. Xiao, Z., et al.: Tell me about yourself. ACM Trans. Comput.-Hum. Interact. **27** (2020). https://doi.org/10.1145/3381804

The Similarity of Virtual Meal of a Co-eating Agent Affects Human Participant

Jui-Ying Wang[1] and Tomoo Inoue[2] (✉)

[1] Graduate School of Comprehensive Human Sciences, University of Tsukuba, Tsukuba, Japan
[2] Institute of Library, Information and Media Science, University of Tsukuba, Tsukuba, Japan
inoue@slis.tsukuba.ac.jp

Abstract. In co-eating with real people, similar food consumption was found to benefit food intake and some subjective feelings. While co-eating agents have the potential to be caregivers or companions, the discussion of meal similarity between participants and agents is lacking. In this study, to achieve better social facilitation and the sense of eating together by a co-eating agent, we focused on the effects of meal similarity on eating amount and subjective feelings. We developed co-eating agents which can eat three types of food and conducted a laboratory-based artificial co-eating experiment. The results showed that participants perceived the meal similarity and the sense of eating together to be higher when the co-eating agent eats similar virtual food. In addition, a relationship was found between food tastiness and the difference of eating amount between the conditions. We propose that creating similar foods for co-eating agents can improve the feeling of togetherness in artificial co-eating and have the potential to facilitate eating when the food is preferred.

Keywords: co-eating agent · dietary similarity · digital commensality

1 Introduction

Co-eating is an important social activity for humans and plays a role in a good quality of life [1]. Due to lifestyle changes, such as an increase in one-person households globally [2], people face difficulties in co-eating because they are in different places, have irregular mealtime, or do not have a co-eating partner [3]. Some technologies have been adopted to support co-eating, such as co-eating through video calls or co-eating with an agent. However, whether these kinds of co-eating can provide companionship remains a question. For example, a survey showed that many people feel a gap between real-life and remote co-eating [4].

In a real-life co-eating, it is common for people to share meals with friends and family members [5], or order a similar type of food in a restaurant as a kind of strategy for promoting affection [6]. In addition, a study showed that meal similarity positively affected closeness and trust in face-to-face co-eating [7]. Another study suggested preparing similar food in remote co-eating as a way to enhance social facilitation and the sense of eating together [8].

H. Takada et al. (Eds.): CollabTech 2023, LNCS 14199, pp. 115–132, 2023.
https://doi.org/10.1007/978-3-031-42141-9_8

Other than eating with real people, agents were also used for co-eating. Some themed restaurants place dolls of characters as companions. Based on programming characteristics, some agents can monitor the food remains and encourage people to eat more varied and balanced by conversation [9, 10]. Since the co-eating agents can function independently, there is a potential to assist in the care of humans and provide companionship for those who are busy and have irregular mealtime. It is considered that co-eating agents can be applied in a wide range.

However, due to the physics-based constraints or the limitation of the number of food 3D models, the meal similarity between users and agents is usually low. In the cases of physical agents, most do not eat together or have their food. To break this, Khot et al. made the robots eat the battery and found that the participants thought it interesting [11]. Fujii et al. developed an MR system to simulate eating chocolate with the agent and found that the participants felt the chocolate tasted better and ate more [12]. In the cases of virtual agents, some of them have been developed with food animation and eating animations [13], but there are usually only a few types of food, and the perception of agents' virtual eating still needs more discussion.

Recently, due to the advancement of 3D model generation technology, it is possible to increase the meal similarity between users and agents by generating similar food models. In this study, to reduce the gap between real-life and digital co-eating and achieve better social facilitation and the sense of eating together by a co-eating agent, we aim to explore the effects of agents' meals. Additionally, we wanted to explore whether meal similarity benefited the impression of the agent, which is important for accepting co-eating agents as caregivers or companions. We developed co-eating agents with three types of food models and experimented to investigate the effects of meal similarity. We wanted to explore how people perceive the meal similarity between their physical food and the agent's virtual food and verify if meal similarity's effects on co-eating with agents are consistent with real people, which improves eating amount, feeling of having a meal together [8], closeness and trust [7]. The research questions RQ1–RQ3 were as follows:

RQ1. Does the participant perceive the meal similarity higher when the co-eating agent eats similar virtual food than dissimilar virtual food?

RQ2-1. Does the participant eat more when the agent eats similar virtual food than dissimilar virtual food?

RQ2-2. Does the participant have more feeling of having meal together when the agent eats similar virtual food than dissimilar virtual food?

RQ3. Does the participant have a more positive impression of the agent when the agent eats similar virtual food than dissimilar virtual food?

Though co-eating is seen as promoting the quality of eating, Boothby et al. found that people felt the preferred chocolate was more delicious when eaten with someone else but felt the unpreferred chocolate tasted worse when eaten with someone else [14]. In this study, we also wanted to explore if food preference may infer the effects of meal similarity. The research question RQ4 was as follows:

RQ4. Does the feeling of tastiness relate to the effects of meal similarity on the co-eating experience with the agent?

2   Related Works on Co-eating Agent

For entertainment or care needs, physical robots or virtual characters in the display were used to accompany meals, and their interaction was studied. Niewiadomski et al. discussed the design of non-verbal social interaction of co-eating agents, such as gaze contact, and mentioned those interactions could be developed with either physical or virtual agents [15]. Fujii et al. discussed the timing for starting conversational interaction via voice-user interface by co-eating agents [16]. Besides entertainment, conversational content was also used to encourage eating [9, 10] or augment food information [17]. On the other hand, the design of eating interaction was also studied in some studies, and it is suggested to enhance fun and facilitate eating [11, 12].

3   Method

3.1   Participants

In order to answer the research questions, a within-subjects design artificial co-eating experiment was conducted. In the experiment, a total of 16 students (4 male, 12 female) joined voluntarily, 6 of them were Japanese students, and the other 10 of them were international students from 6 different countries. Most students were from Eastern countries, and only one was from Western countries. The average age was 24 (SD = 4.15), ranging from 19 to 33. Participants were recruited through social networking services and a recruitment website. Every participant received a 600-yen Amazon gift card for participation.

3.2   Meal Similarity and Food

In order to investigate the effects of meal similarity in artificial co-eating, there were "same meal item" and "different meal item" conditions in the experiment. To avoid the effects of the taste of food [18], participants' meals were consistent in both conditions, while agents' meals were inconsistent. Dark chocolate was served as the meal in this study because it is low in sugar, low in the glycemic index, and easy to preserve. Agents' meals were virtual, which were made by 3D model software.

In the same meal item condition, the meal of the participant and agent were similar, the participant ate dark chocolate, and the agent also ate dark chocolate. In different meal item condition, the meal of the participant and agent were dissimilar, the participants ate dark chocolate, but the agent ate Kasutera (Japanese sponge cake), a less healthy snack, or vegetable dips, a healthier snack (Fig. 1). Three types of the snacks were all common in Japan, which were available from convenience stores. One piece of dark chocolate (5 g) contains 1.6 g of sugar, one piece of cake (42 g) contains 42 g of sugar, and a bowl of vegetable dips (50 g) contains 2 g of sugar.

The chocolate for participants was 72% dark chocolate. Considering hygiene issues, the chocolate is with the package. The three types of virtual food for the agents were made in 3D models using 3ds Max ® (Fig. 2).

Fig. 1. The images of the agent and her food. Left: The agent eats dark chocolate in the same meal item condition. Middle: The agent eats cake in the different meal item condition. Right: The agent eats vegetable dips in the different meal item condition.

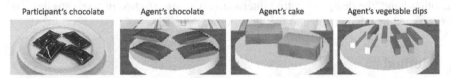

Fig. 2. The image of the food. Left to right: participant's chocolate, agent's chocolate, agent's cake, agent's vegetable dips.

3.3 Co-eating Agents

In this study, we developed two virtual co-eating agents, which could eat and chat with the participants. Agent 1 was called Toko, a girl with a brown ponytail, and Agent 2 was called Marie, a girl with straight black hair (Fig. 3). They were developed with Unity® and the character models are from © Unity Technologies Japan/UCL. These character models' actions could be edited by moving skeleton joints and the expression could be edited by changing the shader. Considering the behavior realism, we adopted basic breath and wink behavior for the agents. We made the agents' eyes refocus when the agents were on standby for over two seconds. In addition, we also developed lively eating actions for the agents. In addition, we also developed lively eating actions for the agents. On the other hand, the appearances of models were CHIBI style. CHIBI style was one of the cartoon styles, which was cute, and the head-to-body ratio was about 1:2. Though cartoon style is lower in appearance realism, it is considered suitable for social tasks [19]. In addition, the agents were young females, which were preferred over older or male agents at first glance in previous research [20].

Fig. 3. The image of the two agents (Left: Agent 1; Toko, Right: Agent 2; Marie).

Eating Actions. The eating actions of the agents were set as a conditional repeating sequence of the "Home position," "Preparation," "Hold," "Stroke," and "Recovery" (Fig. 4). A cycle of eating was about 45 to 50 s, and the agents ate 6 to 7 times in co-eating. Sound effects and cartoon symbols, such as stars and flowers (Fig. 5), were attached to make it easier for the participants to notice the agents' eating actions. During the eating, the amount of the virtual food on the plate was decreased so the participants could see how much was eaten by the agent (Fig. 6). The amount of chocolate, cake and vegetables was 4 pieces, 2 pieces and 8 pieces, respectively. And one piece of the chocolate, cake and vegetables was eaten in 2 bites, 4 bites and 1 bite, respectively. The description of each eating action period of the agent was as follows:

- Home position: The agent held her hands down and didn't hold any food in her hands.
- Preparation: The agent reached for food on the plate and/or held the food in the right hand near the chest. When food was not eaten up, the "Preparation" period restarted after the "Storke" period when the agent kept holding the food in hand. After the aforementioned restarted the "Preparation" period, there was half the chance of entering the "Recovery" period and the other half of the chance of entering the "Stroke" period again.
- Stroke: The agent bit the food. In addition, to emphasize the agent's chewing after biting, the agent's head was nodding, and eyes opened and closed. After the "Stroke" period, it entered the "Recovery" period if the food in hand is eaten up and entered the "Hold" period if not.
- Recovery: The agent's position recovered to the home position. If the previous period was "Stroke," the agent moved the right hand from mouth to chest and then moved it down. If the previous period was "Hold," the agent put the food back on the plate and then moved the right hand down.

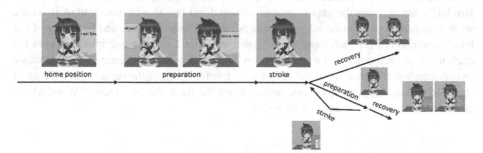

Fig. 4. The process of the agent's eating actions.

Conversation. As a companion, the agents chatted with the participants through dialogues and communication panels. Agents' dialogues were pre-scripted, and the sound was created through Google Text-to-Speech speech synthesis. Agent 1 had an American accent, and Agent 2 had a British accent. Through the conversation, agents talked about their hobbies, recent health goals, and plans for the weekends and discussed the

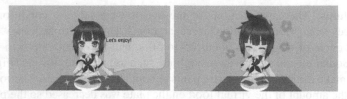

Fig. 5. The images of cartoon symbols after picking up and eating food.

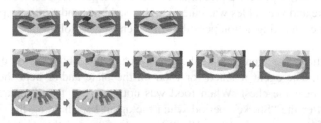

Fig. 6. The process of chocolate, cake, and vegetable dips decreases during the co-eating.

food impression with the participants. The agents asked some questions, and the participants answered by clicking or typing through the communication panel. There was an ice-breaking before starting co-eating.

The ice-breaking period took about 2 min. The agent said hello to the participant, introduced herself, and asked the participant's name. The participant also said hello to the agent and told his/her name through the communication panel (Fig. 7).

The co-eating period took 5 min. If the conversations were over before 5 min, agents would keep eating in the left time. During this period, there were some daily life conversations about food (Fig. 8). Sharing the impression of food was common in co-eating with strangers and provided a chance for participants to perceive different levels of food similarity not only by the appearance of virtual food but also by the taste of it. There were four aspects of conversation about food: smell, taste, texture, and likability of the food. The choices for each topic were shown in Table 1. And pre-scripted answers for each topic of each condition were shown in Table 2. For showing empathy, there was a two-dimensional branching of the dialogue as the feedback of the participant's liking of the food. When the participant said he/she liked the food, the agent said, "Wonderful." If not, the agent said, "I regret to hear that."

Fig. 7. The images showing the communication panel during ice breaking period.

Fig. 8. The images showing the communication panel during co-eating period.

Table 1. Choices for each topic

Topic	Option
smells like	1: No floral flavors 5: Floral flavors 1: No fruity flavors 5: Fruity flavors
taste like	salty/bitter/sweet/sour/warming/chilling/simple/complex/gentle/strong/fresh/fatty. (Choose some suitable adjectives.)
texture	smooth/rough/soft/hard/crumbly/tender/chewy/gummy/dry/moist. (Choose some suitable adjectives.)
likability	1: bad 5: good 1: unpleasant 5: pleasant 1: favor 5: not favor

Table 2. The pre-scripted answer to each topic for each snack

Topic	Pre-scripted answer for each snack
smells like	Chocolate: I slightly feel some flavors like flower Cake: I feel some flavors like egg Vegetable: I feel some strong flavors like grass
taste like	Chocolate: I feel bitter, a little sweet, and maybe kind of gentle Cake: I feel sweet, kind of warming, and maybe a little fatty Vegetable: I feel kind of chilling, fresh, and maybe a little simple
texture	Chocolate: I feel hard, but also smooth and kind of moist Cake: I feel soft, tender and kind of smooth Vegetable: I feel hard, rough but also kind of moist
likeable	Chocolate, Cake, Vegetable: I think my snack is kind of good and I like it Said "Wonderful." beforehand, when participant like the food (average >= 3). Says "I regret to hear that." beforehand, when participant do not like the food (average < 3)

3.4 Environment

The experiment was conducted in a lab at a university. The experimental environment was as shown in Fig. 9. The participant sat in front of a table during the experiment. On the table, there was a large screen (32 inches) showing the agents, a keyboard, and a mouse for interacting with the agents. In addition, there were four pieces of chocolate with packages on a plate, a cup of water, disinfectant alcohol, and Kleenex that participants could use as they liked. Two cameras recorded the experiment.

Fig. 9. The image of the experimental environment.

3.5 Data Collection and Analysis

To answer the research questions, the data of perceived meal similarity, eating amount, impression of the co-eating, and impression of the agent were collected. The eating amount was counted by the experimenter after each co-eating session. Because chocolate could be broken in half, the smallest unit was 0.5 pieces. Perceived meal similarity, impression of the co-eating, and impression of the agent were measured via questionnaires and an interview. The questionnaire contained 7-point Likert scale questions, as shown in, Table 3 and a free description question. The interview was semi-structured with some behavior events questions, as shown in Table 4.

Perceived Meal Similarity and Impression of Co-Eating. A 7-point Likert scale questionnaire (1: strongly disagree, 7: strongly agree) was used for investigating "perceived meal similarity" (CE1-CE3), the feeling of "tastiness" (CE4-CE6), and the feeling of "having meal together" (CE7-CE9). 3 items were adapted from the questionnaire in food similarity research [7, 8], 3 items were self-made for measuring perception of food similarity when eating with an agent, and the other 3 items were self-made for making each aspect had at least three items.

Impression of Agent. A 7-point Likert scale questionnaire (1: strongly disagree, 7: strongly agree) was used for investigating "closeness" (Cl1–Cl4), "trust" (Tr1–Tr4), "social presence in aspect of reality" (SP1–SP5), and "social presence in the aspect of companionship" (SP6–SP12). In "social presence in the aspect of reality," items were about whether participant saw the agents as real beings [21]. In "social presence in aspect of companionship," items were about whether participants and agents maintain attention to each other [22]. The items were adapted from the questionnaire in two food similarity research [7, 8], human-robot interaction research [23, 24], and the items were adapted from the questionnaire in two social presence research [21, 22].

Statistical Analysis. Nonparametric analysis was used because some of the items were not normally distributed according to the Shapiro-Wilk normality test. To answer RQ1, RQ2, and RQ3, the Wilcoxon rank-sum test was used to compare eating amount and subjective feelings between the "same meal item" and "different meal item" conditions, as the data were paired. To answer RQ4, we calculated the average level of feeling of "tastiness" in the two conditions and calculated the values of eating amount and subjective feeling under the condition of "same meal item" minus the values under the condition of "different meal item." We used Spearman's rank correlation coefficient to investigate the relationship between tastiness and the effects of meal similarity on eating amount and subjective feeling.

Table 3. Questionnaire

Category	Item
Perceived meal similarity	CE1: I felt the agent was eating similar snack with me
	CE2: I could find something in common in agent's snack and mine
	CE3: I felt the agent's snack tasted like mine
Tastiness	CE4: During the meal, I felt this snack favorable
	CE5: During the meal, I felt that I liked the flavour of this snack
	CE6: During the meal, I felt that the snack was delicious
Having a meal together	CE7: I felt like I was eating with the agent
	CE8: I enjoyed the snacks with the agent
	CE9: I **did not feel isolated** when I was eating with the agent
Closeness	Cl1: I felt close to the agent
	Cl2: I felt the agent likable
	Cl3: I would like to spend more time with the agent
	Cl4: I do **not** see myself being friends with the agent.*
Trust	Tr1: I thought the agent was communicating honestly
	Tr2: I trust the agent can provide me with good suggestions
	Tr3: I will follow the advice the agent gives me

(continued)

Table 3. (*continued*)

Category	Item
	Tr4: I will trust the agent if the agent gives me advice in the future
Social presence in aspect of reality	SP1: When staying with the agent, I felt like staying with a real person
	SP2: I sometimes felt like the agent was actually looking at me
	SP3: I can imagine the agent as a living creature
	SP4: I often realized the agents was **not** a real living creature.*
	SP5: Sometimes it seemed as if the agent had real feelings
Social presence in aspect of companionship	SP6: Agent was easily distracted.*
	SP7: I was easily distracted.*
	SP8: The agent tended to ignore me.*
	SP9: I tended to ignore the agents.*
	SP10: I sometimes **pretended** to pay attention to the agent.*
	SP11: The agents sometimes **pretended** to pay attention to me.*
	SP12: The agent paid close attention to me

The question has * mark was reverse score question
The words "did not feel isolated", "not" and "pretended" were bold and underline in the questionnaire to reduce misunderstanding

3.6 Experimental Procedures

The experiment consisted of three sessions and lasted about 40 min in total. Within-subjects-design was used to avoid the effects of personal differences in acceptance or familiarity with technology. The participants eat with the agents in two sessions. One session eats with Agent A, and the other eats with Agent B. To minimize the order effects, such as feeling less hungry or getting familiar with the co-eating procedures in the later sessions, the eight combinations (2 orders * 2 agents * 2 different snacks used in the different meal item condition) were randomly assigned to each participant. Each combination was assigned two times. The following procedures were as follows:

1. Explain the experiment to the participant in writing and orally, then obtain the signatures on a consent form.
2. Let the participant and an agent have ice-breaking for 2 min, and then eat with the agent for 5 min (in the same meal item condition or different meal item condition).
3. Let the participant fills in the questionnaire.

Table 4. Interview in experiment

Topics	Items
General	1. Overall, what do you think about these two co-eating? Why? 2. Is there any most memorable parts of to co-eating?
Eating together	3. (If CE1-CE3 items are high) Please describe a time when you felt that the agent was eating similar food./(When CE1-CE3 items are low) Please describe a time when you felt that the agent was eating dissimilar food.* 4. (If CE7-CE9 items are high) Please describe a time when you felt like that you were eating with the agents./(When CE7-CE9 items are low) Please describe a time when you felt like that you weren't eating with the agents
Closeness	5. What feelings do these two agents bring out in you? 6. (If Cl1-Cl4 items are high) Please describe a time when you felt close to the agents./(If Cl1-Cl4 items are low) Please describe a time when you felt not close to the agents.*
Trust	7. You have communicated with two agents. What feelings do those communication bring out in you? 8. (If Tr1-Tr4 items are high) Please describe a time when you felt trust in agents./(If Tr1-Tr4 items are low) Please describe a time when you felt not trust in the agents. *
Social presence	9. What did you pay any attention to in the two co-eating? Why? 10. (When SP1-SP5 items are high) Please describe a time when you felt that the agent is similar to a person./(When SP1-SP5 items were low) Please describe a time when you felt that the agent is not similar to a person.*
Free description	11. (Check the free description.)

*If the first and second session trends are different, ask about each situation

4. Let the participant and the other agent have ice-breaking for 2 min and eat with that agent for 5 min (in a condition different from step 2).
5. Let the participant fills in the questionnaire.
6. Conduct the interview.

4 Results

4.1 Perceived Meal Similarity

According to the 7-point Likert scale questionnaire, the medians of perceived meal similarity in the same and different meal item conditions were 6.7 and 1.3 (Fig. 10), respectively. Among participants attainted to the different meal item condition, the mean of perceived meal similarity between their chocolate and the agent's cake was 2, and the mean of perceived meal similarity between their chocolate and the agent's vegetable was 1.2. A Wilcoxon rank sum test was conducted to compare perceived meal similarity between the same and the different meal item conditions. It was significantly different between the conditions ($N = 16$, $W = 0$, $p = 0.000$). It suggested that participants have higher perceived meal similarities in the same meal condition.

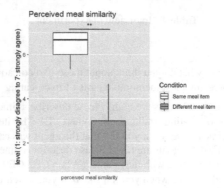

Fig. 10. Box plot of perceived meal similarity

4.2 Eating Amount and Impression of Co-Eating

Out of the four given chocolates, the medians of pieces of chocolate eaten was 3 ($Q_{1/4}$ = 1.75, $Q_{3/4}$ = 4) in the same meal item condition, and 2 ($Q_{1/4}$ = 1, $Q_{3/4}$ = 3) in the different meal item condition (Fig. 11). To compare eating amount between the same and the different meal item conditions, a Wilcoxon rank sum test was conducted. However, there were no statistically significant differences.

According to the 7-point Likert scale questionnaire, the participants had a generally positive attitude toward "tastiness" (Md_s = 5.8, Md_d = 5.6). They also had a generally positive attitude toward the feeling of "having meal together" (Md_s = 5.8, Md_d = 5.3). A Wilcoxon rank sum test was conducted to compare the impression of the co-eating between the same and the different meal item conditions. It was significantly different in "having meal together" between the conditions (N = 14, W = 16.5, p = 0.026). It suggested that participants felt the sense of eating together in the same meal condition.

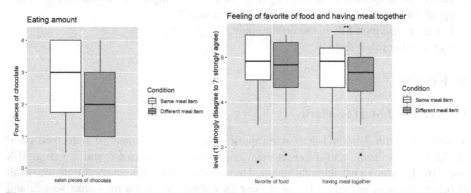

Fig. 11. Left: Box plot of eating amount. Right: Box plot of the feeling of "tastiness" and feeling of "having meal together."

4.3 Impression of the Agent

According to the 7-point Likert scale questionnaire, the participants had a generally positive attitude toward "closeness" ($Md_s = 5.5$, $Md_d = 5.4$) and "trust" ($Md_s = 5.3$, $Md_d = 4.5$). Besides, they had a neutral attitude toward the feeling of "social presence in the aspect of reality" ($Md_s = 4.2$, $Md_d = 4.3$) and a positive attitude toward the feeling of "social presence in the aspect of companionship" ($Md_s = 5.4$, $Md_d = 5.2$). A Wilcoxon rank sum test was conducted to compare the impression of the co-eating between the same and the different meal item conditions. However, there were no statistically significant differences (Fig. 12).

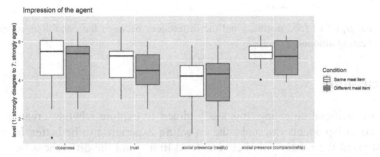

Fig. 12. Box plot of impression of the agent

4.4 The Relationship Between Tastiness and the Differences Between the Conditions of Eating Amount and Subjective Feeling

According to the average level of "tastiness" in the two conditions for each participant, there are three participants did not think the chocolate was tasty ($M < 4.5$), five participants slightly thought the chocolate was tasty ($4.5 <= M < 5.5$), one participant thought the chocolate was tasty ($5.5 <= M < 6.5$), and other seven participants strongly thought the chocolate was tasty ($6.5 <= M$).

The scatterplot of food tastiness and the differences between the conditions of the subjective feeling and eating amount was shown in Fig. 13. The x-axis showed the average feeling of "tastiness," and the y-axis showed the absolute value of the levels in the same meal item condition minus those in the different meal item condition. To explore if the participants had more positive experience in the same meal item condition when they thought the food was tastier, Spearman's rank correlation coefficient tests were conducted. Results showed that the average feeling of "tastiness" in the two conditions moderately positively correlated with the difference of "eating amount" between the two conditions ($rho = 0.60$, $p = 0.01$).

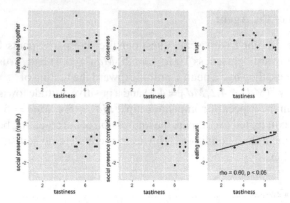

Fig. 13. Scatterplot of food tastiness and the differences between the conditions of subjective feeling and eating amount.

5 Discussion

To improve artificial co-eating, this study aimed to explore whether creating similar food for co-eating agents can make the co-eating experience to be better. In addition, we investigated the relationship between food liking and the differences between the conditions of eating amount and subjective feeling.

5.1 Perceived Meal Similarity

To answer RQ1 ("Does the participant perceive the meal similarity higher when the co-eating agent eats similar virtual food than dissimilar virtual food?"), we developed co-eating agents with three types of virtual food and investigate the perceived meal similarity through the questionnaire. The results showed that people perceived a higher meal similarity when the agent ate similar virtual food. According to the interview, when asked, "Please describe a time when you felt that the agent was eating similar food," most of the participants answered the time when snacks looked similar ($N = 15$), such as the package or the color of chocolate, in the same meal item condition. In addition, about half of them answered that they realized the taste ($N = 8$) through the conversation. Besides, some participants thought the nutrition ($N = 1$) or the chewing sound was similar ($N = 2$). On the other hand, in the different meal item condition, some participants still thought there were some common points between the food, such as they are both sweet ($N = 2$) or sound hard ($N = 1$). In summary, participants may perceive whether agent foods are similar to their food through visual cues, audio cues, and shared information about foods in conversations.

5.2 Eating Amount and Impression of Co-eating

To answer RQ2-1 ("Does the participant eat more when the agent eats similar virtual food than dissimilar virtual food?") and RQ2-2 ("Does the participant have more feeling of having meal together when the agent eats similar virtual food than dissimilar virtual food?"), we counted the eaten chocolate and investigated the perceived meal similarity through the questionnaire. About eating amount, the medians of pieces of chocolate eaten was 3 in the same meal condition, and it was 2 in the different meal item condition. However, there were no significant differences between the two conditions. Compared to previous online co-eating research [8], the medians are higher in the same meal condition in both studies, which showed a tendency to eat more when the partner ate the same food. However, the statistical results were different. Some of the possible reasons were that the diversity of the meal was lower, mealtime was shorter, and participants were less in this study. Besides, the amount of food eaten was measured in this study, and times of putting food into mouth were measured in the previous research through video analysis.

Regarding the feeling of having a meal together, the results of the questionnaire showed that people felt the sense of eating together in both conditions, and the feeling was stronger when the agent ate similar virtual food, which was consistent with the previous online co-eating research [8]. When being asked "Please describe a time when you felt like that you were eating with the agents." some participants cited the importance of agents' eating speed, patterns, or synchronizations ($N = 7$). For example, a participant mentioned that "I felt eating together when the agent took the food at the same time" (No 4). It is interesting that some participants even said that they would wait for the agent to eat and then eat at the same time. In addition, some participants mentioned that they felt eating together when they have enjoyable communication ($N = 4$). However, there are some participants thought they could not feel eating together because the agent is just a procedural artifact ($N = 3$). On the other hand, some participants pointed out that they felt the feeling of eating together more when they had the same food ($N = 6$). For example, a participant mentioned, "When eating the same thing, I matched the agent's eating more unconsciously, which made me feel like we are eating together." (No 5), "[When eating the same meal] I waited for her to open the package and ate together." (No 16), "[I felt the sense of eating together more] because we had something in common. For example, we felt the same way about food." (No 14). It suggested that the eating speed of the agent should be set to be similar to a human's speed that the user could follow, and agent conversations about how food feels should resonate with users.

5.3 Impression of the Agent

To answer RQ3 ("Does the participant have a more positive impression of the agent when the agent eats similar virtual food than dissimilar virtual food?"), we collected information on subjective feelings through a questionnaire. The results of the questionnaire showed that people generally felt the agent was close, and trustworthy and felt the social prescience in the aspect of companion. However, they have a neutral attitude toward the feeling of social presence in the aspect of reality. This means they cannot tell if they think the agent is like a real creature or has a real feeling. In addition, there were no statistically significant differences in the impression of the agent between the two conditions. Notably, pre-scripted dialogues and repeated eating actions of agents were used in this experiment. Thus, the agents' impression of food and eating speed did not adjust to the participants' situation, which was considered unlike real-life co-eating.

5.4 Tastiness and Difference of Eating Amount Between the Conditions

Lastly, to answer RQ4 ("Does the feeling of tastiness relate to the effects of meal similarity on the co-eating experience with the agent?"), we used Spearman's rank correlation coefficient. We found the relationship between food liking and the difference of eating amount between the conditions. When participants thought the food was tasty, they tended to eat more in the same meal item condition. On the contrary, when participants thought the food was not tasty, they tended to eat less in the same meal item condition. In previous research, it is suggested that having an eating partner may make people more focused on the eating experience, which will be an advantage if the food is preferred but a disadvantage if the food is not preferred [14]. Therefore, though there were no significant differences of eating amount in the two conditions in this study, the results may be different with more preferred or less preferred food.

5.5 Limitations

There were some limitations in this study. The diversity of the meal and mealtime was limited in this study compared to previous studies. More studies are needed to explore whether creating similar virtual food could encourage people to eat other kinds of nutritious food, such as a healthy lunchbox, over a longer time. Besides, the agent was pre-scripted, and participants interacted with it through mouse and keyboard. Although this setting avoids errors, it limits free interaction. Lastly, the number of participants was small, and we planned to conduct experiments with more participants in the future.

6 Conclusion

In this study, we wanted to reduce the gap between real-life and digital co-eating and achieve better social facilitation and the sense of eating together by a co-eating agent. We explored the effects of agents' meals and developed two co-eating agents with three types of food. The results showed that participants perceived the meal similarity and the sense of eating together to be higher when the co-eating agent eats similar virtual food. In addition, a relationship was found between food tastiness and the difference of eating amount between the conditions. We propose that creating similar foods for co-eating agents can improve the feeling of being together in artificial co-eating and have the potential to facilitate eating when the food is preferred.

References

1. Choi, M.J., Park, Y.G., Kim, Y.H., Cho, K.H., Nam, G.E.: Eating together and health-related quality of life among korean adults. J. Nutr. Educ. Behav. **52**, 758–765 (2020)
2. Ortiz–Ospina, E.: The rise of living alone: how one-person households are becoming increasingly common around the world. Our world in data (2019)
3. Ministry of Agriculture, Forestry and Fisheries: Shokuiku promotion policies: Fy2017 (white paper on shokuiku) (2017)

4. Ceccaldi, E., Huisman, G., Volpe, G., Mancini, M.: Guess who's coming to dinner? surveying digital commensality during covid-19 outbreak. In: Companion Publication of the 2020 International Conference on Multimodal Interaction, pp. 317–321 (2020)
5. Oh, A., Erinosho, T., Dunton, G., Perna, F.M., Berrigan, D.: Cross-sectional examination of physical and social contexts of episodes of eating and drinking in a national sample of US adults. Public Health Nutr. **17**(12), 2721–2729 (2014)
6. Cavazza, N., Guidetti, M., Butera, F.: Portion size tells who i am, food type tells who you are: specific functions of amount and type of food in same-and opposite-sex dyadic eating contexts. Appetite **112**, 96–101 (2017)
7. Woolley, K., Fishbach, A.: A recipe for friendship: similar food consumption promotes trust and cooperation. J. Consum. Psychol. **27**, 1–10 (2017)
8. Wang, J.Y., Kubota, S., Inoue, T.: Effects of meal similarity on interpersonal synchronization in three-party remote dining. Front. Comput. Sci. **4**, 838229 (2022)
9. McColl, D., Nejat, G.: A socially assistive robot that can monitor affect of the elderly during mealtime assistance. J. Med. Devices **8**(3), 030941 (2014)
10. Randall, N., Joshi, S., Liu, X.: Health-e-eater: dinnertime companion robot and magic plate for improving eating habits in children from low–income families. In: Companion of the 2018 ACM/IEEE international conference on human–robot interaction, pp. 361–362 (2018)
11. Khot, R. A., Arza, E. S., Kurra, H., Wang, Y.: Fobo: towards designing a robotic companion for solo dining. In: Extended Abstracts of the 2019 CHI Conference on Human Factors in Computing Systems, pp. 1–6 (2019)
12. Fujii, A., Kochigami, K., Kitagawa, S., Okada, K., Inaba, M.: Development and evaluation of mixed reality co-eating system: sharing the behavior of eating food with a robot could improve our dining experience. In: 2020 29th IEEE International Conference on Robot and Human Interactive Communication (RO–MAN), pp. 357–362 (2020)
13. Takahashi, M., Tanaka, H., Yamana, H., Nakajima, T.: Virtual co-eating: making solitary eating experience more enjoyable. In: Munekata, N., Kunita, I., Hoshino, J. (eds.) ICEC 2017. LNCS, vol. 10507, pp. 460–464. Springer, Cham (2017). https://doi.org/10.1007/978-3-319-66715-7_63
14. Boothby, E.J., Clark, M.S., Bargh, J.A.: Shared experiences are amplified. Psychol. Sci. **25**(12), 2209–2216 (2014)
15. Niewiadomski, R., Bruijnes, M., Huisman, G., Gallagher, C.P., Mancini, M.: Social robots as eating companions. Front. Comput. Sci. **4**, 909844 (2022)
16. Fujii, A., Okada, K., Inaba, M.: Relationship between eating and chatting during mealtimes with a robot. In: Stephanidis, C., Antona, M., Ntoa, S. (eds.) HCII 2021. CCIS, vol. 1498, pp. 249–256. Springer, Cham (2021). https://doi.org/10.1007/978-3-030-90176-9_33
17. Weber, P., Krings, K., Nießner, J., Brodesser, S., Ludwig, T.: FoodChattAR: exploring the design space of edible virtual agents for human-food interaction. In: Designing Interactive Systems Conference 2021, pp. 638–650 (2021)
18. Williams, L.E., Bargh, J.A.: Experiencing physical warmth promotes interpersonal warmth. Science **322**(5901), 606–607 (2008)
19. Ring, L., Utami, D., Bickmore, T.: The right agent for the job?: the effects of agent visual appearance on task domain. In: Bickmore, T., Marsella, S., Sidner, C. (eds.) Intelligent Virtual Agents: 14th International Conference, IVA 2014, Boston, MA, USA, August 27-29, 2014. Proceedings, pp. 374–384. Springer International Publishing, Cham (2014). https://doi.org/10.1007/978-3-319-09767-1_49
20. ter Stal, S., Tabak, M., op den Akker, H., Beinema, T., Hermens, H.: Who do you prefer? The effect of age, gender and role on users' first impressions of embodied conversational agents in eHealth. Int. J. Hum. Comput. Interact. **36**(9), 881–892 (2020)

21. Heerink, M., et al.: A field study with primary school children on perception of social presence and interactive behavior with a pet robot. In: 2012 IEEE RO-MAN: The 21st IEEE International Symposium on Robot and Human Interactive Communication, pp. 1045–1050 (2012)
22. Lubold, N., Walker, E., Pon-Barry, H.: Effects of adapting to user pitch on rapport perception, behavior, and state with a social robotic learning companion. User Model. User-Adap. Inter. **31**(1), 35–73 (2020). https://doi.org/10.1007/s11257-020-09267-3
23. Ghazali, A.S., Ham, J., Barakova, E., Markopoulos, P.: Persuasive robots acceptance model (PRAM): roles of social responses within the acceptance model of persuasive robots. Int. J. Soc. Robot. **12**(5), 1075–1092 (2020)
24. Ghazali, A.S., Ham, J., Barakova, E., Markopoulos, P.: Assessing the effect of persuasive robots interactive social cues on users' psychological reactance, liking, trusting beliefs and compliance. Adv. Robot. **33**(7–8), 325–337 (2019)

Work-in-Progress Papers

Towards a Design Toolkit for Designing AR Interface with Head-Mounted Display for Close-Proximity Human-Robot Collaboration in Fabrication

Yi Zhao[✉][iD], Lynn Masuda[iD], Lian Loke[iD], and Dagmar Reinhardt[iD]

The University of Sydney, Sydney, Australia
{yi.zhao1,rin.masuda,lian.loke,dagmar.reinhardt}@sydney.edu.au

Abstract. Industry 5.0 puts forward clear requirements for improving the interactive experience of human-machine collaboration, but few design tools currently exist to assist designers to think through how to design human-robot interactions, with a focus on turn-taking, coordination and communication of the interactive intention flow. We present a design toolkit for designers to explore, specify, analyse and document the unfolding interaction between human(s) and robot(s) through a model of interaction where the roles of leader and follower shape the forms of collaborative behaviour. We illustrate our preliminary design toolkit in action and demonstrate how it can be used to aid in exploring new augmented reality applications in robotic fabrication.

Keywords: Design Toolkit · Augmented Reality · Human-robot Collaboration · Robotic Fabrication · Industry 5.0

1 Introduction

The next wave of the fifth industrial revolution will need to standardise and optimize the experience of interaction for human-robot collaboration, especially in the field of interaction experience design within a close-proximity scenario [5]. A cyber-physical system (a support technology of Industry 4.0) enables the robot to act as an agent linked to the virtual and physical world. Through various sensors and the artificial intelligence (AI) algorithm, the robot can perceive the world and give feedback to the real world via its own behaviours [4]. Therefore, in order to integrate the human factor into the cyber-physical system, an increasing number of researchers focus on Augmented Reality (AR) Interface design for head-mounted display (HMD) [12]. AR provides a method for operators to interact with digital information in real time, as it is a medium that can combine virtual information with the perception of the individual human from a real environment. For close-proximity HRC tasks, human operators can

Supported by DMaF Lab, The University of Sydney.

view information from cyber-space in the HMD, including robot status, tasks procedure, and attributes of other devices participating in the task, and as a result, make rational interaction choices based on the real environmental conditions. This process allows the human agent to participate deeply in production and manufacturing under the premise of ensuring safety, which is an important feature emphasised in Industry 5.0.

However, considering the current high threshold for hardware and software programming capabilities in developing an AR-based HRC system, it takes a lot of time for the programmer to create a fully functional interaction system [10]. This blocks rapid iteration and optimization around interaction experience. To address this problem, our research aims to investigate appropriate design tools to assist designers of human-robot interactions with AR interfaces. In Sect. 3.1, we use the Research-for-Design (RfD) methodology [3] to develop an HRC design toolkit for AR interface with HMD especially based on the behavioural logic of the industrial robot, guiding users without robotic development experience to conceptualise and prototype the AR interface for HRC task. It is constructed with the human-robot leader-follower (HRLF) model, looking at the flow of interaction intention behind the relationship roles. It is worth noting that the proposed design toolkit is generally applicable for designing AR interface with HMD in robotic fabrication. It is not for special-purpose HRC industrial applications. Notwithstanding, this design toolkit can be customised for different fabrication scenarios. In Sect. 3.2, following the Research-through-Design (RtD) approach [14], we design a typical scenario of robotic fabrication—using small granules to build an aggregate architecture model with human—to demonstrate how it can be used to analyse and design a complete augmented reality (AR) interface. The contribution of this paper is a preliminary design toolkit that can effectively design and iterate HRC tasks in the AR collaboration for the fabrication scenario. It combines the characteristics of industrial robots to help developers focus on the interaction design of collaborative behaviours by using HMD.

2   Related Work

Lack of in-depth consideration of context and user experience is a common weakness in HRC, as engineers tend to provide the "satisficing" outcomes meeting all requirements instead of the best results balancing the technological innovation and user experience of HRC [1]. To bridge this gap, researchers advocate bringing methodologies from human-computer interaction (HCI) to the HRC community: Lupetti et al. (2021) [6] suggest adding a reflection section at the early stage of the project development. Such initial reflection activities allow for an investigation of robot users' needs and requirements through sketching and prototyping, thus generating intermediate-level knowledge for the HRC community [6].

To illustrate this, Cloud Remote Control (CRC), developed by the Association for Robots in Architecture, provides an online collaboration platform enabling designers to work with KUKA robot(s) from anywhere remotely. In a sample workshop, an immersive AR prototyping environment is coupled with a fabrication robot to build steel structures. Using the HoloLens, participants place the position of hologram steel with their design ideas to design the prototype of the robot assembly path. Through the AI function, this prototype can be turned into a fabricable trajectory for the KUKA robot. Although visualization and simulation play an important role in promoting the cooperation of interdisciplinary researchers and engineers, the design of the interactive user experience in HRC has not fully benefitted from the established concepts, methods and theories from the HCI field, such as human-centred design principles [13]. More specifically, a research gap exists in how to design AR interfaces for close-proximity user collaboration in robotic fabrication.

3   Methodology and Main Procedure

We use RfD and RtD methodologies to design two research stages, scaffolding the entire study flow for this paper. In Stage 1, RfD can help us gather existing theoretical materials from HRC, HCI and AR design guidelines effectively, finding valuable content that contributes to the construction of a new design toolkit for AR interaction with robotics. The final design toolkit is iterated by these key findings, containing the human-robot leader-follower (HRLF) model. In Stage 2, the RtD is used to create an AR-based HRC case study by this new design toolkit. We aim here to validate the use of the proposed design toolkit in robotics fabrication scenarios. This application process includes AR prototype design, testing, and implementation, where the result can generate intermediate-level knowledge for HRC/HRI community.

3.1   Stage 1: Construction of Design Toolkit

The HRC design toolkit will support designers (interaction designers) to formulate concrete expression (textualization and visualization) of intention

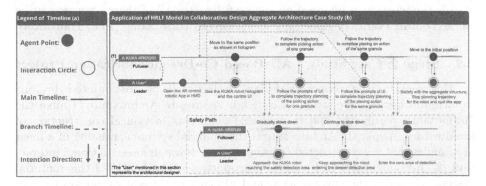

Fig. 1. (a) Legend of key elements from human-robot task timeline; (b) Task timeline of AR-based co-design robotic fabrication system

communication between humans and robots. We believe that, in the Industry 5.0 era, the robot will act as working companion with human, thus, the concept of turn-taking from human-human communication [9] is introduced in the design toolkit, helping designers demonstrate the intention communication between the human and robot. This concept is integrated by HRLF model, containing three communication modes: (1) human as leader to start turns (the flow of intention from human to robot); (2) robot as leader to start turns (the flow of intention from robot to human); (3) adaptive state (both human and robot can be leader to initiate the turn-taking intention). Once the designer selects one of the HRLF modes, according to its direction of the main intention flow, each key interaction node can be visualized through the human-robot task timeline. As shown in Fig. 1(a), the timeline includes five key elements: "Agent Point", "Interaction Circle", "Main Timeline", "Branch Timeline" and "Intention Direction". Designers can expand the selected HRLF interaction mode by freely combining these elements to assign the interaction role for human(s) and robot(s). For the finalisation of details in specific interaction nodes, we provide guided questions, inspired by Microsoft's AR design guidelines [8].

This series of questions can unfold the "Turn-taking" activity, prompting thinking on the available options and the implications of choices for timeline and intention (The detailed content of guided questions will be shown in Stage 2—Case Study Fig. 2). Turn-taking focuses on the design of the handover of action in the interaction nodes. Namely, the designer should clearly understand whose turn it is (leader); how to transmit the interactive information to the interacting agent (follower), and how to identify if the other party receives and understands the interactive intention, etc. The guided questions begin with Turn-taking (Start). Subsequently, at the end of an interactive task, we hope the designer can also clarify the corresponding expression of intention. It can be completing the entire task or enabling both parties to enter the next task node to advance the overall interactive process. However, independent of scheme selection, the designer assigns how the leader communicates with the follower if the task is accomplished; how to transmit this information (combining with the intention type configured previously); how to determine that the follower receives and understands the interactive information successfully, etc. All of these answers can be worked out in a series of guided questions for the Turn-taking (End/Transition).

3.2 Stage 2: Case Study - AR-Based Co-Design Fabrication Project

In this section, the proposed design toolkit will be instantiated by one robotic fabrication case study—Co-design Aggregate Architecture. Unlike the "immutable, permanent and controllable" concepts in typical construction of architecture, Aggregate Architecture is the material system consisting of a mass of granules that are constructed together merely through loose frictional interaction [2]. Reconfigurable and uncertain properties are hallmarks of this material system. However, the current local and global robotic fabrication system has explicit planning definitions and methods, which cannot satisfy the design and planning requirements for this evolving structure. This building system requires an interactive mode that supports users (architectural designers) to continuously observe and adjust the planning sequence during construction with granules. Coupling robotic fabrication with HRI through AR-based co-design systems can be a viable solution. With HMD, users would be able to view the virtual scene in the fabrication environment including the robotic workspace and grabbable granules. In this virtual scene, their hands can be tracked by the mesh display. With the guidance of a series of AR pop-up user interfaces, they can pick up a hologram granule from the designated place and put it in another place in the robotic workspace to help the physical robotic arm complete trajectory planning.

According to the design toolkit introduced in Sect. 3.1, we apply the task timeline and guided questions from the HRLF model to complete the entire prototype design. Considering that the purpose of this case is to demonstrate the contribution of an AR-assisted interaction system to build aggregate construction, we select a typical combination of HRC project—a single human with a single robot. As discussed, a user is responsible for observing and planning the building process, so we assigned the user a leader role in the HRLF model to initiate the interaction turn, with a KUKA KR6R900 as a follower to receive the interactive content.

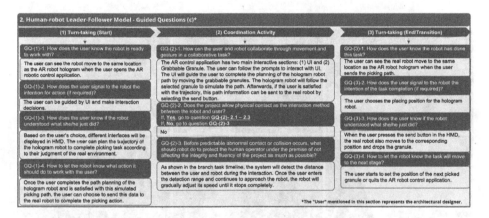

Fig. 2. Guided questions for specifying Interaction Details of AR-based co-design robotic fabrication system

Thus, Fig. 1(b) shows the task timeline for interaction of a user with HMD to co-create an aggregate construction with a robot via an AR user interface (UI). The user opens the AR robotic control application and chooses a pick-and-place task of one granule with the robot through the guidance of AR UI and repeats this action until the construction work is completed. By following Malik and Bilberg (2019)'s [7] reference model and Wang et al. (2020)'s [11] HRC overview, the "Speed and Position Monitoring" is chosen as safety specification, the branch timeline—grey dashed frame below the main timeline—describes how the robot reacts if the operator accidentally approaches it. As this safety guideline needs to be followed throughout the interaction, it is necessary to ensure that the user and robot remain within a safe distance in each interaction node.

The guided questions are used to clarify the interaction details of each node in the pick-and-place task Fig. 2. The content of "(1) Turn-taking (Start)" explains how the user operates the AR robotic control application in HMD to plan the path for the picking task of one granule. "(2) Coordination Activity" enriches the details for the transition interaction between the picking and placing path planning of the same granule and clarifies the safety behaviour norms when the user collaborates with the robot. "(3) Turn-taking (End/Transition)" is responsible for the position choosing of the placement. The combination of these three interaction processes constitutes how the user plans the trajectories of the hologram robot in HMD to control the real robot completing a pick-and-place task. Through repeating these operations, an aggregate architecture can be built from a mass of granules. With the above interaction design, we built the system with the Microsoft MRTK toolkit in Unity 3D to design the AR UI for HoloLens, with the capacity of the ROS Sharp library to import and create the hologram KUKA robot displayed in the HMD. The first-generation HoloLens and KUKA KR6R900 have been selected as manipulation hardware in this case study, due to equipment availability in our lab.

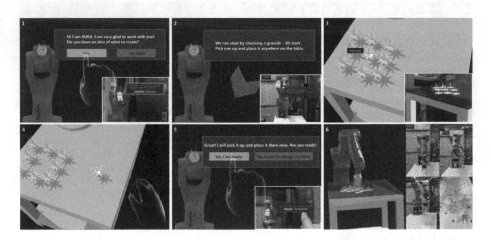

Fig. 3. Interface and Interaction Process for AR-based co-design robotic fabrication system

A user wearing HoloLens stands in a safe area to participate in the design and fabrication task of aggregate architecture with KUKA robot. Through the HMD, the user can not only see the AR elements of the entire robotic control system, including a hologram KUKA robot, AR-guided UI and hologram grabbable granules (we use multiple 3D stars as the operation object) but also can see the physical granules (3D stars) and KUKA KR6 robotic arm. By using the default air-tapping selection gesture, the user can complete the pick-and-place trajectory planning of one granule for the robot through the guidance of the AR UI and complete the construction of a pile of aggregate architecture by repeating this operation. The specific interaction process is shown in Fig. 3, illustrating a combination of the perspective of the HoloLens and the demonstration content. It clearly shows that as the leader, the user is responsible for the initiation of each interactive task with the robot. The interaction process is carried out according to interactive nodes set in the task timeline (Fig. 1) and the screen content of each frame is mapped to content of each interaction node. Details of this content are combined with the interaction designer's reflection and answers to the guided questions on turn-taking and coordination (Fig. 2).

4   Discussion

For successful collaborations between humans and industrial robotic arms, the use of design tools for interaction designers to explore, specify, analyse and document planned interactions between human(s) and robot(s) through a model of interaction where the roles of leader and follower shape the forms of collaborative behaviour is required. Our proposed design toolkit offers such a tool for visualising and thinking through the turn-taking and coordination of collaborative activity between humans and robots. The case study demonstrated the toolkit in action for a single human user and single robot, working together to create an aggregate architecture with an AR interface. In this example, the human user was designated as the leader. However on reflection it is worth noting that in Fig. 3 it sometimes seems like the robot is leading, as the instructions in the AR UI prompt the user what to do next. This observation raises questions about the role of the AR UI—is it an extension of the human, or the robot? Should this case actually be an example of Adaptive where the robot and human take turns leading?

This case study was limited to conducting a small-scale construction simulation with a few granules, and the AR-based robotic control system can only allow the operator to plan the trajectory for the robot to achieve pick-and-place task. Future work will use the presented design toolkit to explore how to apply these design processes to the construction of more intricate architecture. Initial feedback on the usability of the AR interface was provided by the second author, a robot technician who supplied the use case as a real-world application that is currently difficult to simulate in traditional robotic fabrication tools (Grasshopper/Rhino). We plan to apply for ethics approval for user testing with students and design practitioners where participants can interact with physical robots directly whilst wearing HMD to view the AR interface. Both qualitative and quantitative data will be collected during user testing and analysed to evaluate the usability of the prototype AR interface and the design toolkit.

5   Conclusion

To address existing challenges of HRC design methodologies and AR-based fabrication applications, we presented an AR-HRC design toolkit to explore and specify the interaction design and AR interface with HMD. It comprises a task timeline and a set of guided questions to support interaction designers in coordinating the interaction process between humans and industrial robotic arms in the context of fabrication and manufacturing, through identifying and exploring the next level of detailed specification for how turn-taking and coordination are achieved when human and robot take on roles of leader and follower. This has been illustrated with a case study on AR-based co-design fabrication, involving a novel method for users to collaborate with a fabrication robot for a pick-and-place task by guidance of an augmented reality user interface. Our example demonstrated one possible solution for how to make visible to human operators the evolving safety risks in the dynamic fabrication process through AR interface, although this design space is yet to be fully explored. Future work includes further testing and validation of the toolkit through inviting other designers to use it for similar robotic fabrication tasks.

References

1. Bartneck, C., Belpaeme, T., Eyssel, F., Kanda, T., Keijsers, M., Šabanović, S.: Human-Robot Interaction: An Introduction. Cambridge University Press (2020)
2. Dierichs, K., Menges, A.: Aggregate architecture: simulation models for synthetic non-convex granulates. In: Proceedings of the 33rd Annual Conference ACADIA, vol. 301 (2013)
3. Frayling, C.: Research in art and design (royal college of art research papers, vol 1, no 1, 1993/4) (1994)
4. Gannon, M.: Human-centered interfaces for autonomous fabrication machines (2017)
5. Leng, J., et al.: Industry 5.0: prospect and retrospect. J. Manuf. Syst. **65**, 279–295 (2022)
6. Lupetti, M.L., Zaga, C., Cila, N.: Designerly ways of knowing in HRI: broadening the scope of design-oriented HRI through the concept of intermediate-level knowledge. In: Proceedings of the 2021 ACM/IEEE International Conference on Human-Robot Interaction, pp. 389–398 (2021)
7. Malik, A.A., Bilberg, A.: Developing a reference model for human-robot interaction. Int. J. Interact. Des. Manuf. (IJIDeM) **13**, 1541–1547 (2019)
8. Sean-Kerawala: Instinctual interactions - mixed reality. https://learn.microsoft.com/en-us/windows/mixed-reality/design/interaction-fundamentals. Accessed 05 Jul 2023
9. Skantze, G.: Turn-taking in conversational systems and human-robot interaction: a review. Comput. Speech Lang. **67**, 101178 (2021)
10. Suzuki, R., Karim, A., Xia, T., Hedayati, H., Marquardt, N.: Augmented reality and robotics: a survey and taxonomy for AR-enhanced human-robot interaction and robotic interfaces. In: Proceedings of the 2022 CHI Conference on Human Factors in Computing Systems, pp. 1–33 (2022)
11. Wang, L., Liu, S., Liu, H., Wang, X.V.: Overview of human-robot collaboration in manufacturing. In: Wang, L., Majstorovic, V.D.., Mourtzis, D., Carpanzano, E., Moroni, G., Galantucci, L.M. (eds.) Proceedings of 5th International Conference on the Industry 4.0 Model for Advanced Manufacturing. LNME, pp. 15–58. Springer, Cham (2020). https://doi.org/10.1007/978-3-030-46212-3_2

12. Yin, Y., Zheng, P., Li, C., Wang, L.: A state-of-the-art survey on augmented reality-assisted digital twin for futuristic human-centric industry transformation. Robot. Comput. Integr. Manuf. **81**, 102515 (2023)
13. Zhao, Y., Loke, L., Reinhardt, D.: Preliminary explorations of conceptual design tools for students learning to design human-robot interactions for the case of collaborative drawing. In: 2022 17th ACM/IEEE International Conference on Human-Robot Interaction (HRI), pp. 1135–1139. IEEE (2022)
14. Zimmerman, J., Forlizzi, J.: Research through design in HCI. In: Olson, J.S., Kellogg, W.A. (eds.) Ways of Knowing in HCI, pp. 167–189. Springer, New York (2014). https://doi.org/10.1007/978-1-4939-0378-8_8

Competition or Cooperation: Classification in a VR Environment Based on Sensor Data

Yoshiko Arima(✉) ⓘ and Yuki Harada ⓘ

Kyoto University of Advanced Science, Kyoto, Japan
arima.yoshiko@kuas.ac.jp

Abstract. This study investigated activity during a joint Simon task in a VR environment to develop an analysis tool for collaboration teams using Metaverse software. In this pilot study, we distinguished between competition and cooperation during the task and explored the relationship between the classification model and performance on the joint Simon task. This study consisted of two phases: creation of the body movement classification model and adaptation of the model to the joint Simon task. In Phase 1, data from 6 participants (three pairs) were used to construct a machine-learning classification model. The other two participants provided test data for the model. Using random forest models, we classified two categories of pair movements: cooperation (synchronization) or competition. This model yielded an accuracy rate of 88.8% in classifying the test data. In Phase 2, as a case study, we applied this model to the joint Simon task. The results suggested that competition elicited better performance than cooperation. In conclusion, the classification model successfully distinguished subtle movements in the VR environment. This model could be used to analyze the state of pairs during collaborative tasks.

Keywords: VR · Human Activity Recognition · Machine Learning · Joint Simon Effect

1 Background

1.1 Collaboration in the VR Environment

With better management of the COVID-19 pandemic, some companies that shifted to fully remote work are now returning to in-person work. Face-to-face team communication is considered the most efficient way to communicate. However, remote work remains important for the revitalization of rural areas and as a new avenue of work. Therefore, it is important to identify the factors that facilitate efficient remote work. From this perspective, the present study attempted to classify sensor data during cooperative work in a VR environment using machine learning.

This study aims to develop a system for effective collaboration in a VR environment. As a pilot study, we examined which features to focus on to explore more effective collaborative relationships using the Simon task. The Simon task detects we-modes [1], that is, cognitive modes with shared goals.

H. Takada et al. (Eds.): CollabTech 2023, LNCS 14199, pp. 144–151, 2023.
https://doi.org/10.1007/978-3-031-42141-9_10

1.2 Machine Learning Classification

Machine learning algorithms are particularly useful for image classification and text analysis, but they can also be applied to signal data. A variety of sensor data can be obtained from the VR environment. For example, it is possible to estimate body movements from the position and rotation of the head-mounted display (HMD) and the controller. Furthermore, we can infer attention and arousal from gaze and pupil size, respectively.

However, interpreting human interactions from these data can be difficult. Usually, methods suitable for analysis time-series data such as LSTM are used to analyze sensor data [2], but in this study, we first employed random forest models to select features that useful for classification from a large number of features.

We used raw data without filtering to identify important features for classifying interpersonal behavior in VR environments. For this purpose, we employed the joint Simon task in a VR environment. We divided this task into smaller stages, such as before and after stimulus presentation, and searched for segments that could be classified as cooperative behaviors.

1.3 Joint Simon Task

The Simon task [3] is a stimulus-response competitive task in which a match between the spatial position of the stimulus and the response key influences behavior. In the classic task, participants push a left or right button based on the physical feature of target stimuli (e.g., color) presented on the left or right side of a screen. Responses are slower when the spatial locations of the button and target are incongruent than when they are congruent, even though the location is irrelevant to the task (i.e., the Simon effect).

The Simon effect disappears in the go/no-go task, in which participants respond to only one physical feature of targets. However, when the stimulus-response correspondences are individually assigned to individuals within a pair, the Simon effect reappears, even if the task is the same as the go/no-go task performed [4]. This phenomenon is called the joint Simon effect and has been explained by shared representations of stimulus-action rules [5] or spatial recognition of stimuli and responses [6]. The joint Simon task has been used as a communication task to investigate the effect of social factors on cognitive performance [7].

In this study, the percentage of correct responses and reaction time in the joint Simon task were used as performance indicators of cooperative behavior within pairs.

1.4 Research Question

The purpose of this study was to select features that discriminate between cooperative and competitive states within pairs from various sensor data in a VR environment. For this purpose, in addition to the usual Simon task, we also established a cooperative condition (in which pairs were instructed to touch the target at the same time in the same task) and a competitive condition (in which they were instructed to touch the target faster than their partner) and examined whether machine learning could classify the two successfully. We also examined, as a case study, which features led to higher performance when a machine-learning model used to classify competition or cooperation was applied to data from the joint Simon task.

2 Methods

2.1 Participants

Eight participants (age: 19–21 years, university students, six males and two females) were recruited. The participants were divided into four pairs, and each pair performed the experiment. Before the experiments, the participants were informed about the ethical standards for psychological research, and they signed an informed consent form.

2.2 Device and Stimulus

A VR system was set up in two separate rooms. Each system was composed of a head-mounted display (VIVE Pro Eye), two controllers (VIVE controller 2018), two base stations (SteamVR Base Station 2.0), and a personal computer.

A VR environment was created with Unity (2021.3.1f1) using a server-client network using "Netcode for GameObjects." In this environment, pairs of participants entered the same virtual space and interacted with each other. The VR environment contained two avatars, two buttons, a display, and a mirror (Fig. 1). The avatars could move according to six coordinate data (three positions and three rotations) obtained from the HMD and two controllers. Avatar motion was executed by the asset "Final IK". The avatar's appearance was box shaped, with no individual features. The two buttons were red and green and arranged in front of the avatars. The buttons could acquire touch responses from the avatar's hand.

The sequence of experimental trials was as follows. The experimenter pressed the space key to start the trial. After three seconds, a black fixation cross "+" was presented at the center of the display to guide participants' attention. Subsequently, a target square (red or green) was presented on the left or right side of the display. The participant's task was to touch the button corresponding to the target color regardless of the target location. Different color-button correspondences were assigned to each participant: one participant touched the "R" button in response to the red square, and another participant touched the "G" button in response to the green square. After the touch, there was a brief intertrial interval, and the next trial began. The color and location of targets were randomized across trials.

2.3 Procedure

This study was conducted as a part of a larger project; however, only procedures relating to the present purpose are reported. After practice and other experiments, the participants performed the joint Simon task, cooperation task, and competition task. The trial sequence of the joint Simon task is shown in the device and stimuli section. In the cooperation task, participants touched the button based on the target color while synchronizing their motions with each other. The competition task was identical to the cooperation task except that participants were asked to touch the button quicker than their partner. All tasks were composed of 16 trials.

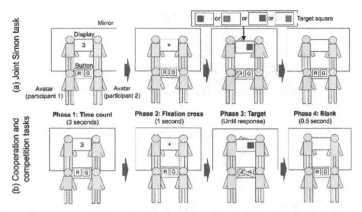

Fig. 1. A semantic illustration of a trial sequence. *Note.* (a) Joint Simon task. Participant 1 touched the "R" button when the red target was presented, and Participant 2 touched the "G" button when the green target was presented. (b) Cooperation and competition tasks. Both participants touched the buttons corresponding to the target colors.

2.4 Sensor Data

For the sensor data obtained regarding movement along the three axes, the square root was taken, excluding the line of sight. We used the following indices: head position, head rotation, left/right controller position, left/right controller rotation, XYZ direction of gaze, and left/right trend size. Depending on their room in the laboratory, participants within a pair are referred to as the host and the client. Specifically, the pair data were sent as streaming data from the client side computer to the host side computer. There were no other differences between the host side and the client side in the experiment.

The temporal signal was sampled at variable rates (average of 80 Hz). The task was divided into Phases 1 to 4 (time count, fixation cross, target, and blank). This study reports the results of Phase 1 as the countdown stage. The countdown was identical among the three sessions and involved data from the time spent looking at the countdown (i.e., "3, 2, 1"). Therefore, it was a suitable interval for analyzing the raw data because it is unlikely to produce large outliers. We aimed to capture the subtle movements in preparation for competitive or cooperative sessions.

The delay time required to send data from the client-side computer to the host-side computer could have affected the results. This should have to be taken into account as an influence of host-side features in the classification.

3 Results

3.1 Selection of Features

Figure 2 describes the distributions of the main features measured in the VR environment. The distribution of gaze data was similar between the competition and cooperation sessions (A and B). These results reflect the context of the countdown stage, which required standing still and gazing at the focal point. However, the distribution of hand rotation showed several peaks and differences between competition and cooperation.

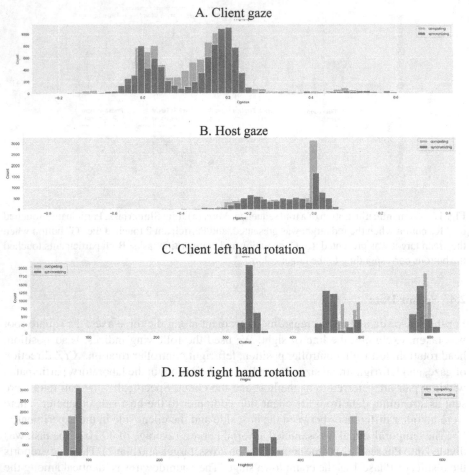

Fig. 2. Representative distributions of main features. *Note.* Orange: competing session data. Blue: cooperating session data

3.2 Random Forest Classification

We applied a random forest model to the selected features. For cross-validation, data from three pairs of the eight participants were used as training data, and the remaining pair was used as test data.

In a random forest model, a set of decision trees is established from randomly sampled subsets of the training data. Each decision tree is trained independently and makes a prediction based on a subset of features randomly selected from the total set of features. The final prediction is then made by aggregating the predictions of all the decision trees. The random forest model yielded the following parameters in order of importance for each feature: (0.16, 'Hrightrot'), (0.15, 'Cleftrot'), (0.14, 'Hleft'), (0.1, 'Hright'), (0.07, 'Hleftrot'), (0.07, 'Chead'), (0.06, 'Hhead'), (0.05, 'Hheadrot'),

(0.04, 'Cleft'), (0.02, 'Crightpupil'), (0.02, 'Cright'), (0.02, 'Cgaze'), (0.01, 'Hright-pupil'), (0.01, 'Hgazez'), (0.01, 'Hgazey'), (0.01, 'Hgazex'), (0.01, 'Cleftpupil'), (0.01, 'Cheadrot'), (0.01, 'Cgazez'), (0.01, 'Cgazey'), (0.01, 'Cgazex').

Figure 3 presents the result of a decision tree model targeted to the classification of cooperation or competition. The right hand rotation of the host side was crucial. This implies that we can predict cooperation or competition according to the opposite hand to the hand needed to respond. At the second level, host-side head rotation affected the classification model. When applying the random forest model to the test dataset, the confusion matrix between the predictions of the model and the observed data reached 88%, and the F1-score was .8925 (Precision = .8066, Recall = .9988).

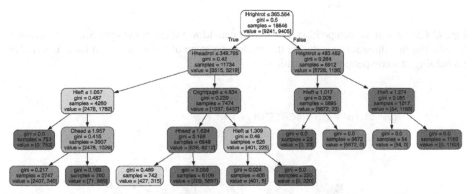

Fig. 3. A decision tree model. *Note.* This model is an example of a decision tree. The target was the behavioral category: (0) competing or (1) cooperating. The indication of each box represents from the first line, branching condition, Gini's Diversity Index, sample size, and Classification Summary, respectively.

3.3 Classification in the Joint Simon Task: A Case Study

Using the classification model produced by Phase 1 for identifying cooperation and competition, we classified the countdown stage in the joint Simon task. Figure 4 shows data from the first three seconds.

Figure 5 depicts the mean correct responses and reaction time (second) on the joint Simon task in each pair. Pairs 1 and 2, which had a decreasing probability of competition during the countdown stage (Fig. 4), exhibited worse performance than Pairs 3 and 4, which showed an increasing rate.

The black bars represent the mean accuracy rate (correct responses) during the 16 trials. The Y-axis shows the percentage of correct answers for the black bars. The gray bars represent the mean reaction time (RT) during the 16 trials. The Y-axis shows seconds for the gray bars.

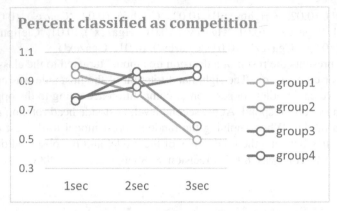

Fig. 4. Changes in the competition ratio during countdown stage of the joint Simon Task. *Note.* X-axis: the first three seconds during the countdown stage of the joint Simon task. Y-axis: The probability of a competition classification.

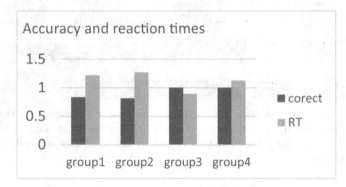

Fig. 5. Percentage of correct responses and reaction time (second) for each pair.

4   Discussion

Application of a random forest model to the raw data showed that the countdown stage, which occurs before stimulus presentation, could be used to discriminate between cooperation and competition. Rotation of the hands or head tended to contribute more than their positions or the gaze direction. Interestingly, the raw data that contained relatively little movement were able to discriminate between Competition and Cooperation with 88% accuracy.

Furthermore, when the model was applied to the Simon task, two patterns were shown: an increase in features of competition or a decrease in features of competition. Pairs that exhibited the former tended to have better accuracy and reaction times on the Simon task. It is possible that in the state considered cooperative, the participants were consciously attending to their partner's movements to match them, which may have delayed their response to the task. On the other hand, in the state considered competitive, participants may have been more focused on the task, and in that state, they were able to cooperate subconsciously, which may have increased their performance.

To scrutinize these results, it would be necessary to use different tasks and increase the sample size. These results suggested that the classification of behavior in relation to performance should be viewed as a time-series pattern. We plan to apply an LSTM to our data; however, we should consider the data slice width carefully to compensate for this transmission time lag. This study represents an attempt to analyze a small amount of data. However, it provided important insights into the variable selection and analysis methods. We plan to gather additional data to select filtration and analysis methods.

References

1. Gallotti, M., Frith, C.D.: Social cognition in the we-mode. Trends Cogn. Sci. **17**, 160–165 (2013). https://doi.org/10.1016/j.tics.2013.02.002
2. Arima, Y.: Effects of chest movements while sitting on Navon task performance and stress levels. BMC Dig. Health (2023). https://doi.org/10.1186/s44247-023-00011-6
3. Simon, J.R.: Reactions toward the source of stimulation. J. Exp. Psychol. **81**(1), 174–176 (1969). https://doi.org/10.1037/h0027448
4. Sebanz, N., Knoblich, G., Prinz, W.: Representing others' actions: just like one's own? Cognition **88**(3), B11–B21 (2003). https://doi.org/10.1016/s0010-0277(03)00043-x
5. Dolk, T., Hommel, B., Prinz, W., Liepelt, R.: The (not so) social simon effect: a referential coding account. J. Exp. Psychol. Hum. Percept. Perform. **39**(5), 1248–1260 (2013). https://doi.org/10.1037/a0031031
6. Müller, B.C.N., et al.: When Pinocchio acts like a human, a wooden hand becomes embodied Action co-representation for non-biological agents. Neuropsychologia **49**(5), 1373–1377 (2011). https://doi.org/10.1016/j.neuropsychologia.2011.01.022
7. Stenzel, A., Chinellato, E., Bou, M.A.T., Del Pobil Á.P., Lappe, M., Liepelt, R.: When humanoid robots become human-like interaction partners: corepresentation of robotic actions. J. Exp. Psychol. Hum. Percept. Perform. **38**(5), 1073–1077 (2012). https://doi.org/10.1037/a0029493

Effect Analysis of Facemask on Emotions' Communication Between Japanese People

Yoko Nishihara[1(✉)], Azumi Inoue[1], and Junjie Shan[2]

[1] Ritsumeikan University, 1-1-1, Nojihigashi, Kusatsu, Shiga 5258577, Japan
`nisihara@fc.ritsumei.ac.jp`
[2] Ritsumeikan Global and Innovation Research Organization, 1-1-1, Nojihigashi, Kusatsu, Shiga 5258577, Japan

Abstract. This paper reports the effect of a facemask on emotions' communication between Japanese people through experiments with participants. In the experiments, we made participants in pairs and asked them to speak about their own episodes with emotion to another. The relationships of the pairs included "first-meeting" and "friends." The participants picked out emotions on their own and spoke about their episodes with the emotions in Japanese. We separated the pairs of participants into two groups. Group A (18 pairs, 36 participants) was asked to communicate without a facemask, while Group B (18 pairs, 36 participants) was asked to converse with facemasks on. The results were compared between the two groups to reveal the effect of the facemask. From experimental results, we found that the effect of emotion conveyance would reduce for friend-pairs if they wore facemasks.

Keywords: Emotions' communication · Facemask · Relationship of speakers · HCI

1 Introduction

As soon as the World Health Organization declared an emergency, the movement of one-third of the world's population (2.6 billion people) was restricted and controlled by their respective governments [3], aiming to prevent further spread and to minimize the risk of COVID-19 infection. In Japan, wearing a facemask has become mandatory both indoors and outdoors. People's activities also were restricted. For example, practicing with facemasks was recommended for school class choruses. Even if, at lunchtime, they were recommended not to talk. Many people had to wear their facemasks more often for daily activities.

Speaking with a facemask caused problems in people's communication [1]. Most common complaints include trouble hearing others and grasping their intention. The facemask covers a large part of the face, which makes it difficult for people to understand the other's emotions. If a person says something wearing a facemask, it is a challenge to distinguish whether he/she is in anger or in jest. If it turns out that emotions are difficult to convey with a facemask

H. Takada et al. (Eds.): CollabTech 2023, LNCS 14199, pp. 152–159, 2023.
https://doi.org/10.1007/978-3-031-42141-9_11

covered, a device that could use other information such as heartbeats, voices, or partial expressions recognition to detect emotions can come into play to support the emotions' communication. However, it is not clear how much emotion is conveyed in communication by wearing a facemask. Moreover, there are several types of emotions. It is also unclear which emotions can be easily conveyed by wearing a facemask and which cannot.

This paper reveals the effects of wearing a facemask on emotions' communication in Japanese. We conducted experiments with participants and found the effects from experimental results. We set a hypothesis and verified the hypothesis from the experimental results.

- If people communicate emotions wearing facemasks on, their emotions are conveyed less than without facemasks.

To verify the hypothesis, we conducted experiments and asked participants to speak about their own episodes with emotions in Japanese. In the experiments, the participants speak their own episodes with emotion. The participants are separated into two groups. Group A was asked to speak without a facemask, while Group B was asked to speak with facemasks on. Experimental results are compared between the two groups to find how wearing a facemask affects emotions' communication. In the study, we were mandatory to wear a facemask in talking face-to-face to prevent the spread of Covid-19. However, we need communication data in which people talk without a facemask. Therefore, we used a video conference system in our experiments.

Collaboration is considered to be the cooperation of two or more individuals/groups to achieve a specific goal. It is expected that those involved in the collaboration often have discussions. Some of them have difficulty in removing their masks for psychological or physical reasons. Speaking with a facemask caused problems in understanding emotions. If we could gain insight into the emotions that are difficult to convey, we might use this knowledge to study a collaboration technique that takes them into account.

1.1 Related Work

Due to the prevention of Covid-19 infection, people must wear a facemask worldwide. New research relating to facemasks has been conducted. For example, deep learning models for detecting facemasks [8] and deep fake images in which people wear a facemask [7] have been studied. Image processing studies have been widely conducted. In this paper, we try to find the effects of facemasks on emotions' communication.

In communication, emotions should be conveyed to others to build good relationships. If few cues are given for emotion recognition, it is challenging to grasp people's emotions precisely. Many studies have found that emotions were less conveyed, and emotion recognition has more trouble in text-based communication like e-mail and text-chatting than in-person communication [2, 5]. Video conference systems were heavily used as a communication tool during the Covid-19 epidemic. The video conference systems were expected to achieve people's communication equivalent to face-to-face communication because the systems allowed people to see their face each other. However, emotion recognition on video conferencing was complex due to various reasons [11]. Social networking services would provide users with functions to design user spaces representing their emotions, which makes emotions' communication much easier [10]. The facemask covers most of the face and disturbs people from hearing others' voices. The cues of emotions' communication wearing a facemask are not enough for emotional recognition. This paper reveals how much the facemask reduces the effect of emotion conveyed from experimental results with participants.

The types of emotions are various. For example, Ekman showed six types of emotion [4], and Plutchik showed a circle of emotion [9]. Plutchik's circle represents the intensity of emotion, which means the emotion of "love" is stronger than the emotion of "like." Therefore, we guess some emotions are easily conveyed while others are not. This paper reveals which emotions are not affected and which emotions are affected by wearing a facemask in emotions' communication.

Some existing studies have shown the extent to which emotions can be read from masked facial expression images and videos [1,6]. Both studies reported that wearing a facemask affected emotions' communication. On the other hand, few studies have examined the effect of facemasks on emotions' communication, taking into account the relationship between speakers. This study attempts to evaluate the influence of facemasks in emotions' communication, taking into account the speakers' relationship.

2   Experimental Design

This section describes experiments with participants.

2.1   Experimental Procedures

The experiments with participants were conducted as follows.

1. The experimenter makes every two participants a pair.
2. In the pair, one participant picks out an emotion on his/her own and talks about his/her own episode with the emotion in Japanese.
3. After 2., the other participant picks out an emotion and talks about his/her own episode with the emotion in Japense.
4. The procedure 2 and 3 are conducted several times.

In procedure 1, we also separated these pairs into two types through the participants' relationships: first-meeting or friend. This is because we thought that the relationships between participants could also affect emotions' communication. The participants' pairs were separated into groups: Group A and B.

Group A:
In Japanese without facemask via video-conference software

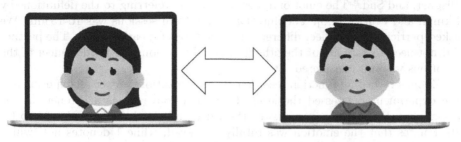

Group B:
In Japanese **with facemask** via video-conference software

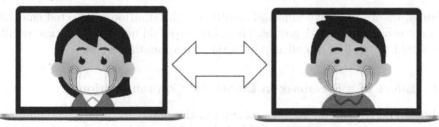

Fig. 1. Conversation setting of each group

Table 1. Relationships and number of participant pairs

Relationship	Gr. A: w/o facemask	Gr. B: w/ facemask
First meeting	12 pairs	12 pairs
Friends	6 pairs	6 pairs

– Group A: Communication **without** a facemask
– Group B: Communication **with** facemasks on

Table 1 shows the number of participant pairs per relationship and group. Each group had 12 pairs (24 participants) of "first-meeting" participants and six pairs (12 participants) of "friends" participants. In total, 36 pairs (72 participants) joined the experiments. The participants used a video conference system (Zoom) in the experiments. This is because we were mandatory to wear a facemask in talking face-to-face to prevent the spread of Covid-19. The participants used their own personal computer with a camera and a microphone. They were asked to sit in front of the camera and show their upper body.

In procedures 2 and 3, the participants picked out an emotion type from 10 types of emotions "Joy, Like, Happy, Peaceful, Excited, Surprise, Anger, Fear, Disgust, and Sad." The emotion types were set by referring to the definitions by Ekman and Plutick [4,9]. The duration of the total sessions was 10-15 min. We asked participants to select different emotion types for each session. The partner did not need to care about the other's selected emotions. The order effect of the emotions was not considered.

Zoom's recording function recorded the conversations. After all experiments, the experimenter assessed the level of emotion conveyed as a listener. In the assessment, the experimenter viewed the video and rated it on a scale of 1 to 10. 10 denotes that the emotion was totally conveyed, while 1 denotes not, which means the experimenter as a listener could not recognize the speaker's emotion. We averaged the scores per relationship and group.

3   Results

Though we obtained experimental results, the distribution of selected emotions was not consistent in both groups. Therefore, we could not find statistical results. We would try to find a tendency from the experimental results.

3.1   Effect of a Facemask in Emotions' Communication

Tables 2 and 3 show the average scores and the difference between communications with/without a facemask. Table 2 shows friend-pairs' results, while Table 3 shows the results of the first-meeting pairs. In pairs of friends, the average of Group A was 7.31 while the average of Group B was 5.95. On the other hand, in the pairs of first-meeting, the average of Group A was 6.84 while the average of Group B was 6.84. The pairs of friends are known each other well. They might be more familiar with conveying emotions through each others' facial expressions rather than speaking words. Therefore, the pairs of friends without a facemask conveyed their emotion strongly than those with facemasks on. The results indicated that it was more difficult for friends to communicate their emotions to each other when wearing facemasks. The hypothesis might be verified if emotions' communication happened between friends. As future work, we will collect more communication data in which the distribution of emotions is consistent in both groups.

3.2   Distribution of Selected Emotions in the Experiments

Next, we discuss the distribution of emotions selected by the participants. Table 4 shows the numbers and rates of selected emotions by the participants of the friend and first-meeting. The top 3 emotions were "joy," "like," and "happy." Their rates were more than 10%. Three emotions belong to positive emotions. If the emotions are conveyed to others, their conversations will keep a positive atmosphere. Meanwhile, when people express their "disgust" towards something,

Table 2. Experimental results in **friends**. The score was the average given by an experimenter who evaluated each communication as a listener. The score was between 1 to 10.

	Gr. A: w/o facemask	Gr. B: w/ facemask	Difference
Joy	6	7.2	−1.2
Like	7.9	4	3.9
Happy	7.3	6.9	0.4
Peaceful	9.3	5.7	3.6
Excited	7.5	5.9	1.6
Surprise	8.3	5.3	3.0
Anger	6.3	6	0.3
Fear	6.3	6	0.3
Disgust	6.2	7.5	−1.3
Sad	6.6	5	1.6
Average	7.31	5.95	1.22

Table 3. Experimental results in **first-meeting** The score was the average given by an experimenter who evaluated each communication as a listener. The score was between 1 to 10.

	Gr. A: w/o facemask	Gr. B: w/ facemask	Difference
Joy	6.3	5.7	0.6
Like	6.1	7.6	−1.5
Happy	7.9	5.2	2.7
Peaceful	6.7	10	−3.3
Excited	3.3	10	−6.7
Surprise	10	7	3.0
Anger	7.9	5	2.9
Fear	4	6.5	−2.5
Disgust	9.6	6.9	2.7
Sad	6.6	6.4	0.2
Average	6.84	6.84	−0.19

they are more willing to gain empathy from others. Therefore, it is a better choice to share "disgust" with friends of similar senses than strangers.

Meanwhile, the pairs of friends selected the emotion "disgust" more (15%) than the pairs of first-meeting (8%). An example of the episode about "disgust" by the pairs of friends was about their private information in a familiar place (e.g., they were disagreeable with their family members). The first-meeting pairs might be afraid to talk about private information to the others. Meanwhile, when people express their "disgust" towards something, they are more willing to gain

Table 4. Number and rate of selected emotions by participants

Emotion	first-meeting		friends	
	number of selected	rate	number of selected	rate
Joy	24	16%	26	18%
Like	22	15%	19	13%
Happy	15	10%	17	11%
Peaceful	7	5%	3	2%
Excited	13	9%	3	2%
Surprise	10	7%	5	3%
Anger	13	9%	8	5%
Fear	9	6%	10	6%
Disgust	22	15%	12	8%
Sad	8	5%	39	27%

empathy from others. Therefore, it is a better choice to share "disgust" with friends of similar senses than strangers.

The pairs of friends selected the emotion "sad" less (5%) than those of the first-meeting (27%). An example of the episode about "sad" by the pairs of first-meeting was about their difficulty of job hunting. This shows that people are more likely to share their depression with strangers than with friends. This is because, when facing familiars, people are more unwilling to reveal their failures. But for strangers, there are fewer social connections or benefits involved between each other. Sharing failures and frustrations with strangers comes with less social risk. Therefore, the pairs of first-meeting selected "sad."

4   Conclusions and Future Work

This paper conducted experiments with participants to explore the effect of face-masks on emotions' communication between Japanese people. Every two participants were paired and asked to talk about their own episodes in Japanese with emotion to another. Half of the pairs talked without a facemask, while the rest spoke with facemasks on. The averages of degrees of emotion conveyed were compared between the facemasks on or out. Relationships of the participants were also considered (first-meeting and friends). In total, 36 pairs (72 participants) joined the experiments.

From experimental results, we found that the effect of emotion conveyance would reduce for friend-pairs if they wore facemasks. Meanwhile, there was no significant difference in emotions' communication between the pairs of first-meeting with/without a facemask.

As future work, we try to conduct experiments again as face-to-face communication not via video conference system. The distribution of emotions should be similar in both groups for the purpose of quantitative analysis. Each emotion should be taken by itself and analyzed.

References

1. Carbon, C.C.: Wearing face masks strongly confuses counterparts in reading emotions. Front. Psychol. **11**, 566886 (2020). https://doi.org/10.3389/fpsyg.2020. 566886. https://www.frontiersin.org/articles/10.3389/fpsyg.2020.566886
2. Choi, S., Yamasaki, T., Aizawa, K.: Typeface emotion analysis for communication on mobile messengers. In: Proceedings of the 1st International Workshop on Multimedia Alternate Realities, pp. 37–40. AltMM 2016, Association for Computing Machinery, New York, NY, USA (2016). https://doi.org/10.1145/2983298.2983305
3. Dey, N., Mishra, R., Fong, S.J., Santosh, K.C., Tan, S., Crespo, R.G.: COVID-19: psychological and psychosocial impact, fear, and passion. Digit. Gov.: Res. Pract. **2**(1), 3428088 (2020). https://doi.org/10.1145/3428088
4. Ekman, P.: An argument for basic emotions. Cogn. Emotion **6**(3–4), 169–200 (1992). https://doi.org/10.1080/02699939208411068
5. Hancock, J.T., Landrigan, C., Silver, C.: Expressing emotion in text-based communication. In: Proceedings of the SIGCHI Conference on Human Factors in Computing Systems, pp. 929–932. CHI 2007, Association for Computing Machinery, New York, NY, USA (2007). https://doi.org/10.1145/1240624.1240764
6. Kastendieck, T., Zillmer, S., Hess, U.: (un)mask yourself! effects of face masks on facial mimicry and emotion perception during the COVID-19 pandemic. Cogn. Emot. **36**(1), 59–69 (2022)
7. Lee, S., Ko, D., Park, J., Shin, S., Hong, D., Woo, S.S.: Deepfake detection for fake images with facemasks. In: Proceedings of the 1st Workshop on Security Implications of Deepfakes and Cheapfakes, pp. 27–30. WDC 2022, Association for Computing Machinery, New York, NY, USA (2022). https://doi.org/10.1145/3494109. 3527189
8. Mao, P., Hao, P., Xin, Y.: Deep learning implementation of facemask detection. In: The 2nd International Conference on Computing and Data Science. CONF-CDS 2021, Association for Computing Machinery, New York, NY, USA (2021). https:// doi.org/10.1145/3448734.3450794
9. Plutchik, R.: The nature of emotions: human emotions have deep evolutionary roots, a fact that may explain their complexity and provide tools for clinical practice. Am. Scientist **89**(4), 344–350 (2001). http://www.jstor.org/stable/27857503
10. Semsioglu, S., Karaturhan, P., Akbas, S., Yantac, A.E.: Isles of emotion: emotionally expressive social virtual spaces for reflection and communication. In: Creativity and Cognition. Association for Computing Machinery, New York, NY, USA (2021). https://doi.org/10.1145/3450741.3466805
11. Tausif, M.T., Weaver, R., Lee, S.W.: Towards enabling eye contact and perspective control in video conference. In: Adjunct Proceedings of the 33rd Annual ACM Symposium on User Interface Software and Technology, pp. 96–98. UIST 2020 Adjunct, Association for Computing Machinery, New York, NY, USA (2020). https://doi. org/10.1145/3379350.3416197

Extracting User Daily Routine Activity Patterns from UWB Sensor Data in Indoor Environment

Muhammed Rahim Fawad and Tessai Hayama[✉]

Nagaoka University of Technology, Kamitomioka Nagaoka, Niigata 1603-1, Japan
t-hayama@kjs.nagaokaut.ac.jp

Abstract. In recent years, location-based technologies for ubiquitous environments have transformed individuals' current location data into valuable assets. To establish advanced indoor location-based services, highly accurate positioning technology is required to precisely recognize and predict the movements of humans and objects. Hence, we proposed a method for extracting a user's activity patterns from time-series ultra-wideband (UWB) tag data in indoor environments. The proposed method consists of three steps: 1) estimate the user's stay regions from the user's location history using UWB sensors attached to the user, 2) assign each stay region to significant indoor activities, and 3) mine the activity patterns and their characteristics of the user from the sequence of indoor activities. In our experiments, we confirmed that the proposed method performed better in recognizing activity regions indoors and that the activity patterns of each member in the laboratory were discovered in a practical environment using the proposed method.

Keywords: Human Activity Recognition · Indoor Location-Based System · Human Activity Pattern Analysis · Sensor Network

1 Introduction

In recent years, location-based technologies for ubiquitous environments have transformed an individual's current location information into a valuable asset, improved organizational productivity, and provided unprecedented services such as inventory monitoring in warehouses, real-time traffic updates for routing and navigation, and indoor and outdoor property surveillance. The Global Positioning System is commonly used in outdoor environments to find the position of a person or an object by using a network of satellites to detect the location ; however, in indoor environments, it fails because of the absence of signals inside the building. To establish advanced indoor location-based services, highly accurate positioning technology is required to precisely recognize and predict the movements of humans and objects in an indoor environment. For example, if the location and activity of people in indoor environments, their interactions with people and objects, and their activity frequency and patterns could be detected, advanced context- or location-based services could be realized.

Conventional indoor positioning technologies using wireless sensors are based on Wi-Fi, RFID, and Bluetooth. Wi-Fi is easy to set up in indoor facilities and has a low error of less than 230 m; however, it is susceptible to noise [1]. RFID and Bluetooth are not suitable for precise indoor position estimation because of large errors of more than 3000 mm [2,3]; thus, they have been used for room-by-room recognition of targets. Recently, indoor location estimation using ultra-wideband (UWB) sensors has also been considered. Although indoor measurements using UWB sensors can provide highly accurate location estimation with errors of 100–200 mm [4], further improvements are required to reduce the effects of measurement errors in indoor environments due to the problems of Non-Line-of-Sight (NLOS) and reflection caused by metallic objects and obstacles. As a result, high-precision target tracking systems using UWB sensors have yet to be addressed in indoor location estimation.

Hence, we proposed a method for extracting users' activity patterns from time-series UWB tag data in indoor environments. In our experiments, we confirmed that the proposed method performed well in recognizing activity regions indoors and that the activity patterns of each laboratory member were detected in a practical environment using the developed system.

2 Developing System to Extract User Activity Patterns

2.1 System Overview

The developed system sequentially acquires and accumulates the positions of UWB sensors installed indoors and finds the locations where the UWB sensors are stationary and the transition of their positions. Furthermore, the characteristics of movement based on the accumulated indoor location information are extracted and presented for each UWB sensor. To realize this system environment, we developed a stay region extraction method that identifies the indoor stay position without being affected by the error of the UWB sensors and an activity pattern extraction method from the sequential stay region data. In the developed system environment, it is possible to grasp the indoor behavior of a person and his/her daily activity patterns by attaching a UWB sensor to the person and using a database that contains data on indoor locations and symbols.

As depicted in Fig. 1, the developed system consists of UWB anchors and tags installed in the four corners of a room and a location information storage server. The indoor two-dimensional coordinate position of the UWB tag is calculated by trilateration [5] with the three nearest anchors, which are determined based on the communication time between each of the four anchors and the tag. In the communication between an anchor and a tag, the quality factor (QF) is derived, which is the confidence level of the distance measurement between the tag and the anchor in the range of 0–100, based on the signal strength and error rate of the communication; a low QF score indicates a high probability of NLOS. The coordinate position of each tag, along with its UWB sensor ID and QF, is sequentially transmitted from the UWB sensor tag to the location information storage server via Bluetooth and is registered in the database with a timestamp on the server.

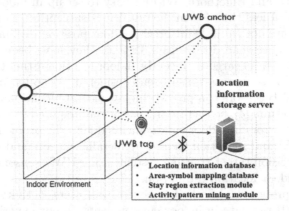

Fig. 1. Developed System Composition.

The location information storage server comprises a location information database, an indoor area and symbols mapping database, a stay region extraction module, and an activity pattern mining module. The indoor region-symbol mapping table is manually created based on indoor symbols that indicate target action at each location. Regarding the data processing module, the stay region extraction module extracts the target location(s) for each UWB sensor ID from time-series location information contained in the location information database. It avoids the influence of position errors of the UWB sensor The activity pattern mining module extracts the activity pattern(s) for each UWB sensor ID from the time-series data of the stay regions extracted by the stay region extraction module. It outputs the diagrams to understand the characteristics of the activity for each UWB sensor ID.

2.2 Data Processing Modules

Stay Region Extraction Module. To reduce the effects of NLOS and metallic reflections [6], this module takes as input the time-series data of positions of a UWB tag and performs three processing steps: First, the input data are filtered by the QF value of the UWB sensors, stay regions of the UWB tag are identified from the filtered time-series data of positions of the UWB tag using a time-based clustering algorithm [7], and then each stay region is assigned to a symbol. It is expected that the QF filtering reduces the effect of NLOS on the UWB sensor, and the time-based clustering algorithm removes large position errors caused by metallic reflection.

In the time-based clustering algorithm, the time-series of the location data is clustered along a time axis; if a new location is further away from the previous location, the new location is considered to belong to a different cluster from the cluster of the prior location, as depicted in Fig. 2. The algorithm starts with the input of a time-series of location information with timestamps, a time parameter, and a distance parameter, then creates clusters of the location data, and identifies stay regions using the clustering data. In the clustering process, the location is called up sequentially from the time-series of location data, and if the location is closer to the prior location, i.e., smaller than the distance parameter, the location is involved in the same cluster as the prior.

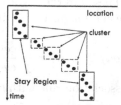

Fig. 2. Illustration of Time-based Clustering Algorithm.

Activity Pattern Mining Module. Activity pattern mining is an algorithm for discovering frequent activity patterns and episode rules [8]. An activity pattern is a subset of frequent actions in an action history and is represented by a directed graph. Episode rules indicate meaningful relationships among the discovered episodes. In this study, the algorithm is adapted to process the action history of UWB tags. The processing steps of the activity pattern mining algorithm primarily consist of four steps, namely, generating frequent episode candidates, recognizing frequent episodes, pruning, and discovering episode rules, using an ordered set of time-stamped stay regions as input. The details of the steps are described below.

1. Generating frequent episode candidates: Episodes are generated using the transitive reduction of partial order based on an action history, which is a set of stay regions and transitions between them; episodes are generated as frequent episode candidates when their frequency is higher than the threshold. Stay regions and their transitions are represented as a directed graph whose nodes indicate the stay regions, and nodes at the input/output of a node are also included in the episode graph. If there is an injective mapping of two episodes, the episodes are merged to create a new episode.
2. Recognizing frequent episodes: The frequency of occurrence of each episode can be calculated using Eq. (1). Each episode is mapped to the action history of the stay regions, as depicted in Fig. 3. If the frequency of occurrence of an episode in the action history is higher than the threshold, the episode is recognized as a frequent episode.

$$freq(\alpha) = \frac{|[T_i|T_i \in L \wedge \alpha \subset T_i]|}{|L|}. \tag{1}$$

Here, α, T_i, i, and L represent an episode, an action history of user i' stay region, and an action history of all users' stay regions, respectively.

3. Pruning: A frequent episode is excluded if its number of actions defined by Eq. (2) is smaller than the set parameters.

$$ActFreq(A) == \frac{|[T_i|T_i \in L \wedge A \subset T_i]|}{|L|}. \tag{2}$$

Here, A indicates a frequent episode.

4. Discovering episode rules: These are the association rules for episodes. Rules with low episode confidence and magnitude ratings, as defined in Eqs. (3) and (4), are excluded.

$$conf(\beta \Rightarrow \alpha) = \frac{freq(\alpha)}{freq(\beta)}. \tag{3}$$

Here, $\beta \Rightarrow \alpha$ indicates an association rule with $\beta \prec \alpha$ stating that after seeing β.

$$mag(\beta \Rightarrow \alpha) = \frac{size(\alpha)}{size(\beta)}. \tag{4}$$

Here, $size(\alpha)$ denotes the number of stay regions in an episode α.

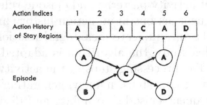

Fig. 3. Example of Mapping an Episode to an Action History of Stay Regions.

3   Evaluation

3.1   Settings

We conducted an evaluation experiment in terms of the accuracy of the stay region extraction of the UWB sensor and the usefulness of activity pattern mining in the authors' laboratory. The size of the lab room is 5840 mm wide and 10440 mm long, equipped with 17 pairs of desks and chairs, personal computers on each desk, four bookshelves, four whiteboards, a printer, a coffee maker, two refrigerators, and an accessory box. The anchors of the UWB sensor are installed at the four corners of the room at a height of 2700 mm.

In the experiment, we firstly confirmed the distance to the symbol and size of stay regions extracted by stay region extraction with and without QF filtering. Next, we collected 30-day period indoor location data based on the developed environment for the four laboratory members who use the room daily and discussed the mining results of the activity patterns and their characteristics.

3.2 Results

Stay Region Extraction. Table 1 shows the distance to the symbol and size of stay regions extracted by stay region extraction with and without QF filtering from the system history of a UWB tag attached to a user.

As depicted in Table 1, the size of the stay regions was reduced in the case of stay region extraction with the QF filtering; conversely, the distance to symbols was increased. In particular, the sizes of the stay regions detected by QF filtering for Position IDs 1 and 2 were improved by more than 50 mm, and those for the other Position IDs were almost the same, confirming the effectiveness of QF filtering in the NLOS environment. However, the distances between the symbol and stay region extracted by QF filtering for Position IDs 2, 3, and 6 were not increased by more than 40 mm. NLOS objects, which have almost no transparency, such as pillars, are thought to have played a significant role in the errors. To address this issue, it is necessary to consider the installation of new UWB anchors and other countermeasures.

Table 1. The distance to the symbol (mm) and size (mm) of stay regions extracted by stay region extraction with/ without QF filtering.

Location ID	With QF filtering		Without QF filtering	
	Distance to Symbol	Size of Stay Region	Distance to Symbol	Size of Stay Region
1	858.0	3.0	1026.0	128.0
2	690.0	277.0	647.1	317.0
3	547.8	154.0	455.0	137.0
4	162.1	122.0	140.0	131.0
5	547.8	154.0	547.8	154.0
6	278.5	139.0	222.5	139.0
7	133.2	264.0	133.2	264.0
8	140.4	66.0	117.4	66.0
9	196.0	335.0	196.0	335.0
Total	394.9	168.2	387.2	185.7

Activity Pattern Mining. Figures 4, 5, and 6 show the action history of each laboratory member's stay regions, the activity pattern graphs [9] for each user, and the episode rules for each user, respectively.

As depicted in Fig. 4, the stay regions extracted by the proposed method provide information about the characteristics of each user's activities. For example, user A frequently visited the entire room and engaged in various activities, followed by user D, who also engaged in various activities. Conversely, users B and C had a smaller range of indoor activities, and their activities were mostly around their desks. From the figures of the stay regions of users B and C, the

Fig. 4. Illustrations of the Action History of Each User's Stay Regions during 30 Days Extracted by the Proposed Method. The yellow and blue dots indicate the stay regions detected by the proposed method and the center locations of stay regions assigned to a symbol, respectively. (Color figure online)

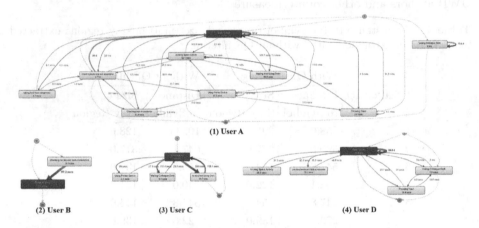

Fig. 5. Activity Pattern Graphs for Each User Created by the Proposed System. The red arrow and rectangle indicate the most frequent transition and activity of each user, respectively. (Color figure online)

proposed stay region extraction method also shows that their location information was removed while they were moving around. As depicted in Figs. 4 and 5, the activities of each user and their transition are understandable concretely from the stay regions of each user. For example, users A, D, C, and B engaged in 9, 5, 4, and 2 activities during the period, respectively. All users appear to have spent the majority of their time at their desks, with brief stops at their colleague's desk, the bookshelf, the accessory box, the beverage area, and the microwave oven. As depicted in Fig. 6, from the sequence of the activities shown in Fig. 5, the episode rules for each user were extracted by the proposed method. The episode rules show the most characteristic activity rules for each user. For example, users A and D were frequently observed visiting colleagues' desks,

Fig. 6. Examples of the Episode Rules for Each User. The red dotted line indicates the association rule. (Color figure online)

whereas users B and C were rarely observed visiting others' desks. Furthermore, user A frequently utilized the drink corner, whereas user C frequently used the microwave oven. Overall, the proposed method is a useful tool for recognizing human indoor behaviors by extracting user activity patterns and characteristic activity rules from the time-series location data of UWB sensors.

References

1. Han, S., Li, Y., Meng, W., Li, C., Liu, T., Zhang, Y.: Indoor localization with a single WI-FI access point based on OFDM-MIMO. IEEE Syst. J. **13**(1), 964–972 (2019)
2. Wang, J., Katabi, D.: Dude, where's my card? RFID positioning that works with multipath and non-line of sight. SIGCOMM Comput. Commun. Rev. **43**, 51–62 (2013)
3. Wang, Y., Yang, X., Zhao, Y., Liu, Y., Cuthbert, L.: Bluetooth positioning using RSSI and triangulation methods. In: IEEE 10th Consumer Communications and Networking Conference (CCNC), pp. 837–842 (2013)
4. Zafari, F., Gkelias, A., Leung, K.K.: A survey of indoor localization systems and technologies. IEEE Commun. Surv. Tutor. **21**, 2568–2599 (2017)
5. Arndt, G.D., Ngo, P.H., Phan, C.T., Gross, J., Ni, J., Dusl, J.: Ultra-wideband angle-of-arrival tracking systems (2010)
6. Jiménez, A.R., Seco, F: Improving the accuracy of Decawave's UWB MDEK1001 location system by gaining access to multiple ranges. Sensors **21**, 1787 (2021)
7. Kang, J.H., Welbourne, W., Stewart, B., Borriello, G.: Extracting places from traces of locations. SIGMOBILE Mob. Comput. Commun. Rev. **9**(3), 58–68 (2005)
8. Leemans, M., van der Aalst, W.M.P.: Discovery of frequent episodes in event logs. In: Ceravolo, P., Russo, B., Accorsi, R. (eds.) SIMPDA 2014. LNBIP, vol. 237, pp. 1–31. Springer, Cham (2015). https://doi.org/10.1007/978-3-319-27243-6_1
9. Günther, C.W., Rozinat, A.: Disco: discover your processes. In: International Conference on Business Process Management (2012)

Semantic Network Analysis of a Learning Task Among Japanese Students of Psychology

Vargas Meza Xanat[1]([✉]) [iD], Shimojo Shigen[2], and Yugo Hayashi[3] [iD]

[1] Institute for the Advanced Study of Human Biology, Kyoto University, Yoshida Konoe cho, Sakyoku, Kyoto 606-8303, Japan
vargasmeza.xanat.8z@kyoto-u.ac.jp

[2] Graduate School of Human Science, Ritsumeikan University, 2-150 Iwakura-cho, Osaka 567-8570, Ibaraki, Japan
cp0013kr@ed.ritsumei.ac.jp

[3] Department of Comprehensive Psychology, Ritsumeikan University, 2-150 Iwakura-cho, Osaka 567-8570, Ibaraki, Japan
y-hayashi@acm.org

Abstract. The complexity of the learning process includes cognitive elements that are difficult to visualize in real time. Collaborative learning adds a social factor. In this study, we examined the case of Japanese university students in a psychology course who first worked individually and then in pairs to draw concept maps using a computer program. We focused on the Interactive Constructive Active/Passive (ICAP) framework of cognitive engagement through semantic and network analysis of the concept maps drawn by the students and their conversations. We drew network graphs to visualize the ICAP indicators across performance groups, uncovering that High Performers employed a wider diversity of nouns, keywords and connections related to the learning task than Low Performers. High Performers were more proactive and emotionally involved in the learning tasks. We confirmed that positive cognitive features are related to positive learning outcomes, providing recommendations for computer-supported collaborative learning (CSCL) systems according to students' needs.

Keywords: computer-supported collaborative learning · ICAP · semantic networks

1 Introduction

Collaborative learning is a body of tools and methods to learn while collaborating, which has two main benefits: cognitive and social [1]. The increasing penetration of technological tools in Higher Education has added another layer of complexity but also an opportunity to enrich learning. However, differences among students require providing tailored help during learning processes. In this paper, we examine the case of Japanese students of psychology who drew concept maps using a computer program. We focus on the ICAP framework of cognitive engagement [2] through semantic and network analysis of the students' concept maps and conversations.

© The Author(s), under exclusive license to Springer Nature Switzerland AG 2023
H. Takada et al. (Eds.): CollabTech 2023, LNCS 14199, pp. 168–175, 2023.
https://doi.org/10.1007/978-3-031-42141-9_13

There are five studies employing data mining techniques in education: assessment of cognition, learning and achievement; learning transfer and discovery of cognitive models; affect, motivation and metacognition; analysis of language and discourse; and others [3]. The KJ and World Café methods were compared, finding that the second method increased usage of relevant keywords [4]. CohMetrix [5] assesses student writing along factors such as cognitive complexity, narrativity, and cohesion. An unsupervised Dynamic Bayesian Network was evaluated on the prevalence of other-oriented transacts, including the effect of power relations [6]. Positive characteristics for cognitive engagement affect collaborative cognitive processes [7]. There are cultural factors perceived as positive among Spanish speakers and as negative among English speakers [8]. However, most research was conducted in westernized environments, with little attention to interrelated cognitive cues available in text and little emphasis on cultural features that may be impacting the learning process.

Research Hypothesis and Objectives. We formulated our hypothesis: H1 Positive cognitive features reflected in the text of concept maps and conversations will be related to learning outcomes. Research objectives were devised as: O1) Provide a quantitative description of cognitive processes during a learning task in a Japanese Higher Education context; O2) Provide a qualitative description of cognitive processes during a learning task in a Japanese Higher Education context; and O3) Determine which interrelated aspects of collaborative learning are associated with learning outcomes.

2 Methods

The experimental task consisted of learning about attribution theory by drawing concept maps with Cmap Tools [9]. The task consisted of six steps: 1) Explanation of concept maps; 2) Reading individually about attribution theory and a case study; 3) Answering an individual pre-test; 4) Drawing an individual Concept Map (ICM); 5) Based on ICMs, pairs of students had a conversation while drawing a Combined Concept Map (CCM); and 6) Answering an individual post-test. 26 university students of Psychology (self-identified as female: 10, male: 16, mean age $= 19.77$, $SD = .4$) participated. The study was approved by the Ethics Committee of Ritsumeikan University, with approval number Kinugasa-Hito-2020–7. Data collected included demographic information, a learning performance score, individual and combined concept maps in.jpg, ICAP measures of conversations during the elaboration of combined maps, and conversations transcriptions taken from video records. The learning performance score (-1 to 2) was calculated by one researcher based on the difference between the scores of pre-tests and post-tests. 15 ICAP indicators divided in 3 dimensions were manually coded by one researcher and a research assistant under a scheme [10] employed in other studies [10, 11]. Conceptual maps were captured as undirected networks in Gephi. Conversations text data of each participant was structured as undirected networks with KH Coder and transferred to Gephi. The learning performance score was used to divide the data into two groups: low performers (scores -1 to 0) and high performers (scores 1 to 2). For O1, each participant conversation was structured as a network and imported to Gephi. The program calculated centrality measures for each ICM, Conversation and CCM, and for concept maps and conversations across performance groups. Table 1 summarizes the measures that were employed:

Table 1. Network centralities and their implications in the context of this study.

Measure	Definition	Implication
Nodes	No. of words in a network	A small no. indicates little activity
Edges	No. of times two words were used together	No edges imply disconnection; few, summarization; and many, trust
Avg. Weighted Degree	Avg. number of ties a word has with other words	Indicates frequently used words
Avg. Harmonic Closeness	Avg. no. of steps to reach all other words in an undirected network	Indicates relevant words
Avg. Betweenness	No. of shortest paths that tie other words in the network passing through a specific word	Indicates bridges between groups of words
Avg. Clustering Coefficient	Avg. measure of how close a word is to become part of a group	Implies trust and redundant information at the word level
Density	Total edges divided by number of all possible edges in a network	High density implies trust and redundant information
Diameter	Avg. of the maximum distance between words in a network	Indicates high socialization
Modularity	Strength of the division between words groups in a network	Identification of distinctive word groups
Avg. Path Length	Avg. of the distance between words in the network	Proximity of words in the conversation/concept map
Weakly Connected Components	Group of words that has at least one connection to other groups	How cohesive the conversation/concept map is

For O2, Visualizations of networks generated with KH Coder and Gephi based on each participant ICM, Conversation and CCM were used to provide an overview of the learning process. Aggregated networks of ICMs, Conversations and CCMs were compared based on modularity across performance groups. For O3, Pearson correlations between ICAP and centrality measures for participants across performance groups were calculated with SPSS. Node level T-tests were conducted in Ucinet for each participant network across performance groups to provide more evidence of differences in centralities correlated with ICAP. We drew aggregated network graphs for ICAP indicators significantly reflected in the networks (at least 0.517, $p \leq 0.048$ for correlations; 0.074, $p = 0.001$ for T-tests).

3   Results

Table 2 shows the centralities of aggregated networks for three learning stages. Please refer to Table 1 to interpret these measures.

Table 2. Summary of centralities in the 3 networks across performance groups.

Measure	ICMs		Conversations		CCMs	
	LP	HP	LP	HP	LP	HP
Number of nodes	86	88	474	608	84	94
Number of edges	97	106	1919	4257	94	116
Average Degree	2.419	2.477	7.767	13.478	2.476	2.638
Average H. Closeness	0.248	0.243	0.339	0.412	0.299	0.253
Average Betweenness	0.051	0.049	0.003	0.002	0.039	0.044
Average Clustering Coefficient	0.006	0.037	0.474	0.571	0.024	0.011
Density	0.027	0.028	0.017	0.023	0.027	0.027
Diameter	14	14	7	6	12	15
Modularity	0.737	0.669	0.001	0.364	0.668	0.639
Average Path Length	6.009	5.285	3.046	2.654	5.042	5.076
Weakly Connected Components	2	1	34	5	4	1

Table 3 suggests that the fourth ICAP indicator (justify, provide reasons) was not correlated with any network centrality, and network measures of HP ICMs were not correlated with ICAP (p > 0.05).

Table 3. Correlation ranges across ICAP dimensions in Low and High Performers.

Low Performers	Centralities	Correlations	Significance
Active	Mostly degree	0.616 - 0.919	0.046 - 0.004
Constructive	Mostly degree	0.612 - 0.754	0.046 - 0.007
Interactive	Mostly degree	0.610 - 0.792	0.046 - <0.001
High Performers	Centralities	Correlations	Significance
Active	Mostly density	0.517 - 0.932	0.048 - <0.001
Constructive	Mostly betweenness and diameter	0.526 - 0.749	0.044 - 0.001
Interactive	Mostly betweenness	0.519 - 0.922	0.048 - < 0.001

Table 4 shows that specific words and groups of words were different during conversations. Differences in degree of ICMs were not significant (p = 0.84).

Table 4. Significant node T-tests in conversation networks (p = 0.001, 1000 permutations).

Centrality	LP	HP	T-test
Degree Mean	7.767	13.478	5.711
Standard Deviation	10.543	20.076	
Closeness Mean	0.316	0.390	0.074
Standard Deviation	0.107	0.084	
Clustering Coefficient Mean	1.186	0.030	1.156
Standard Deviation	5.003	0.279	
Modularity Mean	3.962	6.988	3.026
Standard Deviation	4.367	4.713	
Weakly Connected Components Mean	0.400	0.534	0.134
Standard Deviation	0.350	0.320	

Figures 1, 2 and 3 display conversations subgraphs reflecting 10 ICAP indicators across performance groups. HP includes more conversational words, while LP employ more confusion related terms (e.g. how-do, "how to do?"). The low modularity in LP networks and the presence of a wide variety of words in Fig. 3 corresponding to HP suggests that, while LP talked about a few concepts and relationships between them, HP were better at idea generation. In summary, HP networks were more complex..

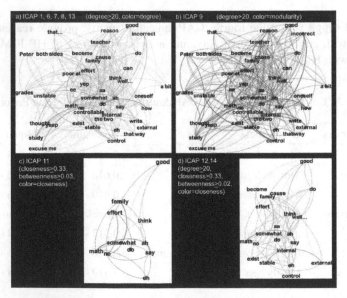

Fig. 1. ICAP in Low Performers aggregated conversations network (tie strength 0.5-3).

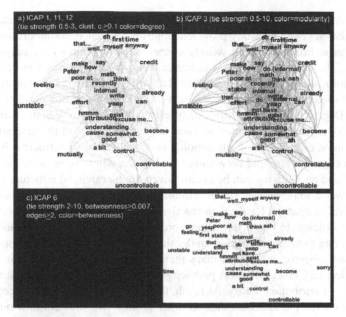

Fig. 2. ICAP in High Performers aggregated conversations network (degree ≥ 40).

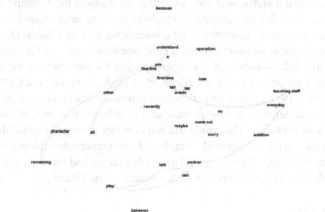

Fig. 3. ICAP 7 in High Performers aggregated conversations network (tie strength 0-3.5, betweenness ≥ 0.003, clustering coefficient ≥ 0.25).

4 Discussion

Degree, closeness, clustering coefficient, modularity and weakly connected components were significantly different (p = 0.001) between HP and LP conversations networks. Clustering coefficient suggested that words that sound similar facilitate knowledge acquisition among American students [12], while closeness centrality indicated fast reachability and access to information in Spanish online classrooms [13]. The importance of degree, density and diameter on educational outcomes was demonstrated through agent simulation [14]. Our study provided empirical evidence to support these centralities' relevance. Modularity and weakly connected components may suggest cultural differences. The qualitative analysis indicates that, while HP showed more vulnerability, negotiation skills and idea generation, LP struggled with socialization. Based on Fig. 1a, LP used mostly negative words and provided few reasons more related to the individual. Degree, Density and Modularity reflected ICAP 3, as seen in distinctive clusters (Fig. 2b), some showing emotion towards the protagonist of the case study, others demonstrating a clear usage of attribution theory keywords. Constructive ICAP 6 was reflected in edges, degree and betweenness in Fig. 2c, where some words acknowledging the self and apologizing can be noted. Given the hierarchical structure of Japanese society, conversations between students of different ages or academic levels might have been negatively impacted. Lastly, Constructive ICAP 7 was reflected in betweenness and clustering coefficient in Fig. 3, depicting words loosely related to the task and including "play", pointing to creativity. Based on density and weakly connected components, HP created more cohesive conceptual maps than LP from the beginning, being proactive during the learning task. The short path length suggests a rich argumentation connecting concepts of attribution theory. As result, there were more relevant concepts and ties in CCMs with HP participation than in other groups. We thus confirm our hypothesis, where positive cognitive features are related to positive learning outcomes. Both concept maps and conversations were crucial to understand in which steps individuals' knowledge acquisition starts, and how socialization impacts the learning process. Our results can be used to design computer-supported learning interventions by suggesting diversifying reasons, more keywords, and connections between them. During the conversation, proactiveness and socialization could be encouraged. As for confusion, it can be addressed through examples of concept maps and for the learning topic. Regarding limitations, our data pertains to a small cohort of students before the COVID-19 pandemic. Controlling for cognitive impairment in future studies is recommended. It would be useful to pair students with those in their same academic year or those of similar age to mitigate power relations. This study did not conduct intercoder reliability for ICAP scores. Given the variety of networks employed, we constructed undirected networks, limiting the analysis range. It is expected to employ larger and more diversified samples of data to model learning networks more accurately in the future.

5   Conclusions

1. High Performers employed a wider diversity of nouns, keywords and connections between them related to the learning task than Low Performers.
2. High Performers were more proactive and emotionally involved than Low Performers.
3. Two Active ICAP (1, 3), two Constructive ICAP (6, 7) and 6 Interactive ICAP (8, 9, 11, 12, 13, 14) were related to outcomes in a collaborative learning task using conceptual maps.

Acknowledgements. This paper was supported by the Institute for the Advanced Study of Human Biology (ASHBi) Fusion Research Grant.

References

1. Chen, W., Tan, J.S.H., Pi, Z.: The spiral model of collaborative knowledge improvement: an exploratory study of a networked collaborative classroom. Int. J. Comput.-Support. Collab. Learn. **16**(1), 7–35 (2021). https://doi.org/10.1007/s11412-021-09338-6
2. Chi, M.T.: Active-constructive-interactive: A conceptual framework for differentiating learning activities. Top. Cogn. Sci. **1**(1), 73–105 (2009)
3. Koedinger, K.R., D'Mello, S., McLaughlin, E.A., Pardos, Z.A., Rosé, C.P.: Data mining and education. Wiley Interdiscipl. Rev. Cogn. Sci. **6**(4), 333–353 (2015)
4. Yasuhara, T., et al.: Studies using text mining on the differences in learning effects between the KJ and World Cafe method as learning strategies. Yakugaku Zasshi: J. Pharmaceut. Soc. Japan **135**(5), 753–759 (2015)
5. McNamara, D.S., Graesser, A.C.: Coh-Metrix: an automated tool for theoretical and applied natural language processing. In: Ishizaki, S., Kaufer, D., Mc Carthy, P.M., Boonthum-Denecke, C. (eds.) Applied Natural Language Processing: Identification, Investigation and Resolution, pp. 188–205. IGI Global (2012)
6. Gweon, G., Jain, M., McDonough, J., Raj, B., Rosé, C.P.: Measuring prevalence of other-oriented transactive contributions using an automated measure of speech style accommodation. Int. J. Comput.-Support. Collab. Learn. **8**(2), 245–265 (2013)
7. Howley, I., Mayfield, E., Rosé, C.P.: Linguistic analysis methods for studying small groups. In: Hmelo-Silver, C., Chinn, C., Chan, C., O'Donnell, A. (eds.) The International Handbook of Collaborative Learning, pp. 184–202. Routledge (2013)
8. Vargas Meza, X., Yamanaka, T.: A video recommendation system for complex topic learning based on a sustainable design approach. Vietnam J. Comput. Sci. **6**(03), 329–342 (2019)
9. Scherp, H.Å.: Quantifying qualitative data using cognitive maps. Int. J. Res. Meth. Educ. **36**(1), 67–81 (2013)
10. Shimojo, S., Hayashi, Y.: Prompting learner-learner collaborative learning for deeper interaction: conversational analysis based on the ICAP Framework. In So, H.J, (ed.) Proceedings of the 28th International Conference on Computers in Education ICCE2020, pp. 177–182. Asia-Pacific Society for Computers in Education (2020)
11. Ohmoto, Y., Shimojo, S., Morita, J., Hayashi, Y.: Investigating clues for estimating ICAP states based on learners' behavioural data during collaborative learning. In: Cristea, A.I., Troussas, C. (eds.) ITS 2021. LNCS, vol. 12677, pp. 224–231. Springer, Cham (2021). https://doi.org/ 10.1007/978-3-030-80421-3_24
12. Goldstein, R., Vitevitch, M.S.: The influence of clustering coefficient on word-learning: how groups of similar sounding words facilitate acquisition. Front. Psychol. **5**, 1307 (2014)
13. Hernández-García, Á., González-González, I., Jiménez-Zarco, A.I., Chaparro-Peláez, J.: Applying social learning analytics to message boards in online distance learning: a case study. Comput. Hum. Behav. **47**, 68–80 (2015)
14. Veillon, L.-M., Bourgne, G., Soldano, H.: Effect of network topology on neighbourhood-aided collective learning. In: Nguyen, N.T., Papadopoulos, G.A., Jędrzejowicz, P., Trawiński, B., Vossen, G. (eds.) ICCCI 2017. LNCS (LNAI), vol. 10448, pp. 202–211. Springer, Cham (2017). https://doi.org/10.1007/978-3-319-67074-4_20

Computational Analysis of the Belt and Road Initiative (BRI) Discourse on Indonesian Twitter

Lotenna Nwana, Ugochukwu Onyepunuka, Mustafa Alassad, and Nitin Agarwal[✉]

COSMOS Research Center, UA - Little Rock, Little Rock, USA
{ltnwana,uponyepunuka,mmalassad,nxagarwal}@ualr.edu

Abstract. The Belt and Road Initiative (BRI) is an ambitious development project to build road and sea infrastructure through parts of Asia, Europe, and Africa that will encourage international trade and development. However, since its launch, a major concern and central research theme has been the possibility of the initiative being a 'debt trap' and an opportunity for China to gain power over countries like Indonesia. Previous research adopting more qualitative approaches have identified negative reactions to the BRI in terms of China's intentions. However, there is a gap in the extant research focusing on the systematic evaluation of the BRI discourse on social media leveraging computational methodologies, particularly content and network analysis. Understanding the structure of the BRI discourse network can reveal key information actors that are driving the propagation of information through the network. As such, we extracted 12,985 tweets from Twitter to understand the different topics being discussed about the BRI in Indonesia. Latent Dirichlet Allocation (LDA) topic model algorithm classified the tweets into topic groups and helped us understand each topic's underlying theme. In addition, the user and user's follower data was analyzed to understand the information flow network and identify the most influential users within the network. While some users speculated on China's good intentions for Indonesia, others argued that Indonesia acts like foreign minions controlled by the Chinese government. Furthermore, we identified key information actors within the network that are important and well-positioned for the diffusion of information across the network.

Keywords: Belt and Road Initiative (BRI) · Network Analysis · Topic Modeling · Social Media · Indonesia

1 Introduction

In 2013, China launched a massive infrastructure project termed the Belt and Road Initiative (BRI) [1]. This was done with a vision of developing an extensive network of energy pipelines, railroads, road networks, and streamlined border crossing to connect the trade routes from China to other parts of Asia, Europe,

H. Takada et al. (Eds.): CollabTech 2023, LNCS 14199, pp. 176–184, 2023.
https://doi.org/10.1007/978-3-031-42141-9_14

and even towards Africa. Overall, the primary aim was to foster international and domestic cooperation, connectivity, and trade in countries within Asia, Europe, and Africa. However, there is growing skepticism that China intends to leverage the initiative to exert its dominance within the international sphere and that particular countries will be "at China's mercy" due to their inability to pay back the loan.

The BRI provides an important opportunity for Indonesia to develop its infrastructure and further establish itself within the global sphere [2]. In 2015, the Indonesian president, Joko Widodo (Jokowi), highlighted the country's need to build roads, railways, and ports that would help boost its operations and the overall economy [3]. Nevertheless, there was limited availability of domestic funds to completely achieve Jokowi's plans for Indonesia [3]. Prior to the launch of the BRI, China's investment in Indonesia was estimated to be minimal; however, since its launch, China's investment in the Indonesian economy has increased considerably, rising to be one of the country's top investors. A large part of this investment is debt; for example, in the development of the 150km Jakarta-Bandung high-speed railway, the China Development Bank offered loans to cover 75 percent of the costs [4]. This, along with other BRI projects, has brought Indonesia's indebtedness to China to over US$22 billion as of March 2022 [4]. With this, growing fears are that Indonesia will likely default on its repayments and face a similar situation to Sri Lanka and Malaysia [4].

This project, as a result, sought to answer two key questions: what are the main discussion points about the BRI in Indonesia, and who are the key actors driving the spread of information on the BRI on Indonesian Twitter? To answer these questions, we utilized the topic modeling technique, Latent Dirichlet Allocation (LDA), to understand the themes that formed part of the BRI discourse on Indonesian Twitter, and developed a user network of BRI Tweeters (users who tweeted about the BRI) to identify the most important users that have the capacity to drive the spread of information.

2   Literature Review

The BRI has seen a burgeoning amount of published research emphasizing its potential effects and impact [5–7]. Yang et al. (2021) adopted an empirical and methodological approach termed cultural framing to analyze the political media discussions around the Belt and Road Initiative [6]. The researchers closely studied 1837 official texts and news articles from six countries (China, USA, India, Japan, United Kingdom, and Australia) to identify and analyze all the frames within the BRI discourse used by multiple key actors relevant to the study. The researchers leveraged deductive analysis to study these frames used by the government officials and elite media actors in the studied countries [6]. Overall, Yang et al. (2021) found that there were opposing perspectives regarding the BRI, which they identified as frames and counter-frames that aid the overall understanding of the BRI [6]. This led to the discovery that while the BRI has numerous benefits, including driving economic benefits and collective decision-making, countries remain cautious about China's hidden agenda and the susceptibility of increasing debt.

Aside from the theoretical-focused approach adopted dominantly in understanding the BRI and China's underlying motivations, researchers have sought to combine computational methodology with the qualitative approach [5,7]. Ya Xiao et al. (2019) applied an evolution of critical discourse analysis (CDA) to understand the similarities and differences that exist between the BRI discourse by the American media and the Chinese media, as well as the reasons for these differences [5]. Based on the high-frequency words analysis, Xiao et al. (2019) found that the Chinese media typically emphasized economic development and infrastructure connectivity, while the American media mainly reported on the political influence and international outlook around the BRI [5]. The researchers confirmed that the American media reported about the BRI from a negative perspective, specifically about China's intention to strengthen its position within the international community. However, over time, they noticed a shift to a more positive perspective attributed to an increasing understanding of China's intent for openness and cooperation [5].

To augment the existing research, this paper employs a computational approach to examine the common themes within BRI conversations on social media (Twitter) as it relates to Indonesia. This paper develops a pathway to understand the communication flow and ascertain the major influencers within the generated user network.

3   Methodology

Data Collection: We collected data on the posts centered around the BRI discourse in Indonesia and metadata about the users who tweeted about these posts using COSMOS custom Twitter API crawler. We chose a date range between January 1st, 2019, and October 28th, 2022, to delve deeper into more recent BRI conversations. Key phrases such as "BRI", "OBOR", "China", "Indonesia", and "Jakarta" were used to collect tweets to align with the research focus, thereby generating a total of 12,985 tweets for analysis.

Topic Modeling - Latent Dirichlet Allocation: Topic modeling is an essential technique in text mining that adopts natural language processing (NLP) for topic discovery (i.e. to discover similar, abstract topic groups in a body of text) [8]. In this research, topic modeling specifies the degree to which each tweet belongs to a topic group by allocating a value between 0 to 1 for that tweet with regard to the topic groups. This is defined as the probability distribution of a tweet belonging to a topic group.

To extract topics effectively, each tweet was broken down into sentences that were further broken down into lowercase words (tokens). In this process, punctuations were also eliminated. Finally, the remaining words were lemmatized and stemmed. Once this is completed, a "bag of words" (BOW) is generated, and the frequency of each word is computed [9]. The LDA topic modeling is executed on the processed data to generate topic groups based on the words and the degree to which each tweet belongs to each group [10]. LDA was utilized because it models the probability distribution of topics in a tweet and the probability distribution of words in a topic, making it more flexible to extract complex relationships between words [10].

Network Analysis: This research work analyzed the relationship between users who tweeted on the BRI and the followers of these users, thereby generating a directed network. Subsequently, modularization, a community-detecting algorithm, was adopted to compute the strength of the connections between nodes, identify the communities within the network, and understand the interrelations [11]. To develop the network, we used Gephi, which adopts the Louvain method for calculating the modularity of a network [12].

Furthermore, a number of methods were combined to help us better understand the network and further deduce the most important nodes in the network. These methods were *Average Degree Centrality*, which computes the number of inward connections to nodes (In-degree) and the number of outward connections from nodes (Out-degree) for each node in the network [13]. *Betweenness Centrality* measures the number of times a node appears on the shortest path between two nodes [11]. It helps to confirm the importance of a node as in the dispersion of information between two nodes. *Closeness Centrality* evaluates the closeness of a node within the network [11].

These methods provide preliminary insight into the nodes that formed the basis for communities in the network [11].

4   Analysis and Results

The results provide useful insights into well-positioned users and the main subthemes around conversations on the BRI in Indonesia.

4.1   Topic Modeling

Following the data extraction, the Latent Dirichlet Allocation algorithm, a generative statistical technique for topic modeling, was adopted to classify the tweets into five topics. Initially, the model was trained on a random number of topics, and based on the coherence score from the elbow method, we ranked the top five topics. For each topic group, the 'top words', as defined by Chuang et al. (2012), were used to deduce the primary idea [14].

Among the overall top five words computed, "Aseng", "Aniesbaswedan", "Pemerintah", "Antek" and "Dilakukan", two of them ("antek" and "aseng") have a negative connotation, and two of them refer to the government (Aniesbaswedan who is the former governor of Jakarta and Pemerintah which translates to 'Government').

The topic modeling showed the main underlying narrative within the discourse that referred to the accusation of the Indonesian government being "loyal servants" or "minions" of the Chinese government. While some opinions defended the Indonesian government as acting solely for Indonesia, others were against the Indonesian government, claiming they were acting for China.

The top words (in their original and translated format) for each topic group are highlighted below:

- **Topic 1** - antek (minion), aseng (a chinese person), bajingan (bastard), pemerintah (government), china, asing, anti, komunis (communist), indonesia
- **Topic 2** - indonesia, ekonomi (economic), china, menguasai (master), road, silk, jokowi, maritime, jinping, laut (sea)
- **Topic 3** - antek (minion), pemerintah (government), dituding (accused), sukuk, pendanaan (funding), pinjam (borrow), aseng (a chinese person)
- **Topic 4**- china, antek (minion), asing (a chinese person), jokowi, indonesia, politik (politics), anies (the former governor of jarkarta)
- **Topic 5** - aniesbaswedan, dilakukan (done), dkijakarta, berantas (eradicate), tengik (rancid), mafia, presiden (president), bajingan (bastard)

We discovered that **topics 1 and 3** overlapped based on the frequency of their overall most salient words. However, a qualitative review of the tweets within these topic groups revealed distinctive elements within them.

Topic 1 had a general negative discursive tone based on the words from the topic modeling and the review of the tweets within that group. Users discussed some of China's vices as speculated on the international scene and attempted to relate them to China's dealings with Indonesia. On the other hand, **Topic 3** was focused on the suspicion that countries would struggle to finance this project and then have to take loans from China, thereby being at China's mercy.

Topics 2, 4, and 5 also revealed aspects of BRI and Indonesian political conversation. **Topic 2** revealed that there is growing discussion on China's intention to control Indonesia's economy via the BRI. **Topic 4** tweets defined how the Indonesian president Jokowi has been described, including as a foreign product (making him a foreign minion), anti-Islam, a Chinese henchman, an invader of foreign Chinese workers, and an affiliate of PKI (an Indonesian communist party). **Topic 5** opinions were geared towards soliciting for the eradication of individuals who were described as mafia-like and "rancid bastards" acting on behalf of Chinese ethnic residents.

Further analysis of the topic groups led to an observation of a good number of negative terms, including "bajingan" (bastard), "antek" (loyal servant/minion), "PKI" (Partai Komunis Indonesia - Indonesian Communist Party), and "Komunis" (Communist). These negative terms were concentrated more in the overlapping topic groups, Topic 1 and Topic 3. Therefore, to understand the extent of negativity of these tweets and the underlying feelings (negative, positive, or neutral), we analyzed the toxicity and sentiments of these tweets. Topic 1 had a frequency count of over 2000 low-toxic tweets, and Topic 3 had a frequency count of over 2500 low-toxic tweets. Although some tweets had $toxicityscores > 0.6$, the frequencies were very low compared to the overall dataset. We, therefore, concluded that Topics 1 and 3 had limited toxicity content.

4.2 Network Analysis

To understand the network and flow of information on the BRI discourse in Indonesia, we developed a directed network flowing from the users who tweeted about the BRI (source nodes), to the followers of these users (target nodes). We also calculated the network's modularity to determine the various communities present.

Overall, the network had 89,874 nodes and 96,322 connections (edges) between the nodes. The modularity assessment generated an average modularity score of 0.516 and detected nine communities within the network, which is represented by the different colors within the network.

As mentioned earlier, we utilized four key techniques within this paper to analyze the network and determine the influential users well-positioned to drive the spread of information. These methods are the average degree centrality (in-degree and out-degree centrality), betweenness centrality, and closeness centrality.

We selected the top 11 source nodes (users) with the highest out-degree and observed 89,868 nodes with at least one as an in-degree value. The out-degree centrality confirmed that these 11 nodes connected to a large number of nodes are top nodes, as any information they send will be received by a significant number of other nodes. Further analysis of these top 11 users revealed that 8 of them did not follow one another. As such, we postulate that information was passed through the connected nodes that intersect between their communities (their followers). In addition, we observed that the remaining three users are connected by an edge, which implies that they follow themselves, with one also noted to be connected to the user with the highest out-degree.

Moreover, we analyzed the connected components of the network to find the number of nodes that could be reached via indirect and direct paths. From this, we found that 99.01% of the nodes are strongly connected and can be reached via direct paths, while the remaining 0.99% are weakly connected components that are linked via indirect paths. For more streamlined information, the betweenness and closeness centrality was also assessed. Based on this, we observed three nodes (users) with the highest betweenness centrality (values greater than zero) and closeness centrality values within the network. This confirms that their features make them the most critical users in the network.

Although the user - 79130206 had a very low betweenness centrality value (0), we considered it influential within the network due to the high significance of its out-degree (six times the next highest out-degree). Given the importance of these four users (source nodes), we explored the topic groups around which these users converse and found they were primarily posting tweets around Topic 2, which focused on the economic discourse about the BRI relating to Indonesia and China, and Topic 5, which focused on citizens lambasting the governor of Jakarta to remove Chinese minions.

We noted a number of sub-topics being discussed with reference to the BRI in Indonesia. There is a balanced exchange on the perception of the economic benefits to Indonesia. However, there is some discourse on the financial implications to Indonesia and the probable chance that Indonesia is acting at the behest of China. In addition, based on the network analysis, we identified three critical users within the network. This results from their position within the network (distance and interceptions) and the number of their connections within the network. To address users' wrong opinions and ensure the spread of information across the network, these three users are vital.

5 Conclusion and Future Work

This research identified and analyzed the topic groups within the BRI discourse in Indonesia, confirming the main themes that formed the basis of the discourse. In addition, a network was generated to identify the communication channel of the tweeters of the BRI topics as well as the important nodes that influence other nodes in the network. The topic modeling revealed differing opinions on China's intentions for Indonesia with respect to the BRI. While some argue that the Indonesian government will be made Chinese minions, others opine that the signs do not point to China's dominance of Indonesia but provide an opportunity for Indonesia's economic growth. Furthermore, the network represented the Twitter users from which the 12,985 tweets originated and the followers of these users. Utilizing out-degree, betweenness, and closeness centrality methods, we identified four important nodes in the network for information transmission. These nodes posted about three topics, with two of them being more dominant, Topic 2 and Topic 5. Topic 2, which centered around the economic implications of the BRI, was directly related to the overarching central theme of the BRI discourse on Twitter. We determined that this is a result of this topic being spread by the influential users within the network.

The majority of the tweets were not in English. In addition, negative words in topics 1 and 3 observed, like "loyal servant", and "minion" in the literal sense, do not have negative connotations; as a result, the toxicity analysis does not tag these as toxic. Subsequent works should involve the analysis of the key users to ascertain whether they are bots, thereby understanding if bots have an influence in driving the spread of information on the overall network.

Acknowledgements. This research is funded in part by the U.S. National Science Foundation (OIA-1946391, OIA-1920920, IIS-1636933, ACI-1429160, and IIS-1110868), U.S. Office of the Under Secretary of Defense for Research and Engineering (FA9550-22-1-0332), U.S. Office of Naval Research (N00014-10-1-0091, N00014-14-1-0489, N00014-15-P-1187, N00014-16-1-2016, N00014-16-1-2412, N00014-17-1-2675, N00014-17-1-2605, N68335-19-C-0359, N00014-19-1-2336, N68335-20-C-0540, N00014-21-1-2121, N00014-21-1-2765, N00014-22-1-2318), U.S. Air Force Research Laboratory, U.S. Army Research Office (W911NF-20-1-0262, W911NF-16-1-0189, W911NF-23-1-0011), U.S. Defense Advanced Research Projects Agency (W31P4Q-17-C-0059),

Arkansas Research Alliance, the Jerry L. Maulden/Entergy Endowment at the University of Arkansas at Little Rock, and the Australian Department of Defense Strategic Policy Grants Program (SPGP) (award number: 2020-106-094). Any opinions, findings, and conclusions or recommendations expressed in this material are those of the authors and do not necessarily reflect the views of the funding organizations. The researchers gratefully acknowledge the support.

References

1. Lall, S.V., Lebrand, M.: Who Wins, Who Loses? Understanding the Spatially Differentiated Effects of the Belt and Road Initiative. World Bank, Washington, DC, Policy Research Working Paper (2019). https://doi.org/10.1596/1813-9450-8806
2. Pratiwi, F.I., et al.: China Belt and Road Initiatives (BRI) in Indonesia's Socio-Economic Security Challenges: A Policy Recommendation. Centre for Strategic and International Studies (2020). https://www.jstor.org/stable/resrep25407.9. Accessed 01 Feb 2023
3. Cheang, K.L.: The struggle to define the Belt and Road Initiative in Indonesia. The Jakarta Post (2019). https://www.thejakartapost.com/news/2019/07/24/the-struggle-to-define-the-belt-and-road-initiative-in-indonesia.html. Accessed 01 Feb 2023
4. Rakhmat, M.Z.: The Political Economy of China-Indonesia Relations in 2022. INDEF (2023)
5. Xiao, Y., Li, Y., Hu, J.: Construction of the belt and road initiative in Chinese and American media: a critical discourse analysis based on self-built corpora. Int. J. Engl. Linguist. **9**(3), 3 (2019). https://doi.org/10.5539/ijel.v9n3p68
6. Yang, H., Gorp, B.: A frame analysis of political-media discourse on the belt and road initiative: evidence from China, Australia, India, Japan, the United Kingdom, and the United States. Camb. Rev. Int. Aff. 1–27 (2021). https://doi.org/10.1080/09557571.2021.1968794
7. Zhang, L., Wu, D.: Media representations of china: a comparison of china daily and financial times in reporting on the belt and road initiative. Crit. Arts **31**(6), 29–43 (2017). https://doi.org/10.1080/02560046.2017.1408132
8. Jelodar, H.: Latent dirichlet allocation (LDA) and topic modeling: models, applications, a survey. Multimedia Tools Appl. **78**(11), 15169–15211 (2018). https://doi.org/10.1007/s11042-018-6894-4
9. Zhang, Y., Jin, R., Zhou, Z.-H.: Understanding bag-of-words model: a statistical framework. Int. J. Mach. Learn. Cybern. **1**(1), 43–52 (2010). https://doi.org/10.1007/s13042-010-0001-0
10. Blei, D.M., Ng, A.Y., Jordan, M.I.: Latent dirichlet allocation. J. Mach. Learn. Res. **3**, 993–1022 (2003)
11. Grandjean, M.: Gephi Introduction (2015). https://serval.unil.ch/resource/serval:BIB_0F0EB41780EB.P001/REF.pdf
12. Onyepunuka, U., Alassad, M., Nwana, L., Agarwal, N.: Multilingual analysis of YouTube's recommendation system. examining topic and emotion drift in the 'Cheng Ho' Narrative. In: Sixth International Workshop on Narrative Extraction from Texts (Text2Story 2023) co-located with the 45th European Conference on Information Retrieval (ECIR 2023). Dublin (2023)
13. Liu, Y., Wei, B., Du, Y., Xiao, F., Deng, Y.: Identifying influential spreaders by weight degree centrality in complex networks. Chaos, Solitons Fractals **86**, 1–7 (2016). https://doi.org/10.1016/j.chaos.2016.01.030

14. Chuang, J., Manning, C.D., Heer, J.: Termite: visualization techniques for assessing textual topic models. In: Proceedings of the International Working Conference on Advanced Visual Interfaces, pp. 74–77. ACM, Capri Island (2012). https://doi.org/10.1145/2254556.2254572

Conducting Morality and Emotion Analysis on Blog Discourse

Stella Mbila-Uma, Ifeanyichukwu Umoga, Mustafa Alassad,
and Nitin Agarwal[✉]

University of Arkansas, Little Rock, Arkansas, USA
{smbilauma,ijumoga,mmalassad,nxagarwal}@ualr.edu
http://www.cosmos.ualr.edu

Abstract. Social media has exploded in its usage, since the advancement of technology with individuals sharing their opinions and beliefs on its platform through text. This has led to the access of tons of text data that researchers can use to further understand human behaviour or user perspective. Emotion analysis is a common text analysis technique used to discover embedded emotion in content. For this research, we compare emotion analysis and morality assessment techniques in discovering embedded user opinions. Our results show that emotion analysis possesses limitations in its result. On the other hand, morality assessment provides a more comprehensive and accurate analysis of text data. For this research, we proposed that both methodologies are not mutually exclusive, and can complement each other to better understand the complexities of human communication and behavior.

Keywords: Text Analysis · Emotion Analysis · Morality Assessment · Blogs · South China Sea · text-data

1 Introduction

With the expansion of technology and the massive spread of social media, researchers have access to tons of text data [5]. But the question is, "How can these researchers interpret human behavior effectively from text data". Emotional analysis has often been used as a text analysis tool to interpret user perspectives from the text. Although this has been effective, the result is not often easily interpretable [9]. This research highlights a better approach to analyzing embedded user opinion in text data using morality assessment.

Morality assessment involves systematically examining and interpreting texts to uncover the moral dimensions embedded within them. As language plays a fundamental role in conveying moral messages, understanding the moral implications and ethical considerations in texts can provide valuable insights into human behavior, societal norms, and cultural values [6].

On the other hand, emotion analysis involves examining the emotional content and expression in the text [3]. It encompasses approaches such as computing feelings, emotion recognition, and sentiment analysis, which aim to identify,

---

The original version of this chapter was revised: the last author's family name and e-mail address was corrected. The correction to this chapter is available at https://doi.org/10.1007/978-3-031-42141-9_21

H. Takada et al. (Eds.): CollabTech 2023, LNCS 14199, pp. 185–192, 2023.
https://doi.org/10.1007/978-3-031-42141-9_15

classify, and quantify emotions in texts or human expressions. Emotion analysis often draws on psychology, neuroscience, and linguistics theories to understand how emotions are experienced, expressed, and interpreted in various contexts.

In this research, we will explore emotion analysis, its limitations, and how morality assessment is better used in understanding embedded user perspectives in text data using the South China narrative [2] as a case study.

1.1   Background of the Data

The South China Sea dispute is a complex and contentious issue involving political, economic, and ethical dimensions. According to [4] Blogging has become a popular channel because users can write extensively on topics that interest or concern them. Due to how extensive a blog post is, it will help in obtaining a deeper insight into the different text analyses being compared [5].

Section 3 explores the methodologies used to analyze text data, including data collection and emotion/morality analysis of south China Sea blog posts. Section 4 presents the obtained results, followed by the conclusion and future directions.

2   Literature Review

The analysis of text data has become a prominent research area in various fields [8]. Two common approaches in text analysis are moral text analysis and emotion text analysis, which involve examining different aspects of text data to gain insights into moral values and emotion states respectively [8].

Moral text analysis and emotion text analysis are two distinct approaches used in text analysis that aim to understand and analyze different aspects of text data [1]. While moral text analysis focuses on identifying and categorizing moral values, ethical principles, and ethical reasoning in text data, emotion text analysis involves identifying and categorizing emotions expressed in text data [3]. Emotion analysis has its strengths in certain research contexts. Emotion text analysis has been used to study emotion expressions in various forms of communication, such as social media posts, customer reviews, and online forums, to understand people's emotions, attitudes, and opinions [3]. Emotion analysis has also been used in social media, health, and business sectors where understanding emotions is crucial [3].

In previous studies, researchers use emotion analysis to gain insights from social media and blogs. This paper demonstrates how morality assessment provides more comprehensive insight as an analytic tool. Also, "from our result, we recommend a combination of both methodologies to provide a more robust framework in interpreting user perspective from text data".

3   Methodology

This section discusses the data used for this research and the methodology employed.

3.1   Data Collection

To begin the data collection, we generated a set of keywords such as ("Permanent Court/Arbitra/rule/ruling/court/tribunal")that were passed into Google crawler after which Google crawler produced target URLs. To discover relevant blog posts, we feed these URLs into Diffbot a web page crawling tool [7] that produced 318 blog posts of which 52 blog posts were found to be relevant and used for further analysis. The next section describes the methodology accessed in this research and how they are employed in text analysis.

3.2   Emotion Analysis

Emotion analysis entails identifying and evaluating the underlying emotions expressed in text data [14]. In the context of the South China Sea narrative context, this methodology was used to discover the distribution of emotions. After the data was collected, the Blog post was passed through a Python script utilizing the Emonet [10] package which is a deep learning-based emotion recognition model that can be used to analyze the Emotion content of text data. The average distribution of emotions(Anger, Anticipation, disgust, Fear, Joy, Sadness, Surprise, and Trust) in each blog post was calculated and visualized to show the distribution of emotion within the collection of blog posts.

3.3   Morality Assessment

To further analyze the results obtained from our emotion analysis, Morality assessment was carried out to gain better insight.

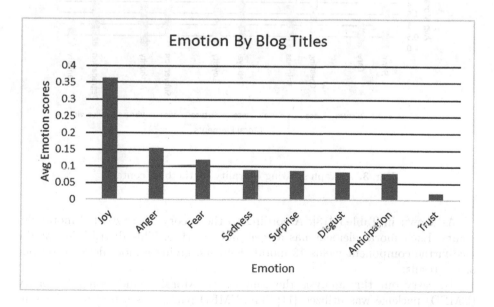

Fig. 1. A graph showing emotion by the blog titles.

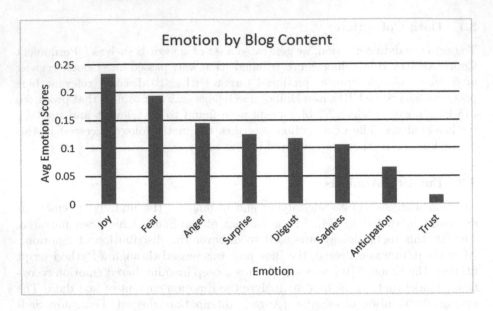

Fig. 2. A graph showing emotion by the blog content.

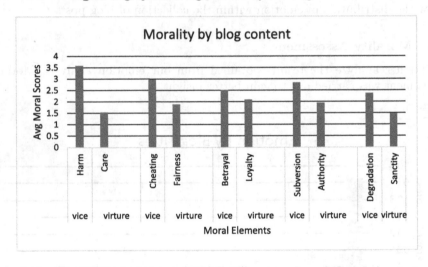

Fig. 3. A graph showing Morality by the blog content.

As shown in Table 1 [13], According to the theory, there exist 6 moral elements. Each moral element has a vice and a virtue. This distribution of the vice-virtue component yields 12 moral elements, giving a more detailed output of the result.

To carry out this analysis the Empathetic Moral Foundations Dictionary (EMFD) package was utilized [11]. The EMFD package is a tool used for sen-

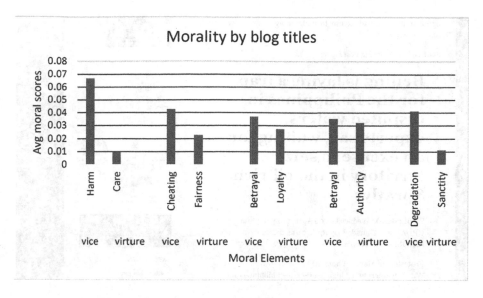

Fig. 4. A graph showing Morality by the blog titles.

Table 1. Moral foundation theory

Virtue	Care	Fairness	Liberty	Loyalty	Authority	Sanctity
Vice	Harm	Cheating	Oppression	Betrayal	Subversion	Degradation

timent analysis that specifically focuses on moral foundations. The average distribution of morals in each blog post was calculated and visualized.

4   Analysis and Results

As discussed earlier, this research aimed to discover the distribution of user perspectives using emotion analysis and morality assessment. Emotion analysis was used to gather insights to accomplish this goal, but its limits required further investigation through morality assessments. Emotional analysis of blog content and titles (Figs. 1 and 2) revealed high occurrence of Joy and low occurrence of trust. Further investigation found contradictory content. To validate user perspective and assess morals, we needed to examine the blog post in detail.

We conducted morality assessments on the blog post to better understand the emotions expressed in a narrative. The combination of those methodologies may provide a complete understanding of the feelings expressed by bloggers about the South China Sea issue. As discussed earlier in the Moral foundation theory, we carried out an analysis highlighting the vice and virtue for each of the moral elements for the blog content and titles displayed in Figs. 3 and 4. We discovered that the moral element with the highest distribution is "Care-Vice(harm)", and the least distributed moral element was "Care-Virtue" for blog

Fig. 5. Blog post showing high joy emotions with no trace of joy [12]

CAN THE U.S. COAST GUARD TAKE ON THE SOUTH CHINA SEA?

AARON PICOZZI AND LINCOLN DAVIDSON   JUNE 20, 2016
COMMENTARY

Fig. 6. Blog post showing high joy emotions with no trace of joy [13]

titles. On the other hand, we discovered that the moral elements for blog content with the highest distribution is "Care-Vice(harm)" and the least distribution is Sanctity-Virtue(Degradation)

To verify our findings, we read through blog posts that expressed these moral elements and found that they aligned with our results as shown in Figs. 5 and 6.

5   Conclusion

The objective of this study was to explore the feasibility of using Emotion and morality analysis interchangeably to analyze blog posts. To achieve this, we analyzed blog posts related to the South China Sea narrative, using both emotion and morality assessments. We used the Emonet package for Emotion analysis and the EMFD package for morality analysis. We analyzed emotions in blog posts and found Joy was dominant. But, after reading them, we discovered a disconnect between computed emotions and actual content. To validate perspectives, we used a morality assessment, which aligned with expressed morals. Emotion analysis alone may not provide a complete understanding of the content of a blog post. Therefore, it is necessary to incorporate morality assessment to gain a more comprehensive insight into understanding underlined user perspective. We plan to combine some methodologies, such as Toxicity analysis to better interpret the 'vice' component of the moral foundation theory.

Acknowledgements. This research is funded in part by the U.S. National Science Foundation (OIA-1946391, OIA-1920920, IIS-1636933, ACI-1429160, and IIS-1110868), U.S. Office of the Under Secretary of Defense for Research and Engineering (FA9550-22-1-0332), U.S. Office of Naval Research (N00014-10-1-0091, N00014-14-1-0489, N00014-15-P-1187, N00014-16-1-2016, N00014-16-1-2412, N00014-17-1-2675, N00014-17-1-2605, N68335-19-C-0359, N00014-19-1-2336, N68335-20-C-0540, N00014-21-1-2121, N00014-21-1-2765, N00014-22-1-2318), U.S. Air Force Research Laboratory, U.S. Army Research Office (W911NF-20-1-0262, W911NF-16-1-0189, W911NF-23-1-0011), U.S. Defense Advanced Research Projects Agency (W31P4Q-17-C-0059), Arkansas Research Alliance, the Jerry L. Maulden/Entergy Endowment at the University of Arkansas at Little Rock, and the Australian Department of Defense Strategic Policy Grants Program (SPGP) (award number: 2020-106-094). Any opinions, findings, and conclusions or recommendations expressed in this material are those of the authors and do not necessarily reflect the views of the funding organizations. The researchers gratefully acknowledge the support.

References

1. Cameron, C.D., Lindquist, K.A., Gray, K.: A constructionist review of morality and emotions: no evidence for specific links between moral content and discrete emotions. Pers. Soc. Psychol. Rev. **19**(4), 371–394 (2015). https://doi.org/10.1177/1088868314566683

2. Adeliyi, O., Adesoba, A., Shaik, M., Agarwal, N.: A multi-method approach to analyze Australia-China geopolitical discourse on YouTube. OSF Preprints (2023). https://doi.org/10.31219/osf.io/pe58w

3. Nandwani, P., Verma, R.: A review on sentiment analysis and emotion detection from text. Soc. Netw. Anal. Min. **11**(1), 1–19 (2021). https://doi.org/10.1007/s13278-021-00776-6

4. Akinnubi, A., Agarwal, N.: Blog data analytics using blogtrackers. SocArXiv (2023). https://doi.org/10.31235/osf.io/497zg

5. Shajari, S., Agarwal, N., Alassad, M.: Commenter behavior characterization on YouTube channels. arXiv (2023). https://doi.org/10.48550/arXiv.2304.07681

6. Gelman, S.A., Roberts, S.O.: How language shapes the cultural inheritance of categories. Proc. Natl. Acad. Sci. **114**(30), 7900–7907 (2017). https://doi.org/10.1073/pnas.1621073114

7. Costa, J.O., Kulkarni, A.: Leveraging knowledge graph for open-domain question answering. In: 2018 IEEE/WIC/ACM International Conference on Web Intelligence (WI) 2018, pp. 389–394. https://doi.org/10.1109/WI.2018.00-63

8. Gentzkow, M., Kelly, B., Taddy, M.: Text as data. J. Econ. Liter. **57**(3), 535–574 (2019). https://doi.org/10.1257/jel.20181020

9. Jain, R., et al.: Explaining sentiment analysis results on social media texts through visualization. Multimed. Tools Appl. **82**, 22613–22629 (2023). https://doi.org/10.1007/s11042-023-14432-y

10. Abdul-Mageed, M., Ungar, L.: EmoNet: fine-grained emotion detection with gated recurrent neural networks. In: Proceedings of the 55th Annual Meeting of the Association for Computational Linguistics (Volume 1: Long Papers), Vancouver, Canada: Association for Computational Linguistics, pp. 718–728. https://doi.org/10.18653/v1/P17-1067

11. https://bigdogdotcom.wordpress.com/2014/04/03/lessons-from-paracels-pt-v-the-panda-trap/

12. https://warontherocks.com/2016/06/can-the-u-s-coast-guard-take-on-the-south-china-sea/

13. Graham, J., et al.: Moral foundations theory: the pragmatic validity of moral pluralism. In: Advances in Experimental Social Psychology, vol. 47, pp. 55–130. Elsevier (2013)

14. Onyepunuka, U., Alassad, M., Nwana, L., Agarwal, N.: Multilingual analysis of YouTube's recommendation system: examining topic and emotion drift in the 'Cheng Ho' narrative (2023)

Gaze-Aware Social Interaction Techniques for Human-Robot Collaborative Shopping

Masaya Iwasaki[1]([✉]), Kosuke Ogawa[2], Tatsuyuki Kawamura[4], and Hideyuki Nakanishi[3]

[1] Graduate School of Engineering Science, Osaka University, Osaka, Japan
iwasaki@irl.sys.es.osaka-u.ac.jp
[2] Graduate School of Engineering, Osaka University, Osaka, Japan
[3] Faculty of Informatics, Kindai University, Osaka, Japan
[4] Consultant, Kyoto, Japan

Abstract. Robots that provide customer service in physical stores are being researched as a means of coexisting with people in everyday situations. One issue with such robots is that their suggestions are usually ignored and may not effectively promote purchasing behavior among customers. This paper aims to investigate whether customers are more likely to accept a robot's suggestion by having the robot use personalized information that can enhance the shopping experience. To investigate the effectiveness of a robot's suggestions, we conducted an experiment in a physical retail store in a real-world environment. The study aimed to encourage customers to pick up products by utilizing their posture information. As a result, the number of customers who picked up the product increased when the robot made suggestions when customers leaned forward to look at the product. This suggests that using a customer's posture information to make suggestions can increase the likelihood of a customer accepting a robot's proposal.

Keywords: Customer Service Robot · Field Experiment · Gaze Awareness · Human-Robot Interaction

1 Introduction

Robots that provide customer service in physical stores have been increasingly utilized to coexist with people in everyday situations. The use of these robots has been expected to reduce labor costs by replacing human salespersons with robots and to provide services such as foreign language assistance and product explanations for foreign tourists. However, the effective utilization of customer service robots for improving sales and promoting products remains unclear, and their potential has yet to be fully realized. One of the reasons for this is that robot suggestions are often ignored and not effectively promoting purchasing behavior among customers. In this study, we aim to explore the potential collaboration between customer service robots and human customers in promoting product sales, investigating effective behaviors for robot suggestions that are more likely to be accepted by customers. As such a proposal, we focused on encouraging customers to pick up a product through the robot's proposal, based on prior research

H. Takada et al. (Eds.): CollabTech 2023, LNCS 14199, pp. 193–200, 2023.
https://doi.org/10.1007/978-3-031-42141-9_16

indicating a higher likelihood of purchase after physically handling a product [1–3]. To encourage customers to pick up a product, we believe that the robot needs to propose it with gaze awareness. The level of attention a customer has towards a product is related to their posture, and we believe that by detecting their posture, we can estimate their level of attention towards the product. Therefore, we aim to investigate whether utilizing personalized information, such as a customer's posture, can enhance their shopping experience and increase the likelihood of accepting a robot's proposal. The purpose of this study is to examine whether using a customer's posture information to make suggestions can increase the probability of a customer accepting a robot's proposal in a physical retail store environment.

2 Related Works

A service robot refers to a robot used in the service industry, excluding industrial robots. Research on service robots includes studies on museum guide robots [4–8], robots used in education settings [9, 10], and robots that perform customer service in hotels and airports [11–13]. Regarding research on customer service robots in retail stores, a study has been conducted where robots were used as salespeople in a shopping mall, providing coupons to increase sales [14]. However, in this study, the robots did not engage with the customers in the store and did not recommend products to them directly. There have been studies on using robots to encourage customers' purchasing behavior, such as those that robotize the product itself and prompt customers to pick it up while it moves [15, 16]. However, since this approach requires robotizing the product itself, it has limitations on applicable products and situations, making it difficult to apply to all products in the store.

3 Experimental Design

3.1 Hypothesis

In this paper, we consider two indicators for estimating attention towards the product: whether the customer is looking at the product and whether they are leaning forward when looking at it. We therefore set the following two hypotheses:

Hypothesis 1: By prompting customers to pick up products while they are looking at them, the number of customers who pick up the products will increase.

Hypothesis 2: By prompting customers to pick up products while they are leaning forward to look at them, the number of customers who pick up the products will increase.

3.2 Conditions

To verify the hypotheses, the following conditions were set: **No gaze awareness condition:** The robot would make a statement "Please try picking up the product" when the distance between the customer and the robot was less than 2 m, as the robot was located approximately 4 m from the store entrance. **Low gaze awareness condition:** When the customer was looking at a product after entering the store, the robot would make a statement "Please try picking up the product that you are looking at now, the [product name]". **High gaze awareness condition:** When the customer was leaning forward to look at a product after entering the store, the robot would make a statement "Please try picking up the product that you are looking at now, the [product name]".

The robot's statements were prepared in Japanese and English, and each condition was performed only once. Some of the customers left the store without meeting the conditions for the robot's statement.

3.3 Experimental Environment

Figure 1 shows the field experiment conducted at "Jintora," a shichimi (Japanese seven-spice) specialty store in a shopping district in Kyoto. This experiment was conducted with the approval of the research ethics committee of our university. Figure 2 is a top-down view of the store where the experiment was conducted, with shelves on both sides. For recording purposes, three obscure recording cameras, one clear recording camera, and one web camera to capture the movement of customers were installed. The clear recording camera was focused on the side of the robot and only recorded the customers who gave consent. Additionally, to enable the experimenters to observe the store during the experiment, a camera for operation was placed behind the robot. In this experiment, Pepper, a humanoid robot, was used as a customer service robot due to its appropriate size and high safety. The experimenter stood at a position where they could see inside the store, observed the store's situation using both camera for operation and naked eye, and operated the robot using a tablet.

3.4 System

Customers' Posture Detection. In this study, we set a condition to make statements when the customer leaned forward while looking at the products. To avoid ambiguity in judging whether the customer took the specified posture or not, we considered the need to use quantitative values for the judgment. Therefore, the customer's posture was determined from the video captured by the webcam using MediaPipe (Fig. 1).

Posture Criteria. We examined the angle (θ) formed between the vector from the waist to the shoulder (A in Fig. 1) and a vertically upward vector (B in Fig. 1) of ten customers who assumed a peering posture before conducting the experiment. Our analysis revealed that a customer was deemed to have assumed a peering posture if the angle θ was 37° or more, which was the average value of all ten customers. In this study, we used the average value as the threshold to detect only those who clearly peered into the display.

4 Results and Discussion

The experiment was conducted for five days in 2022, and 50 groups of customers were served. To exclude groups who left the store quickly, those who spent less than 30 s inside the store were excluded from the analysis, leaving 41 groups for a total of 74 people

Fig. 1. Experimental scene (Left: Customers talking with the robot, Right: posture detection)

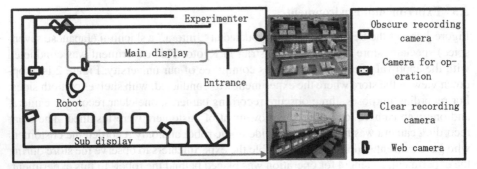

Fig. 2. Layout of the shop with display

(1.8 people/group) as the subject of analysis. Among the 41 groups, 11 groups for a total of 20 participants (1.8 participants/group) in the High gaze awareness condition, 16 groups for a total of 31 participants (1.9 participants/group) in the Low gaze awareness condition, 14 groups for a total of 23 participants in the No gaze awareness condition. The gender distribution of participants in the three conditions was as follows: 5 males and 15 females in the High gaze awareness condition; 13 males and 18 females in the Low gaze awareness condition; and 10 males and 13 females in the No gaze awareness condition. The average time spent in the store was in the High gaze awareness condition was 148 s, 102 s in the Low gaze awareness condition, and 132 s in the No gaze awareness condition. The average time spent looking at the products was 94 s for the High gaze awareness condition, 51 s for the Low gaze awareness condition, and 75 s for the No gaze awareness condition. A total of three people in two groups purchased the recommended product in the High gaze awareness condition, and a total of six people in six groups purchased the recommended product in the Low gaze awareness condition. The wait time from the time the customer entered the store to the time the robot spoke in each condition was 18.9 s in the High gaze awareness condition, 10.1 s in the Low gaze awareness condition, and 18.1 s in the No gaze awareness condition.

The percentage of groups who picked up a product during their store visit for each condition is shown in Fig. 3. From this figure, it was found that 64% of groups served under the high gaze awareness condition picked up a product, while 50% of groups have done so under the low gaze awareness and no gaze awareness conditions. This suggests that serving customers under the high gaze awareness condition is more effective in prompting them to pick up products compared to the other two conditions. However, we did not conduct statistical analysis due to the small sample size in this study.

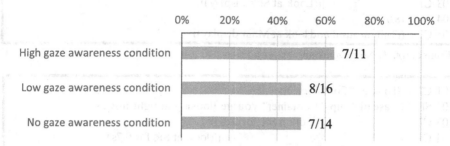

Fig. 3. Percentage of groups who picked up product.

From the perspective of ethnography and conversation analysis, we analyzed the interaction between customers and the robot, examining how the robot's verbal cues at the time when customers showed interest in a product affected their behavior. The interaction was transcribed following the rules below:

(0.0): indicates the length of silence counted in 0.1 s units.
(.): indicates very short silence.
[: indicates the start of overlapping speech or actions by two or more people.
=: indicates that speech continues without interruption.
:: indicates sound stretching, with the number of colons indicating the relative length of the stretching.
(()): notes on actions, gaze, and other nonverbal behaviors.
(h): indicates laughter during speech.

We used the following abbreviations: SR for the robot, and Cx for the customers (with a numerical identifier).

The following are typical examples of customer responses for each condition.

First, an example of a group that responded with no gaze awareness is shown in Transcript 1. Next, an example of a group that responded with low gaze awareness is shown in Transcript 2. Finally, an example of a group that responded with high gaze awareness is shown in Transcript 3.

In Transcript 1, the robot's statement was completely ignored, and the customer did not pick up any products (line 04). On the other hand, in Transcript 2, the customer looked at the robot for a short time (0.8 s), but still did not pick up any products (line 07). Furthermore, as shown in Fig. 3, there was no significant difference in the number of groups who picked up products between the no gaze awareness and low gaze awareness conditions. Therefore, it is possible that the robot's suggestions were not being considered under both conditions. The reason for this could be that most of the

```
01 Cl      ((Move to the center of the store while looking at the main display))
02 SR    Please take the [product in your hands!
03 Cl                      [((Look at Sub display))
04         (8.0)
05 Cl    ((Turn around and look at Main display))
```

Transcript. 1. No gaze awareness condition

```
01 C2    ((Look at "Container"))
02 SR    Please pick up ["Container" you are [looking at right now.=
03 C2                    [((look at SR for 0.8s))
04 C3                                           [((look at SR for 0.7s))
05 C3    =huhuhuhu
06 C2    Thank you.
07 C2    ((Move to Entrance))
```

Transcript. 2. Low gaze awareness condition

```
01 C4    ((Look at "Ichimi"))
02       (5.0)
03 C4    ((Approaching Main display and look into "Ichimi"))
04 SR    Please pick up ["Ichimi" you are looking at right now.
05 C4                  [((look at SR for 3.6s))
06 SR    ((Return her gaze to "Ichimi"))
07 SR    ((Pick up "Ichimi"))
```

Transcript. 3. High gaze awareness condition

customers were always looking at products in the store after they entered, and the robot's statement came when they were already looking at a product, regardless of the condition. Furthermore, in the example shown in Transcript 3, unlike the examples shown in Transcript 1 and Transcript 2, the robot did not make any statements while the customers were just standing and looking at the products. Instead, the robot made a statement when the customers approached the product shelf and peered in. As a result, the customers looked at the robot for a longer time of 3.6 s compared to the other two conditions, and they listened to the robot's statement, ultimately picking up the product (lines 06–07). Previous research [17] suggests that the longer the eye contact between customers and robots, the higher the level of social presence, which indicates the extent to which social interaction with another person is perceived. In previous studies [18], participants who looked at the robot for 1.0 s or more were defined as the sustained attention group, and the social presence of the robot was investigated. Therefore, the same analysis was conducted in this study. As a result, as shown in Fig. 4, the proportion in the high gaze awareness condition was higher than the other two conditions, indicating that the social presence of the robot was enhanced in the high gaze awareness condition compared to the other two conditions. Based on these findings, it can be considered that by making a statement when the customers were in the posture of peering at the products, the robot's social presence was strengthened, leading the customers to accept the robot's statement and pick up the product.

In this study, several limitations were encountered. Firstly, the sample size in this experiment was relatively small. Moreover, the analysis primarily focused on multimodal conversation analysis and behavioral analysis, which limited to investigate customers' impressions. Additionally, the majority of participants were Japanese, and we were unable to explore the impact of cultural differences.

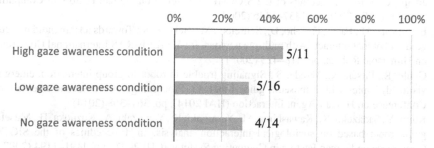

Fig. 4. Percentage of groups who looked at the robot for a long period.

5 Conclusion

In this study, we aimed to investigate whether a customer service robot can promote purchasing behavior by encouraging customers to pick up products through gaze awareness based on their level of attention towards the products. To this end, we conducted an experiment in an actual store, where the robot was used to encourage customers to pick up products. The results showed that the statements made by the robot when customers leaned forward to look at the products enhances the robot's social presence, making its suggestions more easily accepted, resulting in customers picking up the products. This suggests that customer service robots can effectively use customers' personalized information to make proposals that are well received, ultimately promoting purchasing behavior.

Acknowledgments. We would like to express our gratitude to everyone at Jintora, a specialized Shichimi shop, for generously providing us with the experimental space. This research project was supported by JSPS KAKENHI Grant Numbers JP19H00605, JP19K21718, JP18KK0053, JP20H01585, JP22K18548 and Artificial Intelligence Research Promotion Foundation.

References

1. Peck, J., Shu, S.B.: The effect of mere touch on perceived ownership. J. Consum. Res. **36**(3), 434–447 (2009)
2. Reb, J., Connolly, T.: Possession, feelings of ownership and the endowment effect. Judgment Decis. Mak. **2**(2), 107–114 (2023). https://doi.org/10.1017/S1930297500000085

3. Wolf, J.R., Arkes, H.R., Muhanna, W.A.: The power of touch: an examination of the effect of duration of physical contact on the valuation of objects. Judgm. Decis. Mak. **3**(6), 476–482 (2008). https://doi.org/10.1017/S193029750000005X

4. Yamazaki, A., Yamazaki, K., Kuno, Y., Burdelski, M., Kawashima, M., Kuzuoka, H.: Precision timing in human-robot interaction: coordination of head movement and utterance. In: Proceedings of the SIGCHI Conference on Human Factors in Computing Systems (CHI 2008), pp. 131–140 (2008)

5. Yamazaki, K., et al.: Revealing gaugian: engaging visitors in robot guide's explanation in art museum. In: Proceedings of the SIGCHI Conference on Human Factors in Computing Systems (CHI 2009), pp. 1437–1446 (2009)

6. Bennewitz, M., Faber, F., Joho, D., Schreiber, M., Behnke, S.: Towards a Humanoid museum guide robot that interacts with multiple persons. In: 5th IEEE-RAS International Conference on Humanoid Robots, pp. 418–423 (2005)

7. Gehle, R., Pitsch, K., Wrede, S.: Signaling trouble in robot-to-group interaction. emerging visitor dynamics with a museum guide robot. In: Proceedings of the Second International Conference on Human-Agent Interaction (HAI 2014), pp. 361–368 (2014)

8. Kuno, Y., Sadazuka, K., Kawashima, M., Yamazaki, K., Yamazaki, A., Kuzuoka, H.: Museum guide robot based on sociological interaction analysis. In: Proceedings of the SIGCHI Conference on Human Factors in Computing Systems (CHI 2007), pp. 1191–1194 (2007)

9. Tanaka, F., Isshiki, K., Takahashi, F., Uekusa, M., Sei, R., Hayashi, K.: Pepper learns together with children: development of an educational application. Humanoid Robots (Humanoids). In: 2015 IEEE-RAS 15th International Conference on Humanoid Robots (Humanoids), pp. 270–275 (2015)

10. Saerbeck, M., Schut, T., Bartneck, C., Janse, M.D.: Expressive robots in education: Varying the degree of social supportive behavior of a robotic tutor. In: Proceedings of the SIGCHI Conference on Human Factors in Computing Systems (CHI 2010), pp. 1613–1622 (2010)

11. Nakanishi, J., Kuramoto, I., Baba, J., Kohei, O., Yoshikawa, Y., Ishiguro, H.: Can a Humanoid Robot Engage in Heartwarming Interaction Service at a Hotel? In: Proceedings of the 6th International Conference on Human-Agent Interaction (HAI 2018), pp. 45–53 (2018)

12. Heerink, M., Krose, B., Evers, V., Wielinga, B.: Influence of social presence on acceptance of an assistive social robot and screen agent by elderly users. Adv. Robot. **23**(14), 1909–1923 (2009)

13. Kim, S., Kim, J., Badu-Baiden, F., Giroux, M., Choi, Y.: Preference for robot service or human service in hotels? Impacts of the COVID-19 pandemic. Int. J. Hospital. Manage. **93** (2021)

14. Shiomi, M., et al.: Recommendation effects of a social robot for advertisement-use context in a shopping mall. Int. J. Soc. Robot. **5**(2), 251–262 (2013). https://doi.org/10.1007/s12369-013-0180-4

15. Iwamoto, T., et al.: The effectiveness of self-recommending agents in advancing purchase behavior steps in retail marketing. In: HRI 2021: Proceedings of the 9th International Conference on Human-Agent Interaction, pp. 209–217 (2021)

16. Iwamoto, T., Baba, J., Nakanishi, J., Hyodo, K., Yoshikawa, Y., Ishiguro, H.: Playful recommendation: sales promotion that robots stimulate pleasant feelings instead of product explanation. IEEE Robot. Autom. Let. **17**(4), 11815–11822 (2022)

17. Iwasaki, M., Ikeda, M., Kawamura, T., Nakanishi, H.: State-transition modeling of human–robot interaction for easy crowdsourced robot control. Sensors **20**(22) (2020)

18. Iwasaki, M., et al.: Enabling shared attention with customers strengthens a sales robot's social presence. In: HAI 2022: Proceedings of the 10th International Conference on Human-Agent Interaction, pp. 176–184 (2022)

Preliminary Study on Speaker Intimacy Focusing on Topic Continuity

Takuto Miura(✉) and Hideaki Kanai

Japan Advanced Institute of Science and Technology, 1-1 Asahidai, Nomi, Ishikawa, Japan
{s2210162,hideaki}@jaist.ac.jp

Abstract. In recent years, several studies have been conducted to estimate and quantify speaker intimacy based on information obtained from dialogue to improve the usability of dialogue systems. These studies have identified linguistic features (e.g., the presence or absence of honorifics) that contribute to estimating speaker intimacy. However, because these features can only superficially recognize intimacy, intimacy estimation based solely on these features may be less robust. Therefore, this study searched for features that could capture speaker intimacy without being limited by factors such as speaker attributes. In particular, we focused on topic continuity based on the similarity of topics between utterances rather than on-topic content. The results suggest that these features contribute to the estimation of speaker intimacy.

Keywords: Conversation Analysis · Intimacy · Topic Continuity

1 Introduction

In recent years, non-task-oriented dialogue systems, where the user and system interact freely, have attracted much attention. These dialogue systems are expected to be used continuously by users and are required to maintain and build long-term relationships with them. Humans and systems must conduct social conversations that consider the sense of intimacy with the user to establish and maintain long-term relationships [1]. However, existing dialogue systems do not recognize the intimacy that users experience with the system. If the system cannot recognize the intimacy of a user with the system, the system will not notice the user's intention to become intimate with the system, discouraging the user. In addition, the system may not be aware of the user's intention to reject intimacy, and the system may overstep its bounds. The system must quantify and recognize the current level of intimacy with the user to establish and maintain an intimate relationship with a user through conversations [1].

Therefore, we aimed to develop a method for estimating a speaker's intimacy with their partner in a human-to-human dialogue. As a preliminary study of the method, we searched for and analyzed features that could contribute to the method of estimating the level of speaker intimacy in dialogues and verified their significance. We focused on features related to topic continuity based on a study that suggested a significant relationship between speaker intimacy and the total number of utterances on the same

H. Takada et al. (Eds.): CollabTech 2023, LNCS 14199, pp. 201–208, 2023.
https://doi.org/10.1007/978-3-031-42141-9_17

topic [2]. One-on-one dialogue induces spontaneity in the speaker. Human-to-human dialogue induces dialogue that considers the social and psychological distance from the other person that humans implicitly engage. We observed such dialogues to develop a dialogue system that could generate human-like behavior and responses.

Section 2 discusses the related studies and summarizes their positions. Section 3 describes the method for quantifying the features we focus on, and Sect. 4 describes the analysis of the constructed elements. Section 5 describes and discusses the analysis results, and Sect. 6 concludes the paper.

2 Related Studies

2.1 Intimacy Estimation

Various methods have been studied to estimate speaker intimacy in dialogue [3, 4].

Chiba et al. identified useful features from linguistic, prosodic, and visual information in dialogue and implemented a speaker intimacy estimation method using these features [4]. Specifically, the statistical parameters of the features obtained from the dialogue were compared to identify valuable features for estimating speaker intimacy. Subsequently, they proposed a model for estimating speaker intimacy by observing multiple utterances. In this study, an analysis of the relationship between speaker intimacy and linguistic features showed that the presence or absence of honorifics and the number and ratio of questions were text-based features associated with speaker intimacy.

However, there are cases in which honorifics are used even in intimate relationships, such as when the relationship is between an older and a younger person who is an intimate friend. Furthermore, while honorifics may help discriminate between non-intimate and intimate speakers, they may be challenging to discriminate between low- and high-intimacy speakers in intimate speakers. In addition, the number and ratio of questions the speaker asks may be influenced not only by factors related to intimacy with the partner but also by those related to the degree of interest in the partner and the topic. To summarize, linguistic features, such as the presence or absence of honorifics and the number and ratio of questions, can only superficially capture speaker intimacy. Therefore, a method for estimating speaker intimacy based solely on these linguistic features is less robust.

2.2 Intimacy and Topic Continuity

A study investigating speaker intimacy and dialogue suggested a significant relationship between speaker intimacy and the total number of utterances on the same topic [2]. The significance test results in this study indicate that, in a non-task-oriented conversation without an objective, the higher the speaker intimacy, the higher the number of utterances, and the lower the speaker intimacy, the lower the number of utterances.

Therefore, this study focused on the continuity of topics during dialogue and created an index related to the similarity of topics between the current and previous utterances. Topic continuity is a feature of the dialogue structure defined unintentionally by speakers. Therefore, unlike superficial linguistic features, such as the presence or absence of honorifics or the number and ratio of questions, which are easily controlled by the speaker's intentions, they can help estimate speaker intimacy.

3 Creation of Indicators

In this study, indicators of topic continuity were developed based on the similarity between words in an utterance, defined as follows. We decided to use Word2Vec [5], a method for learning word-word relationships based on the probability of occurrence of a word and its surrounding words in text data and assigning a feature vector to each word for topic identification. Figure 1 shows the process of calculating topic continuity. The indicator extracts words from an utterance in a dialogue (0.), calculates the word similarity (1.) and the average of the calculated similarities (2.), and sets a threshold to count topic continuity (3.).

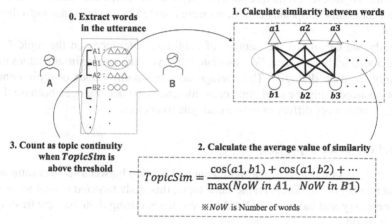

Fig. 1. Process of calculating topic continuity.

Similarly, indicators for topic leaps were developed. Topic leaps have a contrasting relationship with topic continuity regarding the dialogue structure. This study is expected to contribute to estimating speaker intimacy and topic continuity. Counting topic leaps involves changing the threshold and its greater or lesser relationship in Step 3 of Fig. 1.

3.1 Indicators for Topic Continuity

First, to avoid using words unrelated to the topic, the parts of speech used to create the indicators of topic continuity were set in advance. It is necessary to focus on specialized words because finding unique features in an utterance is necessary for topic identification. By contrast, words that appear everywhere and are generic are unlikely to express the characteristics of the utterance for topic identification. Therefore, the parts of speech used were common and proper nouns.

The similarity between all pairs of words in one utterance and those in others was calculated for adjacent utterances in the dialogue. The average similarity between all word pairs was calculated as the topic similarity for the adjacent utterance (1.). The similarity between words was calculated based on the cosine similarity of the word-embedding vectors derived using Word2Vec [5]. We pre-trained Word2Vec using the skip-gram model for the full text of Japanese Wikipedia. This Word2Vec returns a 300-dimensional word-embedding vector for the word-token input.

$$TopicSim = \frac{\sum_a^A \sum_b^B cos(w_a, w_b)}{max(A, B)} \qquad (1)$$

where A: Number of words in one utterance.

B: Number of words in another utterance.

w_q: Feature vectors for the q th word.

$cos(r, s)$: cosine similarity between r and s.

The topic similarity threshold was set. When the similarity between adjacent utterances in a dialogue exceeded a threshold, the topic was counted as a continuation (defined as "topic continuity"). Speaker comments were counted as one utterance until they were replaced.

Finally, we calculated the number of continued utterances on the topic for each topic included in the dialogue. We calculated the average and maximum values of topic continuity for each dialogue. The average and maximum values of topic continuity were normalized using the total number of utterances in each dialogue because the total number of utterances differs from one dialogue to another.

3.2 Indicators for Topic Leap

Based on studies that suggested a significant relationship between speaker intimacy and the total number of utterances on the same topic, this study targeted indicators related to topic continuity and indicators related to topic leaps during dialogue, contrasting with topic continuity.

We performed the same process as in "topic continuity." We counted a topic leap (defined as "topic leap") when the similarity of the topic between adjacent utterances in

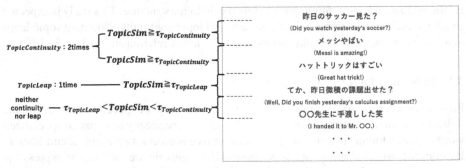

Fig. 2. Example of how topic continuity and topic leap are counted in a dialogue. $\tau_{TopicContinuity}$ is the threshold set for counting topic continuity. $\tau_{TopicLeap}$ is the threshold set for counting topic leaps. Up to the third utterance, $TopicSim$ is higher than $\tau_{TopicContinuity}$, so it is counted as topic continuity; between the third and fourth utterances, $TopicSim$ is lower than $\tau_{TopicLeap}$, so it is counted as a topic leap. Between the fourth and fifth utterances, $TopicSim$ is lower than $\tau_{TopicContinuity}$ and is higher than $\tau_{TopicLeap}$. Thus, it is not counted as either topic continuity or topic leap.

dialogue was less than a threshold value. The number of topic leaps for each dialogue was calculated. The sum of the leaps and minimal topic similarity for each dialogue was calculated. As in "topic continuity," the total number of topic leaps was normalized using the total number of utterances in the dialogue.

Figure 2 shows how topic continuity and leaps are counted in a dialogue.

4 Analysis

Using the average and maximum values of topic continuity, the sum of a topic leaps, and the minimum value of topic similarity described in the previous section, we tested the significant relationships between speaker intimacy and topic continuity and between speaker intimacy and topic leap. Welch's t-test, a type of t-test without correspondence between two countries, was used as the test method. The significance level for all tests was set at 5%. The corpus used for the test was the BTSJ-Japanese Natural Conversation Corpus with Transcripts and Recordings (March 2021) [6]. This is a natural conversation corpus for Japanese people without prior scenarios. We extracted and analyzed chat dialogues between the two speakers from this corpus. Table 1 presents the statistics of the data used in the tests. We used dialogues in which the speakers had never met each other before as dialogues between non-intimate speakers (defined as "non-intimate dialogues"). We used dialogues in which the speakers were acquaintances, such as friends and family members, as dialogues between intimate speakers (defined as "intimate dialogues"). Because [4] defined the relationship between intimate and non-intimate speakers according to whether the speakers met each other, we decided to describe the relationship between intimate and non-intimate speakers similarly.

Table 1. Number of dialogues and the total number of utterances in the test corpus.

	Non-intimate	Intimate	Sum
Number of Dialogues	85	71	156
Number of utterances	30,707	33,552	64,259

5 Results and Discussion

5.1 Analysis of Topic Continuity

The threshold of topic similarity for counting adjacent utterances in a dialogue as topic continuity was set from 0.1 to 0.9 and nine tests were performed in increments of 0.1. Table 2 presents the p-values derived from the test. Only the threshold value for which a significant difference was found in either the average or maximum value is listed.

As summarized in Table 2, when the topic similarity threshold was set to 0.2, there was a significant difference in the average and maximum values of topic continuity

Table 2. Topic continuity test results: Significant differences are indicated with +, while no significant differences are indicated with -.

Threshold	Average	Maximum	Tendency
0.1	0.012 (+)	0.118 (-)	non-intimacy
0.2	0.017 (+)	0.008 (+)	non-intimacy
0.8	0.027 (+)	0.155 (-)	intimacy
0.9	0.017 (+)	0.321 (-)	intimacy

between non-intimate and intimate dialogues. Furthermore, non-intimate dialogues tend to show more topic continuity than intimate dialogues.

When the topic similarity threshold was set to 0.8, there was a significant difference only in the average topic continuity between the non-intimate and intimate dialogues. Furthermore, in contrast to the threshold value of 0.2, the results suggest that topics tend to have more continuity in intimate dialogues than in non-intimate ones.

These results are based on topic similarity, which in turn is based on the similarity between words, and is likely related to the concreteness of the content. For instance, concerning "Atlantic," "pelagic," and "hydrosphere" for "Pacific," while "Pacific" is a concrete word and is highly relevant to "Atlantic," the similarity with other words may not be as high as that between "Pacific" and "Atlantic." By contrast, concerning "Atlantic," "pelagic," and "hydrosphere" for "ocean," "ocean" is a more abstract word than "Pacific." Although it is likely to be similar to all words to some extent, their similarity is not as high as between "Pacific" and "Atlantic." This suggests that more abstract topics are more likely to continue among non-intimate speakers, whereas more concrete topics are more likely to continue among intimate speakers. In a dialogue between non-intimate speakers, basic information such as hometown and age is not shared; thus, they continue to speak about abstract topics. By contrast, in a dialogue between intimate speakers, the aforementioned basic information is already shared among them; thus, they continue to speak about concrete topics, such as common hobbies and jobs.

Consequently, features related to topic continuity are expected to contribute to speaker intimacy estimation. In addition, it is possible to create features with different significance levels by creating the same features with different topic similarity thresholds.

5.2 Analysis of Topic Leap

The threshold of topic similarity for counting adjacent utterances in a dialogue as a topic leap was set from 0.09 to 0.01, and nine tests were performed in increments of 0.01. Table 3 presents the p-values derived from the test. Only the threshold value for which a significant difference was found in either the sum of topic leaps or minimum topic similarity is listed.

As summarized in Table 3, when the topic similarity threshold was set to 0.04, there was a significant difference between non-intimate and intimate dialogues regarding the sum of topic leaps and the minimum topic similarity. Furthermore, the results suggest

Table 3. Topic leap test results: Significant differences are indicated with +, while no significant differences are indicated with -.

Threshold	Sum	Minimum	Tendency
0.04	0.033 (+)	0.006 (+)	intimacy

intimate dialogues are more leap-forward than non-intimate ones. Consequently, features related to topic leaps are expected to contribute to the estimation of speaker intimacy.

Based on tests of topic continuity and topic leap, non-intimate dialogues are more likely to continue on the topic of abstract content and are less likely to leap than intimate dialogues. Intimate dialogues are more likely to continue the topic of concrete content than non-intimate dialogues. In a dialogue between non-intimate speakers, topics tend to develop in a chain based on current topics. By contrast, in a dialogue between intimate speakers, they speak about topics they both know with specific details. Otherwise, the trend is for topic development to leap forward to topics irrelevant to the current topic.

6 Conclusion

In this study, we found possibilities for continuity features or leaps in topics based on topic similarities between adjacent utterances in the dialogue. Significant difference tests indicated that these features differed significantly between dialogues between intimate speakers and those between non-intimate speakers, suggesting that they could contribute to speaker intimacy estimation.

The discussion in this paper suggests that speaker intimacy can be recognized based on the characteristics of topic development. This can help realize a model of a dialogue system that adjusts topic development to improve user intimacy. For example, we attempted to form and maintain user intimacy by designing a model architecture that encourages users who have just started using a dialogue system to switch topics regularly. For a heavy user of a dialogue system, we attempt to improve intimacy by designing a model architecture that continues topics frequently discussed with the user and encourages quick leaps from rarely discussed topics. Through this design, we develop a dialogue system that is comfortable for users regarding psychological distance, including intimacy, and to achieve a dialogue system that encourages long-term use by users.

Future work should include applying state-of-the-art methods for topic modeling and measuring the similarity between utterances. In recent years, methods such as BERT [8] based on Transformer [7], a large-scale language model, have produced innovative performance. We expect to obtain more valuable results by applying these methods to implement topic continuity and leaps. As this study aimed to analyze conversational tendencies and other preliminary studies, Word2Vec, which has a low implementation cost, was used to implement topic modeling and measure the similarity between utterances. In addition, to further generalize the analysis results, future works may include enriching the dialogue data by diversifying the target language and speaker attributes, for example, using other corpora created by other organizations or by creating original corpora through subject experiments.

References

1. Kidd, C.D., Breazeal, C.: Robots at home: Understanding long-term human-robot interaction. In: Proceedings of International Conference on Intelligent Robots and Systems, pp. 3230–3235 (2008)
2. Ura, M., Kuwanara, T., Nishida, K.: A qualitative analysis of conversation in social interaction. Japan. J. Experim. Soc. Psychol. **29**(3), 1–14 (1990). https://doi.org/10.2130/jjesp.29.3_1
3. Pei, J., Jurgens, D.: Quantifying intimacy in language. In: Proceedings of the 2020 Conference on Empirical Methods in Natural Language Processing (EMNLP), pp. 5307–5326, Online. Association for Computational Linguistics (2020)
4. Chiba, Y., Yamazaki, Y., Ito, A.: Speaker intimacy in chat-talks: analysis and recognition based on verbal and non-verbal information. In: Proceedings of the 25th Workshop on the Semantics and Pragmatics of Dialogue, September 20–22, 2021, Potsdam/The Internet
5. Mikolov, T., Sutskever, I., Chen, K., Corrado, G., Dean, J.: Distributed representations of words and phrases and their compositionality. In: Proceedings of the 26th International Conference on Neural Information Processing Systems - Volume 2 (NIPS 2013), pp. 3111–3119. Curran Associates Inc., Red Hook, NY, USA (2013)
6. Usami, M. (ed.): BTSJ-Japanese Natural Conversation Corpus with Transcripts and Recordings (March 2021), NINJAL Institute-based projects: Multiple Approaches to Analyzing the Communication of Japanese Language Learners (2021)
7. Ashish, V., et al.: Attention is all you need. Adv. Neural Inform. Process. Syst. **30** (2017)
8. Devlin, J., Chang, M., Lee, K., Toutanova, K.: BERT: pre-training of deep bidirectional transformers for language understanding. In: Proceedings of the 2019 Conference of the North American Chapter of the Association for Computational Linguistics: Human Language Technologies (Volume 1 Long and Short Papers), pp. 4171–4186 (2019)

Reshaping Group Life: A Transparent and Interpretable Reward Model to Enhance Fairness in Groups

Jia-Wei Liang[✉][iD] and Hao-Chuan Wang[iD]

University of California, Davis, CA 95616, USA
jwlliang@ucdavis.edu

Abstract. Groups can do better than individuals through two mechanisms: aggregation and synergy. Aggregation means bringing knowledge together, and synergy means increasing the effectiveness that comes about through joint action or cooperation. However, we usually measure a group's effectiveness by productivity outcome but disregard the other critical aspects, specifically the experiences and sustainability of the team: does the group member feel fair? Without the sense of fairness, group members do not have a clear metric on how their contributions lead to rewards, and may gradually lose the motivation to engage and contribute. Groups can suffer both in terms of aggregation and synergy. Our goal in this work-in-progress paper is to formulate a user-interpretable and -transparent reward model to operationalize fairness in groups. We apply the model to design a workload tracking dashboard for group members to view and negotiate individual workloads transparently, and to improve fairness both in group procedure and outcome.

Keywords: Group Work · Group Fairness · Fairness Interface Design

1 Introduction

Human work is oftentimes bonded with groups. Many of the past studies have been looking into how group work may benefit individuals by complementing individuals' insufficient resources and capabilities, stimulating interpersonal discussions and inspiring new ideas beyond what separate individuals can think of, as well as all different types of tasks where working in groups can shine [1]. Johnson and Johnson's 5 elements of collaboration [2] share the same concept, and they distinguish group collaboration (work together on a shared goal) from cooperation (ask others for help to achieve individual goals); however, these elements are difficult to measure.

In addition, previous studies have surprisingly yet repeatedly found that although individuals tend to believe in the additional values and effectiveness that group collaboration might offer, the actual productivity gain out of collaboration could be limiting, depending on numerous factors related to the collaborative process and contexts [3].

ⓒ The Author(s), under exclusive license to Springer Nature Switzerland AG 2023
H. Takada et al. (Eds.): CollabTech 2023, LNCS 14199, pp. 209–216, 2023.
https://doi.org/10.1007/978-3-031-42141-9_18

Productivity loss [4], the scenario where the group cannot live up to its full potential due to incidents such as social pressure (individual influences by group), social loafing (group degrades individual's motivation)and production blocking(group blocks individual from offering ideas) [5] can be solved by enhancing individuals' group experience, and fairness plays a crucial role in it [6].

Past studies have been looking into the relations between the outcome of group work and the interaction among group members, such as how frequency and mode of communication impact productivity [7]. However, how interaction impacts fairness in groups, such as understanding each members' value and assigning roles based on agreed terms, as well as how to improve equity among group members are usually disregarded.

A group can only sustain when individuals feel fair about their interactions and collaborations with other members of the group, and only when a group is sustainable, then group effectiveness matters.

Fairness, as perceived by people in their minds and materialized as rules and policies in the world, help prevent the marginalization of individuals interacting with one another within the group, and with people outside of the group. This can lead to a more inclusive, equitable and diverse group working process, which in return can bring better outcomes.

In this work-in-progress paper, we want to propose a socially-transparent interface design for groups, of which the goal is to support fairness-driven collaborations and negotiations in a team. Making the processes of group work transparent and trustworthy is a key factor leading to outcome fairness.

2   Dimensions of Fairness

Speaking of fairness, it has been a topic that intrigues researchers spanning across different communities for a long time. In the study of fair division problems, researchers have been seeking for solutions to achieve the optimal split in resource distribution. The classic cake-cutting algorithm aims to find the perfect unbiased cut. The protocol allows one person to cut the cake into two slices that he or she values equally, and the other person gets the right to pick first [8].

However, these protocols only apply when an object can be clearly quantified, and they usually only works well in a small group. In real life, there are things like *work*, which is difficult to be divided, and the group is usually filled with complicated interest individuals.

Traditional notion of fairness, *the outcome fairness*, focuses on studying the result of joint decisions, considering if the distributions of outcomes are fair or equitable analytically. However, people started to concern not only about the fairness of outcomes, but also the fairness of the process that determine these outcomes. This is how the notion of *procedural fairness* was brought up. Procedural fairness speaks to the idea of fair processes, and how people's perception of fairness in the procedure (e.g., transparency in information and decision making) is strongly impacted by the quality of their experiences of participation and not the end result of these experiences [9]. When procedural fairness is perceived high, people tends to respond more positively on the outcome fairness [10,11].

People are influenced by procedural fairness because it addresses more symbolic and psychological concerns, such as people's needs for self-esteem, self-identity, and affiliation. In a group, decisions made in group collaboration process can have a significant impact on individuals in at least two ways. First, fairness in the decision itself (e.g., what action to take next as a group) can promote trust and cooperation among group members. Second, when individuals feel that their opinions and perspectives are being heard and considered, they are more likely to contribute to the decision-making process and support the final outcome. This is in consistent with Cronin's concept of respect importance in collaborative work [12].

Fairness or *treatment quality* is the key to enhance the effectiveness of work groups and teams. Its importance is even beyond the authority-subordinate relationship [13], cultural diversity, behavioral and cognitive engagement [14]. It can lead to increased productivity, creativity, and satisfaction in a group.

3   Fairness in Group Work

We first consider a hypothetical scenario: "What happens to a hardworking individual in a group that fails to deliver?". It is similar to the notion of *fairness gerrymandering*, in which a classifier appears to be fair on each individual group (a social group in our discussed question), but may badly violate the fairness constraint on one or more structured subgroups (a hardworking individual in our discussed question) [15].

Group fairness traditionally deals with statistical parity among social collectives (e.g., departments and parties). However, when considering fairness in group work, we focus instead on individual fairness in a group context, which ensure individuals share similar working and collaborating conditions receive similar outcomes or rewards.

The input-process-output model of group work [23] is one of the ways to conceptualize the impact of fairness in a group. It identifies the inputs, outputs, and required processing tasks to transform inputs into outputs. It shows the success of a group (its outcome) depends upon inputs or resources which the group has to work with, and the interaction among group members. Research on the psychological experience of fairness suggests that it is a basic form of social evaluation that emerges in interactions with group members and it plays an important role in shaping not only engagement in group life but also in the well-being of individual group members [17]. Unfair treatment can lead to feelings that one is devalued and excluded from the group [18]. It can also lead to disengagement which has the potential to negatively affect a group's outcome including productivity and turnover [19].

In a work group, defining, communicating and grounding what's considered fair among group members is of utmost importance [16]. Relational model also suggest that people's social psychological needs are likely to be satisfied when they interact with others who behave according to the norm of fairness [22]. Moreover, fairness asymmetry [20], which indicates the negative effects of unfairness are substantially stronger than the positive effects of fairness, and social comparisons [21], which means human not only react to their own situation but also others' situations whom we use as references (group members) to compare ourselves with, enlarge these negative feelings.

Developing a group fairness metric can be challenging since fairness is an abstract and potentially sensitive concept that can involve different perspectives and interpretations; however, since fairness perceptions are transferable, we should not neglect its important role in a group and will need to find ways to support the construction and negotiation of fairness norms in groups.

4   Reward Model to Operationalize Fairness in Groups

When people assess the success of a group, it is intuitive to define it in terms of production; however, as discussed in previous sections, it does not take into account how individual members contribute to the work and the rewards received relatively. In our proposed model, we want to make sure we calculate each individuals' contribution, and their corresponding reward.

For simplicity, we assume group reward and individual reward are combined as *Reward*, and we try to draw the group's behavior in a graph as in Fig. 1. The reward in the Y-axis means the outcome or result of an individual's hard work, and the contribution in the X-axis means the time and effort an individual spent. The group behavior, no matter how big or small the group is, will look something not too far away from this graph.

In Fig. 1, the blue line indicates the ideal case where an individual's reward grows correspondingly with their contributions. How many percentage of hard work one puts in result in the same percentage of reward that he or she should get. Whereas the green line represents the real world case, indicating when an individual works "sufficiently" (not making most of the group members unsatisfied), he or she will get a full reward like others for the joint work. We assume this turning point to be 50%, but this number would need further verification.

Our new model aims to provide a result that can possibly fit the gray dotted line. It is an outcome that improved from the current state and is close to the ideal. Before reaching the turning point, an individual has to work hard to gain their reward and trust in the group, and while putting more contributions in, the reward grows faster. Based on our model, we want to propose a transparent interface to facilitate group work, a tool to support negotiations among group members.

Inspired by McGhee's Efficiency Gap [25], we want to use the same concept to identify if the two individuals unfairly assigned their task. The Efficiency Gap is the model that provides a magnitude of divergence between two parties. The original formula is often used in election cases, where people want to see if gerrymandering exists.

The idea behind the formula is that in a hypothetical map with perfect partisan symmetry, both parties would waste the same number of votes. Therefore, a large difference between the parties' wasted vote indicates one party istreated more favorably than the other. An efficiency gap above 7% or below -7% will be considered gerrymandered. The Math formula is as follow:

$$\frac{\text{A's surplus vote + A's lost votes - (B's surplus votes + B's lost votes)}}{\text{total number of votes}}$$

.

The formula calculated the difference between parties' respective wasted votes, divided by the total number of votes in the state. We want to expand it and use the idea of *wasted workload* as a measurement of group fairness.

wasted workload implies an individual do more than what he or she should be doing in a group. They get the same reward as other group members but their contribution is much more. In this case, their extra workload is not counted (wasted). We can calculated the wasted workload by group's peer evaluation result.

Assume there are n people in a group, with each individuals being assigned a number $n_1, n_2...n_n$. The final grade of this group is G, and $g = \frac{G}{n}$ can be simply think of as the individual's minimum contribution in order to reach group fairness.

If the peer evaluation scores they got accordingly are $E_1, E_2...E_n$, then the wasted workload of each individual will be $g - E_1, g - E_2...g - E_n$.

We can then transform McGhee's formula into a indicator *Workload Efficiency Gap* to see if any of the two individuals in a group contribute similarly. For example, if we want to see whether n_1 and n_2 is performing equally, we can use the following formula:

$$c_{1,2} = \frac{(g - E_1) - (g - E_2)}{\text{total points G}}$$

and

$$c_{2,3} = \frac{(g - E_2) - (g - E_3)}{\text{total points G}}$$

and so forth

The $\frac{4}{5}$ or 80% rule [24] is one of the common metrics when defining fairness. It indicates the selection rate of any group should not be less than $\frac{4}{5}$ of the group with the highest selection rate. Continuing with this concept, we know that c should be less than $\frac{1}{5}$ or 20% since it calculated the wasted workload.

5   Application on the Workload Efficiency Dashboard

The primary goal of the *Workload Efficiency Dashboard* design is to provide a workload display that's transparent and intelligible for all users to enhance perceived fairness of the procedure. The initial design of our interface is illustrated

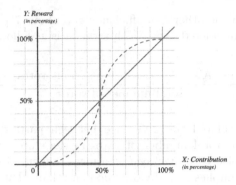

Fig. 1. The blue line is the ideal which means contribution and award grow simultaneously. The green line is more like the reality where if an individual does not perform too unacceptable, they will get the full reward (the percentage will be later confirmed with user study). The gray dotted line will be what our design wants to achieve. (Color figure online)

in Fig. 2. On the left hand side of the interface, it shows all members from the group, n_1, n_2...to n_n, and their peer evaluation scores, E_1, E_2... to E_n. Since there are 4 people in the group (Group A), $g = 100/4 = 25$ is a fair division on how much effort (or equivalent score) one should contribute in a group.

On the right hand side, it shows a time frame of when this score is evaluated so an individual can adjust their behavior in the next time frame, or the group members can discuss and reassign work. The workload efficiency gap calculation is based on the formula we mentioned in Sect. 4.

In Fig. 2, we show an example of reviewing n_2 and n_3. Since their score are $E_2 = 15$ and $E_3 = 20$ accordingly, we can calculate the workload efficiency gap as:

$$c_{2,3} = \frac{(g - E_1) - (g - E_2)}{\text{total points G}} = \frac{(25 - 15) - (25 - 20)}{100} = 5\%$$

The 5% gap indicates that there is an unfairness work distribution among n_2 and n_3. However, it is less than 20% so the unfairness is not that severe. n_2 in the next evaluation time frame should work harder to close the gap.

This interface can act as an agent for group members to motivate oneself or to re-negotiate the work allocation with other group members.

6   Limitation and Future Work

In our work-in-progress paper, we present an initial analysis of the reward model and the application on interface design by assuming (1) individuals in a group to share similar backgrounds; however, culture or gender are other important factors that might affect individual's behavior in a group, and (2) group fairness indicates dividing the workload equally for all group members; however, people

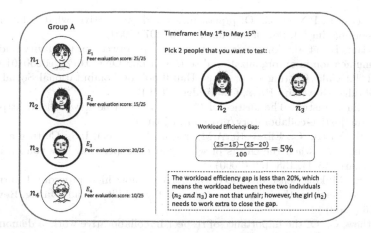

Fig. 2. Initial interface design of the group workload dashboard. The face figures are from Franzi draws. The interface provides a tool that can calculate the Workload Efficiency Gap. First, choose any of the two individuals in a group (in bold circle). Based on the peer review score, the tool will generate a percentage indicating the workload gap between these two individuals.

might have different perception on fairness. Continuing this study, we would like to conduct user studies to better understand individuals' belief and values in different categories. In addition, we will need to validate the model against user behaviors in real group work. For example, what is the threshold that changes the green line with different group configurations and in different contexts of work.

Another aspect that we want to further explore is to better understand and support peer reviewing of self and other's contributions in groups. Fairness in peer reviewing is another interesting issue to consider since our model is grounded on reliable and fair peer evaluation.

References

1. Joseph, M.: Groups: Interaction and Performance. Prentice-Hall Inc, Englewood Cliffs (1984)
2. Johnson, D.W., Johnson, R.T.: Learning together and alone. Cooperative, Competitive and Individualistic Learning (5th ed.). Allyn & Bacon, Boston (1999)
3. Jiaxun, H., Li, C.: Does group work save time? A study of time spent on group verses individual projects in college courses. J. Educ. Bus. 91(6), 308–314 (2010)
4. Mulvey, P.W., Klein, H.J.: The impact of perceived loafing and collective efficacy on group goal processes and group performance. Organizat. Beh. Hum. Decs. Process. 74(1), 62–87 (1998)
5. Robert, K.: Applying Social Psychological Theory to the Problems of Group Work. Theories in Human-Computer Interaction, pp. 325–356. Morgan-Kaufmann Publishers, New York (2002)

6. Elizabeth, J., P.Niels, C.: Of practicalities and perspective: what is fair in group decision making? J. Soc. Issues **65**(2), 383–407 (2009)
7. Arindam, D., et al.: Analyzing the relationship between productivity and human communication in an organizational setting. PLoS ONE **16**(7), e0250301 (2021)
8. Ariel, P.: Cake Cutting Algorithms, Handbook of Computational Social Choice. Cambridge University Press, Cambridge (2016)
9. Procedural Justice, The Justice of Collaboratory, Yale Law School. https://law.yale.edu/justice-collaboratory/procedural-justice
10. Joel, B., Ya-Ru, C., Elizabeth, A.M., Kwok, L., Daniel, P.S.: Culture and procedural fairness: when the effects of what you do depend on how you do it. Adm. Sci. Quart. **45**(1), 138–159 (2000)
11. Joel, B.: Making sense of procedural fairness: how high procedural fairness can reduce or heighten the influence of outcome favorability. Acad. Manag. Rev. **27**(1), 58–76 (2002)
12. Matthew, C.: Of the importance of respect in collaborative work: a demonstration using simulated top management teams (2004)
13. Tyler, R., Huo, J.: Trust in law: encouraging public cooperation with the police and courts. Russell Sage Foundation (2002)
14. Irene, P., Ellen, J., Adriaan, H.: Does the group matter? Effects of Trust, Cultural Diversity, and Group Formation on Engagement in Group Work in Higher Education. Higher Education Research and Development, vol. 41 no. 2, pp. 511–526 (2022)
15. Michael, K., Seth, N., Aaron, R., Zhiwei, W.: Preventing fairness gerrymandering: auditing and learning for subgroup fairness. arXiv:1711.05144 (2018)
16. Reuben, B.: On the apparent conflict between individual and group fairness, conference on fairness, accountability, and transparency (2020)
17. Yuen J.H., Kevin R.B.: why the psychological experience of respect matters in group life: an integrative account. Soc. Personal. Psychol. Compass **2**, 1570–1585 (2008)
18. Yuen J.H., Kevin R.B., Ludwin E.M.: The interplay between fairness and the experience of respect: implications for group life. Research on Managing Groups and Teams: Fairness and Groups, vol. 13, pp. 95–120. Bingley, UK: Emerald Group Publishing Limited (2010)
19. James K.H., Frank L.S., Theodore L.H.: Business-unit-level relationship between employee satisfaction, employee engagement, and business outcomes: a meta-analysis. J. Appl. Psychol. **87**(2), 268–279 (2002)
20. Maryam, K., Isaac, H., Ekaterina, N.: Not all fairness is created equal: fairness perceptions of group vs. individual decision makers. Organiz. Sci. **26**(5), 1301–1315 (2015)
21. Judith B.W., Ellen J.L., Leeat, Y., John C.W.: Frequent social comparisons and destructive emotions and behaviors: the dark side of social comparisons. J. Adult Develop. **13**, 36–44 (2006)
22. Tyler T.R., Lind E., A.A.: Relational model of authority in groups. Advances in Experimental Social Psychology, vol. 25, pp. 115–191 (1992)
23. Joseph, M.: Input-Process-Output Model (1964)
24. Alessandro, C., Riccardo, C., Greta, G., Daniele, R., Ilaria G.P, Andrea C.C.: A clarification of the nuances in the fairness metrics landscape. Sci. Rep. **12**, 4209 (2022). https://doi.org/10.1038/s41598-022-07939-1
25. Eric, M.: Measuring partisan bias in single-member district electoral systems. Legislat. Stud. Quart. **39**(1), 55–85 (2014)

Support How-To Instruction Following via Conversational Agent

Qingxiaoyang Zhu[1]([✉]) [iD], Yi-Chieh Lee[2] [iD], and Hao-Chuan Wang[1] [iD]

[1] University of California, Davis, CA 95616, USA
{qinzhu,hciwang}@ucdavis.edu
[2] National University of Singapore, Queenstown, Singapore
clee@nus.edu.sg

Abstract. People indispensably use instructions shared by one another to work on unfamiliar tasks in daily or professional life. However, personally shared tutorials are often based on personal experiences and represent a collective overview of past encounters, which can be misaligned with the specific work context during the re-enacting time. Drawing inspiration from the effective dynamics observed in conversational instruction-giving and -following between experts and novices, we propose a chatbot system that delivers archived how-to tutorials by providing necessary information in a just-in-time manner, tailored to the needs of the instruction-follower. Our aim is to transform unaided instruction reading activities into conversational instruction-following experiences. We implemented a chatbot system and evaluated it through a between subject study. The results demonstrate a promise of leveraging human-chatbot interaction to support actionable instruction-following.

Keywords: chatbot · instruction-following · how-to tutorial · situated action/plan

1 Introduction

People often share personal experience and tips in the form of tutorials online, which provide instructions for others to follow. Online procedural instruction-following is crucial for people to tackle unfamiliar tasks by referring How-To tutorials archived[1]. However, an informational gap of *context change* could emerge between tutorial-authoring and tutorial-following. After the tutorial is archived, the working space and context associated with the original execution described in the tutorial would disappear, making the tutorial disconnected from the original work context. People who check the tutorial later will need to retarget the described objects, processes, and work states to a later created workspace by re-enacting [10] the tutorial in an new environment [17]. Additionally, knowledge sharers often struggle to convey their expertise in a way that is understandable

---

[1] Sufficient resource is available sharing platforms, such as wikiHow, eHoweHow.

H. Takada et al. (Eds.): CollabTech 2023, LNCS 14199, pp. 217–225, 2023.
https://doi.org/10.1007/978-3-031-42141-9_19

by novices due to the highly abstract nature of their expertise [5] , which may lead to missing information for knowledge receivers. As a result, novice workers may face difficulties in mapping the present work context with the one captured previously, converting the instructions into a sequence of actionable operations, and maintaining an accurate awareness of work progress, due to their limited cognitive and environmental resources (e.g. knowledge, experience, attention) available and accessible [1]. Such *actionability* hurdles impede common users following instructions towards success.

To support instruction-following for novice workers, the HCI community has developed insights to potentially facilitate the process [8,9]. The emergent conversational agents have also been exploratorily applied to support procedural work in general, such as automatically retrieving additional content for the work [6,14] or summarizing alternative plans available online [3]. However, these approaches have not fully considered the situated nature of human work and have not focused on improving the actionability of archived tutorials within the worker's situated context. Additionally, the role of a chatbot as an **Enabler** (e.g. a partner), rather than an **Influencer** (e.g. an advisor) [7], has not been thoroughly explored in this context. It's also not entirely clear what role a chatbot may play in the situationism [15] aspect of work.

In this paper, instead of imposing influences **on** users with domain content, we explore to design chatbots that merely provide a supporting structure from the side and work **with** the user as an **Enabler**. The latter aims to prompt and nudge the user to take the agency to actively explore possible interpretations and actions upon the tutorial, and resolve unclarities and issues discovered in the instruction. The approach is also characterized to be *domain-generic* and *topic-independent* and can be applied to a range of procedural domains. We implemented a chatbot, named ActionaBot, as a planning companion, who systematically prompts and supports novice workers in sensing the work situation (such as the state of work (e.g., "which step are we in?"), worker ("have you finished that step?"), and the work plan ("shall we move to the next step?")). We designed a structured conversational outline for ActionaBot to engage users in activities during the work, confirming the finished steps, suggesting next actions and checking possible errors in completed steps. Human-human collaboration principles, such as developing mutual intelligibility [4] is borrowed and appropriated to fit in ActionaBot. Through an evaluation study involving 26 common users, we assess the effectiveness of Actionabot as an instruction-following companion that benefits the tuotrial actionability, users' awareness of situation and the outcomes of work.

2   ActionaBot Design

ActionaBot aims to convert conventional static How-To tutorials into conversational tutorials and provides step-wise guidance through conversation based on user's task execution situation (next step is given only when user confirms on finishing the current step and proceeds to the next step and support user to conduct the troubleshooting). The ActionaBot consists of a chat interface embedded into the tutorial page(Fig. 1) and a back-end rule-based dialogue system to drive the conversation on step-by-step instructions, including a dialogue management module to manage the dialog flow, a knowledge base module to obtain the outline of the tutorial, a situation tracking module to keep track of the user's progress and a communication strategy module to decide what and how to respond to the user. The modularized system supports extension with alternative tutorial knowledge and communication strategies.

Interface Design. The actionbot interface is an add-on to the conventional tutorial. Figure 1 illustrates an example with a chatting space, where ActionaBot prompts the user to check the current step and decide whether to proceed to the next step (the step-wise instruction is displayed in chat window). Users can engage in conversation with the chatbot by typing in the input field. ActionaBot receives the user's input and sends it to the back-end system to process. Both the user and ActionaBot keep track of the task execution progress, mutually confirm the situation and ground it back into the tutorial space. The chatbot assists the user in locating the appropriate instructions for each step by scrolling through the tutorial.

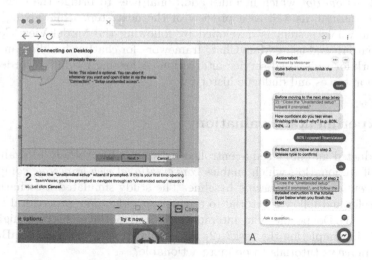

Fig. 1. The chatbot interface of ActionaBot, which is embedded in a sample How-To tutorial. The blue block **A** (on the right side of the figure) indicates the chat window, where the user can talk to ActionaBot while following instructions. The transparent red block (within the message block) shows ActionaBot's response adapts to the user's current execution progress and dynamically loading the step instructions from the tutorial (all content from the underlying webpage and no extra information). Meanwhile, ActionaBot automatically scrolls tutorial for the user to reach an appropriate step after mutual agreement is reached. (Color figure online)

Dialogue Design. The dialogue module is a major component that drives the conversation with the user to mutually understand the task execution situation, specifically which step is currently being performed, whether a step can be completed, what has been achieved, what would be the plan for the next step or collaboratively plan on reviewing the tutorial to debug, and provide situational instruction based on the mutual affirmation. The goal of the dialogue system is to communicate the situation of the task execution with the user, track the working situation and track the tutorial based on users' inputs. To enable a trackable tutorial, we designed a parsing algorithm to convert the original markup wiki-How into a sequence representation of step-wise instructions, which allows the dialogue module to ground the working situation back to the tutorial using step numbers.

To enable the conversational exchange, dialogue acts representing atomic units of a conversation were identified by drawing insights from observations of human conversational instruction-giving in the literature [2,12]. Following dialogue acts were incorporated with ActionaBot for instruction giving: Greeting, Instruction Giving (instruction details), Inquiry (asking about the novice's execution outcomes and feelings), Suggestion (suggesting novice to review instruction, check the outcome, go back and review), Request for User's Action (to execute a step).

Two variations of ActionaBot were implemented, *Base-ActionaBot* and *Context-ActionaBot* which includes additional cues to bridge the conversation with the tutorial, as well as a preview of the next step, while giving instruction. The whole system is developed by following the Model-View-Controller design pattern and using ManyChat[2] framework for chatbot building and Flask[3] framework for web-based service integration. A logging module recorded users' interaction traces and dialogue history.

3   Experimental Evaluation

We conducted an online semi-controlled between-subject study to evaluate our design of ActionaBot, which enables *conversational web browsing*, compared to the *conventional web browsing* baseline. The study simulated a scenario where people refer and follow a tutorial to execute an *unfamiliar* procedural task. We explored: (1) Do people who interact with ActionaBot achieve a higher success rate in completing the task? (2) Does collaboration with ActionaBot make novices perceive tutorials to be more actionable?

Task and Participants Recruitment. We designed a real-time computer operation task to simulate the real situation of novices' instruction-following (with or without chatbot support). Participants with limited computing literacy were invited and asked to install Python 3 or Java[4] on a remote computer with an online archived tutorial given for reference (the validity and quality of the selected tutorial were verified by two researchers). Two topics were used to

---

[2] https://manychat.com/.
[3] https://flask.palletsprojects.com/en/2.0.x/.
[4] https://www.python.org/.

increase the internal validity. The whole task has three major subprocedures, including downloading TeamViewer[5] on a local computer, connecting the local computer to the remote computer using installed TeamViewer, and downloading Python together with testing on the remote computer.

We include participants who have basic skills but limited knowledge of computers in the study as novice workers. Recruitment took place on Prolific platform and within a US university community for generalizability purpose. Participants' computer skills and task-related knowledge were screened through self-evaluation in a pre-survey [16]. A total of 26 participants joined the study[6]. Each participant received US$10 as compensation for their efforts.

Procedure. Based on the purpose of exploring the effect of chatbot support, three experiment conditions were set up as follows and shared the same tutorial content: (1) **Web-Browsing (WB)** Condition: Participants browse the web page and follow the tutorial to take action as they want, which is a conventional and common way of following tutorials. (2) **Web-Browsing + Base-ActionaBot (WA)** Condition: Participants converse with our ActionaBot to get instructions and follow the chatbot's instructions while executing the given task. (3) **Web-Browsing + Context-ActionaBot (WCA)** Condition: Participants converse with our ActionaBot while executing the given task, where the ActionaBot also includes context signaling. Each participant was randomly assigned to one of these three groups, resulting in 7 participants in the WB condition, 8 participants in the WA condition, and 11 participants in the WCA condition (Fig. 2). The experiment was held online and ran for 9 days.

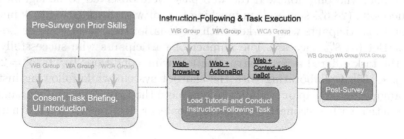

Fig. 2. Online study to evaluate the effects of conversational tutorial

The procedure is illustrated in Fig. 2, participants were first introduced to the task, then conducted the instruction-following experiment. the experimenter was fly-on-the-wall and took observation notes, without intervening in the instruction-following process[7]. Participants were asked to share their screens. They were instructed to keep two windows active, one for ActionaBot and

---

[5] https://www.teamviewer.com/en-us/.

[6] 11 males, 14 females, and 1 unknown.

[7] Researchers addressed logistic questions while avoiding affecting users' behaviors.

the other for task execution. Participants (N=26) took time to complete the instruction-following task. After the task, participants were given a post-survey to respond only based on their experiences and thought processes during the study. A semi-structured interview was conducted immediately following the post-survey.

Measurement. The survey items were mainly used to measure the user's perception, including the actionability of the tutorial [13] (e.g., "the instruction clearly identifies at least one action" and etc., Cronbach's $\alpha = 0.84$), task situational awareness [11] (e.g., "how well did you understand what was going on during the mission" and etc., $\alpha = 0.95$). Each item included multiple questions and we calculated the combined average score of the question cluster for analysis considering the stability [8]. All items used 5-point Likert scales.

4   Results

To answer the first evaluation question, we report whether and how people's behaviors were influenced by the conversational guidance with the ActionaBot, conducting analysis on task outcomes and the dialogue history. To answer the second evaluation question, we use survey data to triangulate the participants' perceptions of how they were affected by the ActionaBot.

4.1   Task Completion

Participants who only followed the web page were observed to be significantly less successful (28.6% success[9]) in finishing the software installation task in comparison to participants who worked with ActionaBot (62.5% success) or Contet-ActionaBot (81.8% success). The number of participants who successfully finished the task differed across instruction following conditions [$\chi^2(1, N = 26) = 4.40$, $p < .05$]. Collaborating with the chatbot system while following instructions augments participants' ability to complete the task. Potential explanation is interaction with ActionaBot triggered people's reflect on the work situation.

4.2   Perception on Conversational Tutorial

Operational Perception Analysis
By working together with ActionaBot, the tutorials were perceived to be more actionable by novice users, compared to the baseline condition in which they have to independently follow the static tutorial without any support (WB). This is supported by the quantitative analysis on the survey item of reported actionability. We analyzed the **combined actionability level** using a linear

---

[8] Cronbach's alpha reported earlier indicates the reliability to derive an average score.
[9] Some factors that can cause failure include skipping steps, missing information, execution errors, and other related issues.

regression model [10]. The assistant level of instruction-following was observed a significant effect on the actionability level of instructions indicating how well the instructions could be converted by people into actions and taken action upon $(F[2, 20] = 4.53, p < .05)$. According to post-hoc (Tukey HSD) analysis, participants in the Context-ActionaBot condition indicated that the instructions were significantly more actionable and more clearly to convert into executable actions $(M = 3.6, SE = 0.25)$ than participants under WB condition $(M = 3.31, SE = 0.25)$.

Improvement on Situational Awareness. We analyzed the *combined situational awareness levels* reported in the survey by conducting linear regression analysis[11]. A significant main effect has been found of the assistance type during instruction-following on the situational awareness score of the instruction-following process (task execution with tutorial reference), where participants working with Context-ActionaBot reported a significantly higher level of situational awareness score, which indicates a better awareness of the situation during following the tutorial to accomplish the task $(F[2, 20] = 3.79, p < .05)$. No sufficient support was found for the effect of computer skill level on situational awareness. We further conducted a post-hoc (Tukey HSD) test to understand the effect of each type of instruction following support. People conversed with Context-ActionaBot reported a significantly higher awareness $(M = 3.70, SE = 0.26)$ of task situations, such as what change has been made, what will happen, which object in the task space is changed, and so on, than people independently referred and followed the archived tutorial page $(M = 2.65, SE = 0.30)$. Although no significant difference has been found on the situational awareness score of Base-ActionaBot versus Web-Browsing, WA group reported a higher situational awareness score$(M = 3.52, SE = 0.31)$ than WB group.

4.3   Conclusion and Future Work

In this paper, we present a novel design to transform archived How-To tutorials into conversational tutorials by integrating a chatbot system called ActionaBot. Our study examines how structured conversations can support instruction-followers in reenacting instructions under dynamic task situations and contexts. By harnessing the principle of mutual intelligibility observed in human-human collaboration, we effectively transfer it to chatbot-human instruction-following. Empirical evidence demonstrates that the seamless integration of archived how-to tutorials into conversational exchanges enhances instruction-followers' awareness of the work situation and enables them to take situated actions that adapt to the changing work context. As such, our approach bridges the gap between static instructions and dynamic work contexts. This research contributes to our

---

[10] LMER(actionability_score ~ assistance_level + computer_skill_level + (1 || uuid)).

[11] LMER(situational_awareness ~ conversational_instruction_following_assistance_level + computer_skill_level + 1||*uuid*), we exclude interaction variable between instruction following condition and computer skill level due to loss of freedom.

understanding of the chatbot's role as an enabler in collaborative instruction-giving and following. To further deepen our understand of the underlined factors that enable actionable instruction-following and derive design implications for human-chatbot interaction, we are continuing qualitative analysis and iterating on the system for empirical studies.

References

1. Bransford, J.D., Brown, A.L., Cocking, R.R.: How people learn: brain, mind, experience, and school. National Academy Press (1999)
2. Carletta, J., Isard, A., Isard, S., Kowtko, J.C., Doherty-Sneddon, G., Anderson, A.H.: The reliability of a dialogue structure coding scheme (1997)
3. Chang, M., Lafreniere, B., Kim, J., Fitzmaurice, G., Grossman, T.: Workflow graphs: a computational model of collective task strategies for 3D design software. In: Graphics Interface 2020 (2020)
4. Clark, H.H., Wilkes-Gibbs, D.: Referring as a collaborative process. Cognition **22**(1), 1–39 (1986)
5. Hinds, P.J., Patterson, M., Pfeffer, J.: Bothered by abstraction: the effect of expertise on knowledge transfer and subsequent novice performance. J. Appl. Psychol. **86**(6), 1232 (2001)
6. Kelleher, C., Pausch, R.: Stencils-based tutorials: design and evaluation. In: Proceedings of the SIGCHI Conference on Human Factors in Computing Systems, pp. 541–550 (2005)
7. Köbis, N., Bonnefon, J.F., Rahwan, I.: Bad machines corrupt good morals. Nat. Hum. Behav. **5**(6), 679–685 (2021)
8. Kraut, R.E., Fussell, S.R., Siegel, J.: Situational awareness and conversational grounding in collaborative bicycle repair (2001)
9. Kraut, R.E., Fussell, S.R., Siegel, J.: Visual information as a conversational resource in collaborative physical tasks. Hum.-Comput. Interact. **18**(1–2), 13–49 (2003)
10. Rae, L.: Knowledge sharing and the virtual organization: meeting 21st century challenges. Thunderbird Int. Business Rev. **40**(5), 525–540 (1998)
11. Salas, E., Prince, C., Baker, D.P., Shrestha, L.: Situation awareness in team performance: implications for measurement and training. Situational Awareness, pp. 63–76 (2017)
12. Scheel, N.P., Branch, R.C.: The role of conversation and culture in the systematic design of instruction. Educational Technology, pp. 7–18 (1993)
13. Shoemaker, S.J., Wolf, M.S., Brach, C.: Development of the patient education materials assessment tool (pemat): a new measure of understandability and actionability for print and audiovisual patient information. Patient Educ. Couns. **96**(3), 395–403 (2014)
14. Speggiorin, A., Dalton, J., Leuski, A.: TaskMAD: a platform for multimodal task-centric knowledge-grounded conversational experimentation. In: Proceedings of the 45th International ACM SIGIR Conference on Research and Development in Information Retrieval, pp. 3240–3244 (2022)
15. Suchman, L., Blomberg, J., Orr, J.E., Trigg, R.: Reconstructing technologies as social practice. In: The Anthropology of Organisations, pp. 431–447. Routledge (2017)

16. Wikiversity: computer skills/proficient/databases – wikiversity (2019). https://en.wikiversity.org/w/index.php?title=Computer_Skills/Proficient/Databases&oldid=1987634. Accessed 20 Mar 2019
17. Zack, M.H.: Managing codified knowledge. Sloan Manag. Rev. **40**(4), 45–58 (1999)

Social Pressure in Co-Manipulation: From Verification of Refrains in Communication During Fusion Avatar Manipulation

Taichi Sono$^{(\boxtimes)}$ and Hirotaka Osawa

Keio University, Yokohama, Kanagawa, Japan
{taichisono0420,osawa.a3}@keio.jp

Abstract. In this study, we analyzed subjective comments on behavioral strategies that indicate negativity toward the partner during joint manipulation of the same avatar by participants who had never met each other before. We validated using the Tele-nininnbaori task: Two participants intervened with asymmetric information about the manipulation and the task for a single arm-shaped object and performed the task while communicating with each other through gestures. In previous studies, researchers have conducted validation between operators who have established some degree of relationship with each other. In this study, we designed a validation experiment in which two first-time participants were the experimenters. We obtained subjective comments on the behavioral strategies of the operators on the side who knew the task's goal but had constraints on the operation in the form of post-experiment interviews, in which they expressed negativity toward the perceptions and actions of the other party. For the mentioned negation behavior strategies, two persons involved in the experiment made assignments to the classification items created by overlooking the strategies all participants took. As a result, we confirmed that the strategy of explicit denial by shaking the object sideways, which has been taken in many previous studies, was hardly used, confirming the occurrence of refrains due to social pressure of communication in multi-person avatar manipulation.

Keywords: Co-operative avatar · Gesture communication · classification and analysis

1 Introduction

As part of collaborative research, researchers are pioneering the field of intervening in multiple operators, rather than just a single operator, in avatars, including robots that exist in remote areas and other locations [1,2]. Implementing multiple operators simultaneously on a single avatar makes it possible for them

---

Supported by JST Moonshot R&D Program "Cybernetic being" Project (Grant number JPMJMS2013).

H. Takada et al. (Eds.): CollabTech 2023, LNCS 14199, pp. 226–233, 2023.
https://doi.org/10.1007/978-3-031-42141-9_20

to complement each other's skills. Multiple operators are incredibly efficient in interactions between people with disabilities or between people who have lost skills, such as the elderly. At the same time, it can be a factor in improving the quality of life of people through avatars.

When multiple people operate avatars simultaneously instead of a single user, they need to coordinate their operation intentions with each other, and the problems associated with this need to be solved. T. Hagiwara et al. call such a method of introducing avatars with multiple operators as "Collaborative Avatar" and conducted a verification study [2]. As a result, they verified that the usability is the same as that of a single operator even when two or more operators are working together and that task performance is improved. In addition, Y. Tanaka et al. verified the effect on task efficiency of giving tactile feedback corresponding to the other person's operation in a Collaborative Avatar [6]. The validation results showed that vibration feedback corresponding to speed increased the efficiency of collaborative work. Increasing work efficiency in collaborative operations helps increase the operator's QoL. In addition, H. Osawa et al. constructed a virtual environment in which multiple operators intervene by dividing the movement of one arm into the manipulation of the position of the entire arm and manipulation of the wrist and finger joint rotation as one of the Collaborative Avatar [5]. H. Osawa et al. then observed behaviors related to the communication of intentions with only the position operator knowing the goal of the task. H. Osawa et al. assumed that the user of the Collaborative Avatar might have limitations in movement and means of communication due to disability or other reasons. In such a situation, the operator with fewer limitations may participate in the work to assist the operator with more limitations. In this case, verifying an operating environment in which asymmetric authority is shared has been conducted as a method for the operator receiving assistance to communicate and perform tasks without losing a sense of independence in work and with only the possible operation details.

On the other hand, these studies are the findings of physical sensations finally obtained by operators who are already skilled and have repeated communication experiences. Suppose the merging operators do not yet know each other. In that case, they need to explore each other's intentions to facilitate these operations and to search for mediation of intentions that do not take the form of aggression toward each other. Ignorance of the fusion partner is a condition of avatar-mediated communication. However, researchers have not examined how social pressure from these intentional manipulators can cause reticence and impede communication in multi-person avatar manipulation. The researchers have not previously examined the effects of social pressure from manipulators in multi-person avatar conditions. In order to introduce avatar technology operated by multiple people more widely in society, it is necessary to consider these issues that need to be considered in advance when communicating with people who have never met each other.

In this study, we designed a robot interface in which strangers collaborated via avatars and measured the changes in communication during interaction to examine the communication pressure in such multi-person avatars. Specifically, using the Tele-nininnbaori task [5], which is a collaborative task with asymmetric role assignment as shown in previous studies, we recruited participants who were unskilled at the task and had never met the collaborators as operators on the side that understood the goal of the task and conducted two types of tasks with a different frequency of intention mediation. We then analyzed the participants' subjective comments on the behavioral strategies taken during the task that indicated negativity toward the collaborators. The results confirmed that fewer participants claimed to have taken behavioral strategies that indicated direct negativity than when the task was performed between operators who had repeated experiences of communicating with each other.

2   Verification

2.1   Purpose

This study aims to investigate the generation of communication pressure in a fusion manipulation in which multiple people intervene in a single manipulation object when the fusing operators do not yet know each other. For the above investigation, we conducted an experiment in which two people who had never met each other before performed a fusion manipulation task focused on communication. To examine the generation of communicative pressure in this context, we investigated the strategy of presenting negations or mistakes to the other's actions or perceptions made by one of the manipulators to the other, based on the participants' mentions. We focus on the strategies of negation and pointing out mistakes because negation and mistakes give a powerful message in communication and, therefore, significantly impact specific pressures in communication.

The Bioethics Committee of the author's institution approved the experiments conducted in this study. (Approval ID: 2022-113)

2.2   Use System

The fusion manipulation system used in this study's validation is the Tele-nininnbaori task, a manipulation task using nonverbal communication of the same object by multiple persons between remote locations, which has been proposed in a previous study [5].The overall picture of Tele-nininnbaori task is shown in Fig. 1.

In Fig. 1, the remote manipulation object is configured as a CG arm model on the screen. The operators are divided into two groups: the Main-operator and the Sub-operator, each of whom is given the configuration of the operating device and the authority and task information as shown in Table 1.

As shown in Table 1, the assignment's goal is assumed to be known only to the Main-operator. In a Tele-nininnbaori task, the operators are not allowed to communicate verbally with each other. Therefore, the Main-operator communicates the content of the assignment to the Sub-operator through nonverbal information

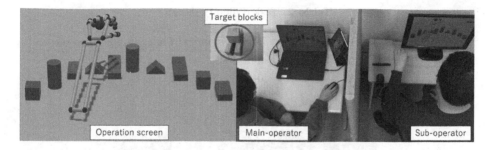

Fig. 1. Overview of Tele-nininnbaori

Table 1. Division of operators in Tele-nininnbaori

Operator	Operating Device	Operating Authority	Task Information
Main-operator	Mouse	Position of arm	goal of task
Sub-operator	Leap Motion	Hand and finger rotation	nothing

using the manipulation objects, and the two operators carry out the job while communicating and mediating their intentions. In the study that proposed the Tele-Nininnbaori task [5], nonverbal communication behaviors observed during the mediation of purposes in the task phase were investigated in a simulation of a building block task, as shown in Fig. 1. The system used in this study for executing the Tele-Nininnbaori task also follows the one used in previous studies. Still, we changed the coordinate system of the arm positions corresponding to mouse operations to make the procedure more intuitive.

2.3 Task Design

We used the building block task, which the proposers also used in a previous study that proposed the Tele-nininnbaori task, to verify the intention-communication behavior performed by the Main-operator in the experiments conducted in this study. The Main-operator was the one who controlled the position and knew the goal of the task, and the Sub-operator was the one who owned the flexion of the fingers. The experiment participant participated in the task as the Main-operator and the Sub-operator was one person on the experimenter's side for all trials. We set up three tasks: one practice task and two main tasks, one of low difficulty and the other of high difficulty. The practice task was the same for some participants, but the main task differed for all participants in all trials. Details of the difficulty settings are shown in Table 2 below. The number of rotations required is the number of times the operators must rotate the building block before achieving the goal. The number of times to put them on is the number of times another block is placed on top of it.

Examples of the various tasks are shown in Fig. 2 below.

Table 2. Task difficulty design

Difficulty	Building blocks	Turns required	Times to put them on
Practice	2	0–1	1
Low difficulty	3	0–1	1
High difficulty	4	1 or more	2

Practice   Low difficulty   High difficulty

Fig. 2. Task examples

The order in which we presented the tasks was always low difficulty followed by high difficulty.

2.4 Participants

The number of participants included in the data was 20, who were not excluded were ten males and ten females each, ranging in age from 19 to 49 years (ave. = 26.2, st.dev = 8.81). The experimenter in charge of the Sub-operator confirmed that they had never met all participants.

2.5 Procedure

After explaining the experiment and giving informed consent, an explanation of the operation on the actual system was given. Then, the practice task was performed an arbitrary number of times by the participants, and the main task was performed twice. After the main task, the participants were asked to answer a questionnaire and also were interviewed at the end of the session. A break was taken after each task.

The maximum duration for the practice task was 5 min, and the maximum period for the main tasks was 10 min. Only for the main tasks, when the whole time limit was reached, the task was terminated at that point. The participant's judgment determined the completion of the task.

The participants and the Sub-operator were introduced to each other only during the explanation of the experiment, and no chatting was conducted to build a relationship between the participants and the Sub-operator.

2.6 Data Collection

Experimental data were collected through questionnaires and interviews. Among the data collected, the central analysis item is the behavioral strategies that indicate negation in the intention-to-mediate behavior questioned in the interviews. This item was collected by asking questions like "Did you perform any behavior that indicated a behavioral error or miscommunication? If so, what did you do?" By analyzing the behavioral strategies that indicate denial, we will examine the occurrence of communication-related pressure.

3 Result and Findings

In this paper, we focus on the classification of subjective mentions of denial behavior strategies obtained through interviews, which indicate behavioral errors or miscommunication, and discuss the refrains that occurred in the denial behavior. Classifications were made for the behavioral negation strategy by the experiment planner and those who participated in the experiment as assistant operators. Table 3 shows the results of the classification and assignment of the denial behavior strategies mentioned by the participants; the participant in ID 1 was excluded from the table because we didn't individually interview them about their denial behavior. The classification items were created based on a generic view of the negative behavior strategies taken by the participants, in addition to the "hand waving" strategy, AP:Sign, which was the most frequently reported negative behavior strategy in previous studies. The assignment of the adverse action strategies the participants took to the classification was based on the list of negative action strategies collected through the interviews. In cases where it was difficult to classify, the audio data from the interviews were used as a supplement. The following rules were established for classification.

– No duplicate classifications were allowed.
– If you think that more than one item falls under one major category, classify them into the one that the participant considered more important in the interview voice

Table 3. Classification of Subjective Comments on Negative Behavioral Strategies

Classification	Name	Name	Detail	Experimenter allocation	Sub-operator allocation
Active presentation	Signs using the metaphor of negation	AP:Sign	using the entire arm of the CG as a negation behavior, mimicking the behavior of swinging the head and hands sideways, which is a metaphor for NO in general		
	Repeat change orders	AP:Repeat	repeating an instruction when the other party's current state or action was incorrect	2,4,10,12,13, 14,15,16,17, 18	4,10,12,13,14, 15,16,18
	Special change orders other than above	AP:Special	taking particular actions that did not fall into the two categories listed above	19	9,19
Passive presentation	Wait for sub-operator to change	PP	not proceeding from one step to the next in the building block assembly process	3,9,20	2,3
Not presentation	Couldn't think of any	NP:Any	not mention the negation behavior strategy	6,8,11	6,8,11,20
	No occasion to point out mistakes	NP:Non	the situation in which the negation should have been made did not occur	5,7	5,7,17

We calculated Krippendorff's α [3] as the goodness of fit between the two classification results, which is 0.708. From the books [4] of the proponents, 0.667 is stated as a lower limit of the number that can be considered a tentative conclusion of the agreement. Therefore, this classification is consistent to some degree.

Overlooking the classification results, it can be seen that AP:Sign, the most common behavior in the previous study that proposed the Tele-nininnbaori task [5], was not observed at all, and instead, AP:Repeat was observed most frequently. The classification results show that participants took none of the strategies revealed in previous studies to indicate to the supporter the difference between the current situation and the direction of rotation by waving the hand sideways. This strategy is although this is the most frequently cited essential communication in previous studies. This difference may be attributed to social pressure in communication. When communicating relative to a person one has never met before, explicitly negating the other person's behavior is sometimes hesitated and becomes a far-fetched negative expression. In the tele-negotiation task in this study, i.e., the joint manipulation of a single object, only the participant knows the goal of the task and can be considered to be in control of the task; it is thought that this social pressure in communication caused the inhibition of action or reticence. In the case of avatars operated by multiple people, the goal of the task is to control the communication.

4   Limitations

There are several limitations to the findings of this study.

The first is a limitation on the difficulty setting. The difficulty level is set by the number of building blocks and processes required in the experimental setting. However, in the actual execution of the experiment, regardless of the above settings, the task's difficulty level may have changed depending on whether the task included triangles or not, as can be inferred from the execution time and participants' mentions. The triangular pillar building blocks have more stable placements than other building blocks. Therefore, the main reason for the tendency for transmission errors when communicating the placement. Some participants should have included the triangles within the two tasks they performed, which may have been a factor in their failure to complete the negative action strategy.

Second, there were cultural limitation. All participants in this experiment were Japanese. In Japan, people tend to be very considerate in their words and actions when communicating with someone they have never met before. Therefore, it is possible that the results of this experiment are unique to Japan.

5   Conclusion

To examine social pressure in multi-person avatar manipulation, we analyzed subjective references to behavioral strategies that indicate negation toward the partner during joint manipulation of the same avatar by participants who had never met each other. We designed a validation experiment for a Tele-nininnbaori task in which two participants [5], who had never met each other before, intervened in a single arm-shaped object with asymmetric information about the manipulation and the task and performed the task while communicating with each other through gestures. The experiment was designed to test the hypothesis that the two first-time operators on the same side of the task know the goal of the task but are constrained in their operation. Then, the mentioned negative action strategies were assigned to the classification items created from a bird's eye view of the strategies taken by all participants, including the negative action strategies taken in the previous study in which the same task was conducted with a certain degree of relationship established. As a result, it was confirmed that the strategy of explicit denial by shaking the object sideways, which had been taken in many previous studies, was hardly taken, confirming the occurrence of refraining due to social pressure of communication in multi-person avatar manipulation.

References

1. Fribourg, R., et al.: Virtual co-embodiment: evaluation of the sense of agency while sharing the control of a virtual body among two individuals. IEEE Trans. Visual Comput. Graphics **27**(10), 4023–4038 (2021)
2. Hagiwara, T., et al.: Collaborative avatar platform for collective human expertise. In: SIGGRAPH Asia 2021 Emerging Technologies. SA 2021 Emerging Technologies, Association for Computing Machinery, New York, NY, USA (2021)
3. Krippendorff, K.: Computing Krippendorff's alpha-reliability (2011)
4. Krippendorff, K.: Content analysis: an introduction to its methodology. SAGE Publications (2018)
5. Osawa, H., Sono, T.: Tele-Nininbaori: intentional harmonization in cybernetic avatar with simultaneous operation by two-persons. In: Proceedings of the 9th International Conference on Human-Agent Interaction, pp. 235–240. HAI 2021, Association for Computing Machinery, New York, NY, USA (2021)
6. Tanaka, Y., et al.: Sensorimotor control sharing with vibrotactile feedback for body integration through avatar robot. IEEE Robot. Autom. Lett. **7**(4), 9509–9516 (2022)

Author Index

H. Takada et al. (Eds.): CollabTech 2023, LNCS 14199, pp. 235–236, 2023.
https://doi.org/10.1007/978-3-031-42141-9

Correction to: Conducting Morality and Emotion Analysis on Blog Discourse

Stella Mbila-Uma, Ifeanyichukwu Umoga, Mustafa Alassad, and Nitin Agarwal(✉)

Correction to:
Chapter "Conducting Morality and Emotion Analysis on Blog Discourse" in: H. Takada et al. (Eds.): *Collaboration Technologies and Social Computing*, LNCS 14199, https://doi.org/10.1007/978-3-031-42141-9_15

In the original version of this chapter, family name and e-mail address of the last author were wrong. This has been corrected. Correctly it should read: "Nitin Agarwal", email: nxagarwal@ualr.edu.

The updated original version of this chapter can be found at
https://doi.org/10.1007/978-3-031-42141-9_15

Printed in the United States
by Baker & Taylor Publisher Services

Printed in the United States
by Baker & Taylor Publisher Services